DATE DUE

BRODART, CO.

Cat. No. 23-221

Arms Control Policy

Arms Control Policy

A Guide to the Issues

Marie Isabelle Chevrier

Contemporary Military, Strategic, and Security Issues

 PRAEGER

AN IMPRINT OF ABC-CLIO, LLC
Santa Barbara, California • Denver, Colorado • Oxford, England

Copyright 2012 by Marie Isabelle Chevrier

Library of Congress Cataloging-in-Publication Data

Chevrier, Marie Isabelle.
    Arms control policy : a guide to the issues / Marie Isabelle Chevrier.
        p. cm. — (Contemporary military, strategic, and security issues)
    Includes bibliographical references and index.
    ISBN 978-0-275-99457-0 (hardcopy : alk. paper) — ISBN 978-1-56720-711-8
(e-book)   1. Arms control—Government policy.   2. Arms control—
International cooperation.   I. Title.
    JZ5625.C49   2012
    327.1'740973—dc23   2012016709

ISBN: 978-0-275-99457-0
EISBN: 978-1-56720-711-8

16   15   14   13   12   1   2   3   4   5

This book is also available on the World Wide Web as an eBook.
Visit www.abc-clio.com for details.

Praeger
An Imprint of ABC-CLIO, LLC

ABC-CLIO, LLC
130 Cremona Drive, P.O. Box 1911
Santa Barbara, California 93116-1911

This book is printed on acid-free paper (∞)

Manufactured in the United States of America

For the loves of my life: Paul, Isabelle, and Zackary

Contents

Acknowledgments

Writing this book has taken me on a long personal journey. The road was not smooth or straight, but I found refuge all along the way from colleagues, friends, and family to whom I owe a debt of gratitude. First and foremost, I want to thank my students and research assistants, especially Ashley Nickels, Jennifer Bridges, Ryan Henry, and Kerri West, for carrying out essential research as well as tedious chores with alacrity and good cheer. Jennifer and Ryan worked with me late at night and Ashley took time away from her precious children when I demanded her time. I hope they learned something worthwhile along the way. My dear friend Ellen Whitford, a self-described grammar nerd, offered excellent suggestions and needed editing on the text. She gave me frequent reminders that the topic was interesting to nonspecialists when I needed it most. My colleague at the University of Texas at Dallas, Professor Denis Dean, kindly produced the bulk of the maps. I was very impressed with his speed and skill.

My interest in arms control stems from graduate school. Tom Schelling, Paul Doty, and Matt Meselson encouraged my learning and set exacting standards and exceptional examples for scholarship. Together they put my feet on the path. My only way of paying them back is to pass on a fraction of what they imparted to me to the next generation.

For many years, I have enjoyed the collegiality and friendship of the Scientists Working Group on Biological and Chemical Weapons. Barbara Hatch Rosenberg, the group's longtime leader, took me under her wing when I was starting out, showed me the ropes at international conferences, and taught me a great deal about successful advocacy. Together with Barbara, the other members of the group, Mark Wheelis, Elisa Harris, Milton Leitenberg, John Gilbert, Jack Woodall, Jack Melling, Lynn Klotz, Kathleen Vogel, Greg Koblentz, Alan Pearson, Jens Kuhn, and David Fidler, provided an intellectual and welcoming community that allowed my own research to flourish. They also taught me virtually everything I know about microbiology, chemistry, and the importance of science to the success of arms control.

International colleagues abound, a few deserve special thanks. Malcolm Dando has been tireless in his devotion to biological arms control and an enduring inspiration. Patricia Lewis opened her house whenever I was in Geneva, and helped me to broaden my perspective on arms control. Her intellect, compassion, and devotion to making the world a better place are stellar in equal measure. Iris Hunger, Angela Woodward, Katherine McLaughlin and Katharine Nixdorff contributed their time and expertise to keeping the BioWeapons Prevention Project afloat when it most needed their attention. We shared dinners, wine, and frustrations. I hold them in the highest regard.

International diplomats sat down with me, explained their craft, and demonstrated their commitment to international peace and security. Ambassadors Jayantha Dhanapala, Tibor Toth, Masood Khan, Bob Mikulak, Larura Kennedy, Adolf von Vagner, and Rolf Ekeus never failed to give me time and answer questions in spite of their full schedules. Other experts in arms control delegations were also instrumental to my work: Bob Matthews of Australia, John Walker and Lorna Miller of the United Kingdom, Ben Stein of South Africa, Volker Beck of Germany, Reto Wollenmann and Ricarrda Torriani of Switzerland, and Ken Ward and Jenny Gromoll of the United States. Robin Coupland and Peter Herby of the International Committee of the Red Cross explained the intricacies of international humanitarian law. In sum, this group of extraordinary individuals helped show me the right fork to follow when the path twisted and turned.

Alicia Merritt and Steve Catalano showed nearly infinite patience and granted me many extensions of the time needed to complete the manuscript. They were tolerant beyond expectation when due to personal concerns or changing jobs and offices I came begging for yet more time. And Steve finally said, 'get it done already,' although not in those exact words. I am grateful for that as well.

Finally, my family and friends gave me support, encouragement, and nudged or shoved me back on the path when I wandered off or sat down to rest. My dearest friends, Elizabeth St. Clair, Sandy Romanow, Becky Ryan, Edna Kiel, and Roxanne Lieb were women I could count on for everything, no matter what. Gabe Meadows, Jeffrey Levine, Deb Gallagher, Cindy and Barry Murphy, Catherine and Doug Eckel cooked meals, shared their homes, and displayed their hospitality; when I needed a lift Gabe sang to me. Carol Emig and Sharon Klots treated me to a spectacular birthday celebration in the midst of the final stretch. Ginny NiCarthy and Leland Hale know the tribulations of manuscripts and each of them pushed, prodded, and sympathized as appropriate. My sisters Darlene Koley and Gail Thomas and many cousins, especially Diana Noonan and Claire Nelson, asked about progress and told me that they were proud of me.

And now, I turn to the last and most important acknowledgements. Zackary, my son, child of my heart, through his fascination with biology, reminded me that I was on the right path and that "my book" was not the most important thing in life. And I always, always, could count on him for a laugh. Isabelle, my delightful, beloved and talented daughter, dutifully shouldered tiresome tasks: checking footnotes, websites, UN resolutions, treaty texts, and the *Chicago Manual of Style*, with nary a complaint. She understood what this was about and never hesitated to fill in when I needed assistance. She also gives the best hugs ever. For Paul, there are not enough words. He edited chapters, made dinner, gave backrubs, filled tubs, forgave egoism, picked me up when I fell, and carried me along the path when I was too weary to travel it on my own.

Finally, a special thanks to the late, great, Stanley Kubrick. I don't remember when I first watched *Dr. Strangelove or: How I Learned to Stop Worrying and Love the Bomb*. The brilliant satire is an enduring testament of the absurdity of the nuclear arms race and a constant reminder that in the midst of serious work we all need to laugh out loud upon occasion.

Acronyms

ABM	Anti-ballistic missile
ACDA	Arms Control and Disarmament Agency
BW	Biological weapons
BWC	Biological Weapons Convention
CBM	Confidence building measures
CCD	Conference of the Committee on Disarmament
CCM	Convention on Cluster Munitions
CD	Conference on Disarmament
CIHL	Customary International Humanitarian Law
CMC	Cluster Munitions Coalition
CSP	Conference of States Parties
CTBT	Comprehensive Test Ban Treaty
CTBTO	Comprehensive Test Ban Treaty Organization
CW	Chemical weapons
CWC	Chemical Weapons Convention
DOD	Department of Defense
EIF	Entry into force
ENDC	Eighteen Nation Disarmament Committee
ERW	Explosive remnants of war
GICHD	Geneva International Centre for Humanitarian Demining
GP	Geneva Protocol
HEU	Highly enriched uranium
IAEA	International Atomic Energy Agency
ICBL	International Campaign to Ban Landmines
ICBM	Intercontinental ballistic missile
ICRC	International Committee of Red Cross
INF	Intermediate-Range Nuclear Forces
ISU	Institutional Support Unit

LTBT	Limited Test Ban Treaty
MAD	Mutual Assured Destruction
MBT	Mine Ban Treaty
MIRV	Multiple, independently targeted reentry vehicles
New START	New Strategic Arms Reduction Treaty
NGO	Nongovernmental organization
NNWS	Nonnuclear weapon states
NPT	Nuclear Non-Proliferation Treaty
NSG	Nuclear Suppliers Group
NWS	Nuclear weapon states
OPCW	Organization for the Prohibition of Chemical Weapons
PTBT	Partial Test Ban Treaty
RevCon	Review Conference
SALT	Strategic Arms Limitation Treaty
SCC	Standing Consultative Commission
SDI	Strategic Defense Initiative
SLBM	Submarine-launched ballistic missiles/ Sea-launched ballistic missiles
SNDV	Strategic nuclear delivery vehicles
SORT	Strategic Offensive Reduction Treaty
START	Strategic Arms Reduction Treaty
TMD	Theatre missile defense
UNMOVIC	United Nations Monitoring, Verification and Inspection Commission

CHAPTER 1

Introduction

Prohibiting the possession and use of weapons, or limiting the size and makeup of weapon arsenals, has been a feature of international relations for centuries. During the Middle Ages, for example, Pope Innocent the II banned the use of the crossbow by Christians against other Christians in Europe's seemingly endless wars. Nevertheless, the scale of warfare that the world witnessed in the 20th century, together with the development of atomic and thermonuclear weapons, provided a profound impetus to search for new ways to control weaponry. For the first time, nations had the capacity to destroy all human life.

Even before the use of nuclear weapons, modern war was so deadly and destructive that nations felt the need to limit weapons of war. During World War I, approximately 10 million soldiers and nearly 7 million civilians were killed. Despite international efforts to fulfill the desire for WWI to be the war to end all wars, less than 30 years later, World War II claimed the lives of more than 60 million people—and more civilians than military personnel perished. WWI brought the horror of poison to the fighting as first the German army and later the members of the Triple Entente, mainly France and Great Britain and later the United States rained down noxious gases on the battlefields of Europe.

Although accurate accounts of civilian deaths in WWII cannot be calculated, the estimates are staggering; they range from 30 million to more than 49 million. Moreover, the effects of weapons used in WWII did not end with the defeat of the Axis Powers. When the United States dropped nuclear weapons on the Japanese cities of Hiroshima and Nagasaki in 1945, the long-term effects of radiation poisoning on its victims and successive generations, as the result of genetic damage, were unknown.

At the other end of the weapons spectrum, land mines laid during WWII are still causing death and serious injury today, overwhelmingly to civilians, including many children. In 2010, land mines caused more than 4,000 deaths and injuries; prior to the Ban Mines Treaty, the number was 26,000 per year.[1] Most of the major and many of the minor conflicts since WWII have left unexploded ordnance and devastation in their wake. Land mines, cluster munitions, and other remnants of war continue to litter the global landscape.

Since WWII, forests of paper have been sacrificed to books and articles about all aspects of arms control; historical, theoretical, technical, and diplomatic treatises abound. Volumes have been written about each of the individual weapons systems from every imaginable point of view. Articles and books have been written about the end of arms control and the future of arms control. So why is there a need for yet another book about arms control?

First, arms control is a dynamic, ongoing enterprise. Many arms control agreements are in force; others remain in effect but have been rendered irrelevant by technological and geopolitical changes; still others are on the drawing board. As agreements such as the Chemical Weapons Convention (CWC) achieve disarmament, other goals become more important in the same way that an exchange of queens elevates the importance of the bishops in a game of chess. Political events promote or impinge on the likelihood that breakthrough arms control negotiations will occur. New dispatches about arms control occur on nearly a daily basis. Since the end of the Cold War, the field has witnessed new approaches, new coalitions, new theories, new leaders, and new processes. Disputes between the superpowers often blocked agreement in multiparty negotiations. Since the breakup of the Soviet Union, multilateral disarmament treaties have been concluded on nuclear testing, chemical weapons (CW), land mines, and cluster munitions. Moreover, the unstoppable march of progress creates new developments in the lethality and deliverability of various weapons systems, upending conventional understandings about the nature of the threat each poses. Keeping abreast of new developments is a daunting task, and each field of arms control has its own experts, vocabulary, and literature.

Second, arms control has broadened as a field. While nuclear weapons arms control dominated the Cold War and, to a certain extent, still does today, the control of many other weapons and the technologies that produce them has characterized much of the post–Cold War period. One dilemma within the arms control field is whether to focus on weapons that have the potential to kill legions of people but have not been used recently or to focus on more commonly used weapons that lead to injury and death on a regular basis. Nuclear weapons have not been used since WWII. Japan used biological weapons against prisoners of war and others in China during WWII, yet the use of biological weapons by a state has not been confirmed since then.[2]

CW have been used sparingly since the massive use of CW in the trenches of WWI. Italy used CW against unprotected Abyssinian troops in the 1930s. The United States used tear gas and chemicals, considered CW by many, for defoliation in Vietnam. Iraq used CW against Iran in their war in the 1980s, and Iran ultimately retaliated with CW use, but never used CW as extensively as Iraq.[3] Other evidence of CW use by national governments includes that of Egypt against Yemen. And of course Nazi Germany killed millions in extermination camps using the chemical Zyklon B. In the meantime, small arms, land mines, cluster munitions, and tactical bombs have destroyed lives on a steady basis. Indeed, antipersonnel land mines have often been described as weapons of mass destruction in slow motion. This book examines both sides of that spectrum and the different theoretical arguments for limiting or banning these weapons.

Third, this book examines the implementation of arms control agreements as well as a description of the agreements and how they were negotiated. Treaty implementation is particularly important and complex in multilateral treaties and can expose weaknesses in treaties that were not foreseen when the treaties were drafted. These weaknesses can lead to disputes or they can be overcome or compensated for in other ways. Implementation of one treaty often informs the negotiation and implementation of future treaties to help those who draft the new treaties to avoid or circumvent implementation difficulties encountered by the earlier treaty. Successful consultation and clarification discussions in the implementation of the CWC, for example, lead the way for similar procedures to become encoded in the language of the Comprehensive Test Ban Treaty (CTBT), and they are included in the proposed Protocol to the Biological Weapons Convention. On the other hand, because the CTBT has not yet been ratified by the requisite states needed to enter into force, the negotiators seeking a treaty to ban the production of fissile material, which is currently under consideration, will perhaps consider less strict provisions for it to enter into force. The CTBT requires all states that possess nuclear weapons to ratify it before it is binding, yet none of the proposed draft treaties to ban further production of fissile material requires all nations that have produced fissile material to ratify the treaty before its provisions would take effect.

Fourth, in the past decade, arms control resources on the Internet have grown exponentially. Statements, documents, working papers, treaty drafts, and texts are now available often at the click of a mouse rather than after long hours in archives or libraries. As with other Internet resources, arms control information on the Internet provides easy access, yet Internet information can be inaccurate or biased, subject to error, and presents an opportunity to drown in a morass of information. As often as possible, I have tried to cite Internet sources for documents, treaty texts, databases, and other information. The Internet sites used in this text are reputable and known for their accuracy. Hopefully, the use of Internet sources may encourage newcomers to the field to dedicate needed time and energy to the enterprise of arms control and disarmament.

Finally, this book attempts to give the newcomer to the field of arms control a way to understand the broad strokes of the subject in one volume. It provides experts or novices in one field of arms control a context to understand how one area of arms control fits into the larger field. It is also able to discuss the relationships among the different arms control measures.

This book has a broad, but necessarily limited, scope. It takes a broad look at arms control and disarmament agreements since the 1960s and their implementation, but does not cover all negotiations or all agreements. It focuses on an important subset: (1) the nuclear agreements between the former Soviet Union and the United States, and those between the Russian Federation and the United States; (2) the multilateral nuclear agreements, specifically the Nuclear Nonproliferation Treaty and the Limited and Comprehensive Test Ban Treaties and the much discussed, but as yet to be completed, Fissile Material Cutoff Treaty; (3) the multilateral agreements banning the other so-called weapons of mass destruction—chemical and biological weapons; and (4) the most recently negotiated multilateral agreements banning land mines and cluster munitions. The Appendix contains a table of the treaties discussed in the book and a summary of their provisions. In doing so, the book examines both bilateral and multilateral diplomacy, weapons of mass destruction, and conventional weapons. The book does not examine regional arms control such as the Treaty of Tlatelolco, which bans nuclear weapons in Latin America and the Caribbean, or other treaties that create nuclear weapon–free zones, nor the Conventional Forces in Europe Treaty, which set limits on tanks, artillery, aircraft, and other weapons in Europe. The book also excludes specialized treaties such as the 1967 Outer Space Treaty and the 1959 Antarctic Treaty. The book does not deal with the Geneva Conventions as a whole, but it does examine several treaties emanating from the Conventions, particularly the bans on biological and chemical weapons, land mines, and cluster munitions. The choices to include or exclude agreements were done to provide a strong overview of the main components of international arms control.[4] The choice was also made to give a strong chronological dimension to the book. The treaties that are discussed in the book span all of the decades since the end of WWII.

The volume looks at both the recent history of arms control and the future of arms control in a complex and evolving international context. It describes the nuts and bolts of treaty negotiation and implementation as well as describing the changing theoretical perspectives on the role of arms control in international relations. It examines dilemmas and controversies that arise in treaty negotiations and obstacles to the effectiveness and success of treaty regimes.

What Is Arms Control?

Definitions and the objectives of arms control have been set forth in different ways by different authors. Hedley Bull, an early and influential contributor to arms control theory, defined arms control as "peace through the manipulation of force . . . through restraints and limits on forces," emphasizing concrete military forces.[5] Nobel Laureate Thomas Schelling and Morton Halperin defined the potential activity of arms control in a very broad fashion with very specific objectives: "all forms of military cooperation between potential enemies in the interest of reducing the likelihood of war, its scope and violence if it occurs, and the political and economic costs of being prepared for it."[6] More recently, Jeffrey Larsen wrote that arms control was "one of a series of alternative approaches to achieving international security through military strategies."[7] Arms control, in these definitions, encompasses disarmament—destroying or disposing of existing weapons or equipment of war—as well as setting restraints on the acquisition, numbers, or composition of weapons and weapons systems. These definitions highlight different objectives of arms control, achieving international security in the third definition; making war less likely, less destructive, and less costly in the second; and, quite simply, peace in the first. In addition, more recent arguments for eliminating land mines and cluster munitions have emphasized the importance of achieving humanitarian goals and protecting basic human rights through arms control.

While arms control may include forms of military or political cooperation such as the 1963 Hotline Agreement, this book examines only measures that concern armaments and that became embodied in bilateral or multilateral treaties or, in the case of the Fissile Material Cutoff Treaty, may yet do so. Nonetheless, the discussion of arms control herein consists not only of the negotiated treaties but also of the norms, expectations, subsequent understandings among parties, the practices of national governments, and the implementation of the agreements. This set of factors can be said to comprise an arms control regime.[8]

Because arms control is dynamic rather than static in nature, it does not end with a completed, signed agreement or entry of a treaty into force.[9] The changing international security and political environments, scientific and technological advances, and the addition of new treaty parties through ratification or accession, all play a role in the ability of agreements to achieve their objectives. Thus, the conflicts and controversies that arise after an agreement enters into force are as relevant as those hammered out through negotiations. This book discusses the major implementation problems, such as the inability of the United States and Russia to meet treaty deadlines to destroy their stocks of CW, and current challenges like the Iranian uranium enrichment program. It also suggests challenges that the different arms control regimes are likely to face in the near future.

International Arms Control Processes

Arms control negotiations occur under different auspices. Bilateral negotiations may be initiated at summits of the nations' leaders or proceed from earlier agreements. Many multilateral negotiations have had their origins or taken place through the Conference on Disarmament (CD). The CD has had several name changes throughout its history. Established in 1960, the assembly was originally called the Ten Nation Disarmament Committee, later expanded to the Eighteen Nation Disarmament Committee (ENDC) in 1962. Further expansions led to the Conference of the Committee on Disarmament in 1969 and finally the CD in 1979. While the CD is independent of the United Nations, strictly speaking, it meets at the UN headquarters in Geneva and has other close connections to the UN. The Conference and its predecessors were created through United Nations resolutions and report to the UN secretary-general.[10] The Conference has a permanent agenda and is supposed to establish a program of work each year. The permanent agenda consists of the following items:

1. Nuclear weapons in all aspects;
2. CW [no longer a component of the agenda since the completion of the CWC on September 3, 1992];
3. Other weapons of mass destruction;
4. Conventional weapons;
5. Reduction of military budgets;
6. Reduction of armed forces;
7. Disarmament and development;
8. Disarmament and international security;
9. Collateral measures; confidence-building measures; effective verification methods in relation to appropriate disarmament measures, acceptable to all parties;
10. Comprehensive program of disarmament, leading to general and complete disarmament under effective international control.[11]

The CD has proved to be a troublesome forum in recent years, recording little success. The Conference operates on the basis of consensus. Because each member state can block a decision, the members of the CD have been unable to agree on a program of work since it completed the negotiations on the CTBT in 1996. Consequently, in recent years, advocates of arms control have worked outside the CD in order to achieve their goals. Both the Ban

Mines Treaty and the Cluster Munitions Treaty were negotiated without the formal involvement of the CD. Patience with the CD is wearing thin among nongovernmental organizations (NGOs), participating nations, and the UN. While there have been some calls for disbanding the CD, it remains the single worldwide negotiating forum for issues of disarmament, and proposals for reforming the body, rather than disbanding it, are likely to receive international support, at least for the time being.

Many, particularly multilateral, arms control negotiations typically progress from working papers that countries submit to the appropriate sponsoring forum, such as the CD, to like-minded governments, or to all interested parties, on various aspects of the negotiations in question to development of the language of the agreement. Each arms control treaty or convention begins with a preamble that sets out the reasons for undertaking the restrictions detailed in the treaty. Following the preamble are several or many articles that specify the obligations that nations that sign and ratify the treaty agree to take on. Arms control treaties can be as short as the Strategic Offensive Reduction Treaty (SORT), less than 500 words and easily fitting on one sheet of paper, or as long as the CWC, which runs to more than 300 pages when its annexes are included. After the language of the agreement is finalized, the treaty is open for signature. After a nation signs a treaty, there is typically an internal process of ratification required to finalize the country's participation in the treaty. Countries that have completed this process are known as member states or states parties of the treaty. States that have signed but have not yet ratified a treaty incur the obligation not to take actions that would undermine the purpose of the treaty. These signatories, of the CWC, for example, are obliged not to use or produce CW because that would undermine the purpose of the treaty, but they are not obligated to establish a national authority to implement other treaty provisions or submit declarations of their CW capacity as required for states that are full parties to the treaty.

After signing a treaty, heads of state take the document back to their capitals for ratification. Treaty ratification procedures vary by country. As required in the U.S. Constitution, the president must submit all treaties to the Senate for its advice and consent. Two-thirds of the senators present must approve a treaty for it to be ratified. After ratification, each country that has signed and ratified a treaty deposits its instruments of ratification with an international office or government specified in the treaty, called a depositary. After a specified period of time or after the number of countries specified in the treaty has deposited their instruments of ratification, the treaty enters into force. When a treaty enters into force, all the obligations set forth in the treaty take legal effect for the states that have signed and ratified the treaty. After entry into force of a treaty, additional states may still become parties to the treaty. States that have signed the treaty can become states parties by ratifying the agreement at any time. States that did not sign the treaty when it was open for signature can accede to the treaty by depositing the appropriate documents with the designated depositary government or international organization. Conversely, states can withdraw from a treaty by following the procedures that are typically set forth in the treaty text. Some treaties are of fixed duration while others are in force indefinitely.

Most arms control agreements share a number of features. All the multilateral arms control treaties discussed in this volume are subject to review at major conferences of member states on a regular basis, typically every five years. All states parties are eligible to participate fully in Review Conferences (RevCons). Additionally, states that have signed but not ratified and states that have not signed may ask to participate as observers. International organizations, such as the International Committee for the Red Cross or the World Health Organization, may participate on a restricted basis. In recent years, NGOs have been permitted to formally address national delegations at some RevCons and have long been allowed or encouraged to observe the public portion of the reviews. States parties, however, are the only participants that can make or block decisions at RevCons.

Preparatory Committees or Conferences, referred to as PrepComs, typically take place approximately six months to one year before a RevCon. PrepComs set the agendas for the RevCons, appoint chairs and cochairs for the main committees of the RevCons, and make decisions on the process of review. NGOs have also participated in PrepComs and other meetings and conferences leading up to the more formal RevCons.

Regarding process, RevCons typically review the operation of the relevant Conventions article by article, considering in detail the language of the treaty. The Conferences review the articles in light of the original treaty language and in view of decisions taken at subsequent RevCons and, if applicable, yearly Conferences of states parties or other formal meetings associated with the treaties. If successful, RevCons issue a Final Declaration or a Final Document at the end of the conference that describes in detail the review, any decisions that delegations made, and actions that the delegations have authorized. Some RevCons, the more recent Non-Proliferation Treaty (NPT) conferences for example, look to the future as well as the past and make recommendations for future action.

Some treaties are also the subject of periodic conferences, or meetings, of states parties that differ from RevCons in several respects. They are typically of shorter duration than review conferences. They can occur on an ad hoc basis or at regular intervals, often yearly. Their agendas differ and are usually more limited than RevCons. Rather than reviewing the entire operation of a treaty, for example, these meetings may discuss only one or two topics relevant to the treaty. A recent yearly meeting of the parties to the Biological Weapons Convention, for example, discussed biosafety and biosecurity, including laboratory safety and security of pathogens and toxins. Participation in these meetings for the most part follows the same rules of procedure as RevCons. At some meetings, governments and NGOs participate in a poster session, highlighting work that they have done in the recent past. Side events, describing new NGO initiatives, scientific breakthroughs, or national legal actions, also take place during RevCons and other official treaty meetings.

Several of the treaties or Conventions discussed in this volume have established formal organizations independent of any member state to implement the requirements that are set forth in the agreements. The International Atomic Energy Agency (IAEA), the Organization for the Prohibition of Chemical Weapons (OPCW), and the Comprehensive Test Ban Treaty Organization (CTBTO) all have dedicated staff and organizational structures that encompass the participation of government representatives, technical professionals, and administrative personnel. Indeed, the CTBTO employs more than 250 people at an annual budget of more than $120 million; however, the treaty has not yet entered into force. In contrast, the Biological Weapons Convention has an implementation support unit of only three people. The Ban Mines Treaty and the Cluster Munitions Treaty do not have dedicated organizations. Each organization has somewhat different responsibilities based on the provisions of the treaties that they have been created to support. Unfortunately, politics sometimes intervenes to prevent the efficient operation of these organizations.

Theory and Law Affecting Arms Control

Several theoretical paradigms and bodies of international law underlie the development and operation of arms control and disarmament. Deterrence theory emerged during the late 1950s and early 1960s, at the height of the Cold War. Proponents of the deterrence theory argue that the practice of deterrence kept the peace between the United States and the Soviet Union and their allies during the Cold War. With nothing less than the survival of the nation at stake, all arms control proposals during the Cold War were considered and evaluated in terms of their effect on security and the status of deterrence. The goal was not so much to limit or abolish weapons but to stabilize the competitive balance and clarify the rules of engagement to reduce the probability that one side or the other would start a nuclear war.

While deterrence theory is fundamental to understanding Cold War era arms control efforts, deterrence alone is not sufficient to explain the complete nonuse of nuclear weapons. Experts on deterrence have also exposed weaknesses in the theory and instances in which deterrence was unsuccessful.

Deterrence theory also has had limited application in regional conflicts.[12] Alternative theories and arguments such as the development of the taboo against nuclear weapons, the role of national leaders, and pure luck are also needed to comprehend this remarkable nonevent. Arms control predates nuclear weapons and encompasses many other instruments of death. Biological and chemical weapons, land mines, and cluster munitions were once an integral part of the military establishments of many countries. The Hague Convention of 1899 and the 1925 Geneva Protocol sought to limit the use of biological and chemical weapons but allowed states to possess them for retaliation or against adversaries who were not part of the agreements. Alternative proposals on land mines and cluster munitions would have placed limits on the types of mines or munitions but not banned their total use and production. In spite of their military utility, however, the very possession and production of all these weapons has been outlawed by international agreement. International humanitarian law has played a significant role in these treaties. This section gives an overview of deterrence theory and alternative explanations of the nonuse of nuclear weapons and discusses the development of international humanitarian law since its origins in the mid-19th century to better understand the forces that inspired and shaped arms control since 1945.

Nuclear Deterrence Theory

Deterrence theory, like arms control, predated nuclear weapons, but the development of the theory and its implementation in practice reached a zenith during the Cold War. During the height of the Cold War, the United States and the Soviet Union were building their nuclear arsenals and, simultaneously, they were aware that such large nuclear weapon stockpiles threatened the very existence of their countries, and perhaps of all life on earth. Thomas Schelling and Morton Halperin, in their seminal work, *Strategy and Arms Control*, describe the central dilemma of nuclear weapons—that, in a nuclear exchange, the advantage clearly went to the state initiating nuclear warfare or the side reacting quickly and strongly to evidence that the other side had launched a nuclear weapon.[13] The ability of each adversary to destroy the other side's retaliatory capability created this advantage. Consequently, both the United States and the Soviet Union shared an interest in avoiding nuclear war, in increasing the time for leaders to make decisions about nuclear war, and in protecting retaliatory forces to reduce or eliminate the advantage in launching first. Reducing the advantage of going first and preserving a robust retaliatory capacity would make each side feel more secure. Thus, arms control theory in the early part of the second half of the 20th century was firmly rooted in a bipolar world with the United States and the Soviet Union as the only truly important players. Safeguarding and improving security were of utmost importance.[14] Deterrence theory called for cooperation among enemies in order to secure and enhance the security of both.

The U.S. nuclear forces were structured and its policy objectives were developed to deter or prevent the Soviet Union from launching a nuclear attack on the United States. If the Soviet Union were to launch such an attack, the United States would have responded with massive retaliation. As a result, the unacceptable consequences of massive retaliation would deter the Soviet Union from a nuclear attack or nuclear war.

A complementary aspect of deterrence theory focused on deterring attacks by conventional forces with the threat of nuclear retaliation. The deterrence effect of the U.S. nuclear forces could extend to the protection of U.S. allies, particularly NATO allies, who were vulnerable to a massive conventional attack by the huge standing armies of the Soviet Union and its Warsaw Pact allies. U.S. policy assured its NATO allies that the United States was willing to use nuclear weapons against such an attack by the Soviet Union on any NATO member, as well as a nuclear attack on any of them. Thus, the United States extended its nuclear umbrella over Western Europe. The purpose of U.S. nuclear doctrine was to deter *any* Soviet attack on its NATO allies. As a consequence of this policy and the vulnerability of Western Europe to the conventional forces of the Soviet Union, the United States has never been willing to publicly renounce the first use of nuclear weapons.

Deterrence depended on the ability of a U.S. retaliatory nuclear attack on the Soviet Union to inflict such devastating consequences that the Soviet Union would not attack the United States or any of its allies. Thus, the United States deployed nuclear missiles on submarines and heavy bombers that would be less vulnerable to a Soviet first strike and would survive to deliver their payload on Soviet cities or infrastructure. The strategy or doctrine of massive retaliation was the nuclear strategy that existed during the administrations of Presidents Truman and Eisenhower, when the United States held a considerable edge over the Soviet Union in nuclear weapons and launch vehicles. The doctrine came to be known in many circles as Mutual Assured Destruction (MAD). Both the United States and the Soviet Union sought nuclear forces capable of surviving a first strike and assuring the destruction of the other, should it be the target of a nuclear first strike.

During the Kennedy administration, especially after the Cuban Missile Crisis, the United States changed its nuclear strategy to a doctrine called Flexible Response. As the name implies, the Flexible Response doctrine was developed in recognition that nuclear war could start with less than a massive first strike and the U.S. president should have a number of options that did not involve destroying cities with nuclear weapons and killing tens of millions of civilians.

Massive retaliation created a paradoxical situation, described by former Secretary of State Henry Kissinger as one where "vulnerability contributed to peace and invulnerability contributed to the risks of war."[15] Nevertheless, Kissinger criticized MAD, arguing that "it is absurd to base the strategy of the West on the credibility of the threat of mutual suicide."[16] In a contrasting point of view, Frank Carlucci, secretary of defense under President Reagan, argued that MAD was never U.S. policy.[17] Carlucci argues that massive retaliation did not equate to mutual assured destruction. The superiority of the U.S. nuclear stockpile in the 1950s and early 1960s meant that the Soviet Union would not be able to assure the destruction of the United States, and the doctrine of Massive Retaliation was replaced by Flexible Response as the Soviet Union began to reach approximate parity with the United States in nuclear weapons.

Deterrence theory is frequently credited with Cold War stability and limited proxy wars during the Cold War era, and with preventing massive destruction on the scale of World Wars I and II, or greater. The United States and the Soviet Union did not go to war over Hungary in 1956, or over the Soviet invasion of Czechoslovakia in 1968, or in Chile in the 1970s. Nor did the United States and China go to war during the Vietnam era. Deterrence is said to be at work in all of these cases.[18] A careful analysis of the role of deterrence, however, paints a more complex picture. Early analysts of deterrence, Alexander George and Richard Smoke, examine numerous cases of the failure of deterrence as early as 1974 and identify a list of conditions that accompanied deterrence failure.[19] Richard Ned Lebow and Janice Stein challenge both supporters and critics of deterrence. They separate the theory of deterrence into several strands: general deterrence, immediate deterrence, and finite deterrence. General deterrence, whether it consists of nuclear or conventional weapons, is meant to preclude a potential adversary from initiating military action because of the reaction that the action is likely to provoke. General deterrence is a long-term strategy of building up one's military and implying retaliation if one's interests are attacked. Immediate deterrence is a short-term strategy of issuing explicit retaliatory threats to halt an imminent attack. It typically comes into play when general deterrence fails.

Lebow and Stein present evidence that the practice of deterrence was, by no means, a resounding success, but rather a very mixed bag. General deterrence, they argue, failed to avert the Cuban Missile Crisis in 1962 and Israel's presumed possession of nuclear weapons did not deter the Egyptian attack on Israel in 1973. Lebow and Stein argue that general deterrence on the part of the United States and the Soviet Union provoked rather than prevented the Cuban crisis. Despite deterrence's role leading up to the confrontation between President Kennedy and Soviet Premier Khrushchev over the placement of Soviet nuclear missiles in Cuba, once the United States discovered the missiles, general deterrence played a role in the leaders' willingness to compromise. Thus, the most serious nuclear crisis during the Cold War ended.[20]

In 1973, general deterrence failed again. Israel's military might did not deter Egypt from initiating war. Indeed, Lebow and Stein state that "Israel's practice of general deterrence . . . convinced Sadat to initiate military action sooner rather than later."[21] Moreover, as the Israeli–Egyptian war played out, there was a possibility that the United States and the Soviet Union might be pulled into the hostilities. Although the UN Security Council passed a ceasefire resolution, largely negotiated between the two superpowers, violations of the ceasefire quickly occurred. The Soviet Union then threatened to intervene in the conflict. The United States responded by raising the defense readiness condition of its armed forces—viewed by the Soviets as an action of escalation. Lebow and Stein argue that Brezhnev never intended to send Soviet troops to support Egypt and the Soviet leadership was "angered, dismayed and humiliated" by the U.S. response. Immediate deterrence—in this case the U.S. move to put its troops on a higher alert status—was irrelevant to the actions of the Soviet Union and "damaged the long-term relationship between the Superpowers." Lebow and Stein conclude that "the strategy of deterrence was self-defeating; it provoked the kind of behavior it was designed to prevent."[22] The Soviet strategic buildup and deployment of missiles in Cuba did not achieve the anticipated restraint on the part of the United States. In contrast, it "intensified American fears of Soviet intentions and capabilities."[23]

To the extent that nuclear deterrence led to superpower stability, it came at a price and had other consequences as well. In the United States alone, the minimum estimated cost of nuclear weapons between 1940 and 1996 was in excess of a whopping $5.4 trillion.[24] Converting to 2010 dollars yields a price tag of more than $7.5 trillion. Add an additional $3.4–70 billion to keep the nuclear weapons development, deployment, and policy secret.[25] More billions are projected to cover the costs of nuclear weapons dismantlement; the care and disposition of fissile material, environmental remediation, and waste management add more than an estimated $300 billion.[26] The monetary cost of other countries' nuclear weapons programs has not been estimated with as much precision as the U.S. cost.

U.S. and Soviet reliance on the deterrence doctrine also contributed to nuclear proliferation. Despite Chinese and Soviet cooperation in the early stages of China's nuclear weapons program, China, a historic enemy of Russia in spite of their related Communist ideologies, developed nuclear weapons at least in part to deter the Soviet Union from any designs it might have on China.[27] Meanwhile, many in India defend its nuclear weapons program as a response to China's nuclear weapons and its unresolved border dispute with China. And Pakistan believed that it needed nuclear weapons to deter India.

Deterrence theory, moreover, is not an adequate explanation for many of the occasions when nuclear weapons might have been used, but were not. Nina Tannenwald makes a strong and convincing case that a so-far robust taboo has arisen against the use of nuclear weapons since the bombings of Hiroshima and Nagasaki laid bare their terrifying power and lasting effects. The existence of the taboo, in tandem with deterrence, Tannenwald argues, does a better job of explaining the nonuse of nuclear weapons than deterrence alone.

There are several flaws in the argument that deterrence, the one theory fits all situations aspect, explains the nonuse of nuclear weapons. Many instances exist when nuclear weapons might have been used and were not that are not explained by deterrence theory. In addition to the examples of the Cuban Missile Crisis and the 1973 Arab–Israeli war, during the war on the Korean Peninsula in the 1950s, the U.S. nuclear arsenal did not deter North Korea from invading South Korea. Similarly, U.S. nuclear power did not prevent China from entering the war on behalf of North Korea. Moreover, the United States did not use its nuclear weapons in the Korean conflict even though neither North Korea nor China possessed a nuclear capability that could deter the United States. The United Kingdom's nuclear arsenal did not deter Argentina from taking possession of the Falklands/Malvinas Islands in 1982. Presumably, the Argentine leadership did not believe the United Kingdom would use nuclear weapons to defend the small islands, and indeed the United Kingdom did not. U.S. threats to come to the aid of Kuwait and the U.S. nuclear arsenal did not compel or persuade Iraq to withdraw from Kuwait in 1991. Some explanation besides nuclear deterrence was likely at play in the Vietnam War, in the Soviet War in Afghanistan, and in the U.S. invasions of Afghanistan and Iraq. In all of the cases, the nuclear powers did not use nuclear weapons and deterrence does not do a convincing job of explaining nonuse.

The mere fact that no nuclear weapons state has used these weapons that are at their disposal could be said to constitute a de facto post-WWII norm against the first use of nuclear weapons. Tannenwald argues that societal pressures, power politics, individual leadership, and a custom of no first use over time have all played a historical role in the development of the no first use taboo. Thomas Schelling devoted his Nobel Prize lecture in 2005 to what he calls the "most spectacular event of the past half century": the nonuse of nuclear weapons. Schelling traces the development of de facto moral aversion to nuclear weapons policy from the early 1950s, eventually achieving "the accumulating weight of tradition against nuclear use." Schelling regards the existence of this taboo or tradition as instrumental in the nonuse of nuclear weapons on several occasions and regards the taboo as an asset to be treasured, "cherished, enhanced and protected."[28]

Acknowledging the existence and operation of a nuclear weapons taboo, we need to see how the taboo has become institutionalized in policy. China and India have declaratory policies in place, stating that they will not use nuclear weapons first.[29]

Most of the other states that possess nuclear weapons, including the United States, United Kingdom, Russia, and France have declared policies that are consistent with their commitments under the Nuclear NPT—that they will not use nuclear weapons against nonnuclear weapons states and that they will use nuclear weapons first only if attacked or invaded by a state that possess nuclear weapons.[30] Pakistan has not publicly declared its nuclear policy, but is believed to have a policy similar to that of the United States and other NPT nuclear weapon states. That is, Pakistan would not use nuclear weapons against nonnuclear weapons states and would initiate the use of nuclear weapons only if invaded or attacked.[31]

Israel, because it has never explicitly confirmed or denied that it possesses nuclear weapons, has no publicly declared nuclear policies. To do so would be an admission that it possesses nuclear weapons. North Korea, however, shortly after its most recent nuclear test in 2009, stated that its nuclear weapons would be "a merciless offensive means to deal a just retaliatory strike to those who touch the country's dignity and sovereignty even a bit," according to the United Kingdom's *The Independent*.[32]

With the exception of North Korea, whose bellicose rhetoric could well be primarily for domestic consumption, the moral revulsion against the use of nuclear weapons has grown in strength and geographic reach over time. Immediately following WWII, states may have pessimistically believed that nuclear weapons would be used in all instances where nuclear armed states had an opportunity to do so. Moral revulsion to other weapons and tactics had certainly been shattered by the strategic bombing and firebombing of cities and troops.[33] Conversely, the taboo against the use of CW was resurrected after WWI. The major belligerents did not use CW in WWII. Following the use of chemical weapons in the Iraq–Iran war of the 1980s, the taboo against such weapons was enshrined and institutionalized in the 1993 Chemical Weapons Convention. Thus, the nuclear taboo may be considered robust by the standard that it has never been violated since its inception. By the standard of declaratory policy and institutionalization, however, it remains in need of enhancement. The nuclear weapons states that have retained the right to use nuclear weapons first, if attacked or invaded, could enhance this precious asset by carefully considering when if ever they would seriously consider the first use of nuclear weapons rather than their often formidable conventional weaponry.

The complete nonuse of nuclear weapons can also be explained, in part, by luck. Numerous incidents during the Cold War could have led to the launching of nuclear weapons based on faulty information from warning systems, communication breakdowns, navigation errors, or incorrect interpretation of what may have originally appeared to be suspicious activity. Luck may also have played a role in the absence of any terrorist group successfully acquiring a nuclear weapon or sufficient weapons-grade nuclear material to construct a weapon.

The near misses include the following. First, in 1968, a B-52 bomber carrying a nuclear payload crashed near Thule Air Base in Greenland. The crew bailed out of the plane after a fire in the cockpit could not be contained. The detonators, containing radioactive plutonium, exploded, but the nuclear weapons contained a safety feature that prevented them from exploding. Although Strategic Air Command personnel responded to the incident by lauding the safety of the nuclear weapon, author Scott Sagan provides evidence that "there were at least three different ways in which the crash of theB-52 on the Thule monitor mission could have inadvertently produced confirmed, but false, warnings that a Soviet attack had been launched."[34] Second, during the Cuban missile crisis, a Soviet satellite exploded. In the United States, some interpreted the explosion as a nuclear missile attack. Third, in 1995, the Russian personnel working with its early warning system informed their superiors of an unidentified missile launch. Norway had appropriately notified the Russian Defense Ministry that it was launching a missile carrying scientific instruments, but the information did not reach those on duty at the early warning station. The Norwegian missile had the earmarks of a U.S. submarine–launched nuclear missile and Russian President Yeltsin activated the electronic device, the nuclear football, allowing him instant online communication with top-level military advisors for the first time in his presidency. Obviously, Russia did not order a missile strike, and once again there are different interpretations of the severity of the near miss.[35] After analyzing numerous incidents, Sagan concludes that "nuclear weapons have been far less safe than has been previously recognized."[36] Nuclear arms control measures during this period generally reflected the need to achieve stable deterrence. Sagan, among others, however, questions the future role of deterrence. He argues that "the attraction some feel for nuclear weapons as an ultimate deterrent must be tempered by a much greater awareness of the risk of accidents. And those who predict that nuclear weapons can be managed safely indefinitely into the future should have to prove their case and not simply refer back to a perfect safety record that never really existed."

The role of deterrence theory has different implications in the 21st century than it did during the Cold War. Will deterrence prevent escalation of Indian–Pakistani conflicts? What role will deterrence play between Israel and Iran if Iran is successful in developing a nuclear weapon? Will other nations in East Asia feel a compelling urge to develop or acquire nuclear weapons to deter a nuclear armed North Korea? And, will the nuclear taboo and luck continue to hold?

International Humanitarian Law

In parallel with security theories that primarily make the case for restraint or limits on nuclear weapons in support of stable deterrence, other arguments for restricting or banning other weapons have emphasized the inhumanity of the use of certain weapons. In his examination of the humanitarian basis for arms control, sociologist Brian Rappert asks the fundamental question, "On what basis then, do individuals identify particular forms of inflicting death and injury as unacceptable whereas others are deemed permissible or at least tolerable?"[37]

At least a partial answer to that question lies in the development of international humanitarian law, also known as the Law of Armed Conflict. International humanitarian law is not limited to restrictions on weapons and methods of warfare. This body of law encompasses many other features, including the definition of combatants, the treatment of the wounded and prisoners of war, the protection of civilian populations, and the protection and disposition of cultural property. Only those portions of international humanitarian law that concern weapons and the methods of warfare are discussed herein. International humanitarian law has been developed and refined over the course of a number of major conferences that have produced several Conventions and Protocols. The most important of these are the Hague Peace Conferences of 1899 and 1907, the Geneva Diplomatic Conference of 1949, and the International Law Convention in New York in 1977.[38]

In 1868, an International Commission met to consult on exploding bullets that had recently been developed. In the text of the resulting 1868 Declaration of St. Petersburg, an international treaty, the Commission "by common agreement fixed the technical limits at which the necessities of war ought to yield to the requirements of humanity."[39] The argument contained in the Declaration stated that weapons that "uselessly aggravate the sufferings of disabled men, or render their death inevitable . . . would be contrary to the laws of humanity."[40] Although the Declaration banned the use of only a single type of ammunition, its supporting argument set the stage for the elimination of entire classes of weapons to follow.

The first Hague Peace Conference of 1899 adopted a Convention with Respect to the Laws and Customs of War on Land. The prohibition of poison or CW dates from this conference. The parties agreed "to abstain from the use of projectiles the sole object of which is the diffusion of asphyxiating or deleterious gases."[41] During WWI, the German army exploited loopholes in the Hague Convention to initiate gas warfare without using projectiles, and the Entente Powers, principally Great Britain and France, soon retaliated in kind with CW of their own as did the United States when it entered the war.

Following the extensive carnage in the war to end all wars, the Geneva Conference in 1925 established the Protocol for the Prohibition of the Use in War of Asphyxiating, Poisonous or Other Gases, and of Bacteriological Methods of Warfare. Like the St. Petersburg Declaration, the prohibition of chemical and biological weapons was based on abhorrence of the weapons themselves rather than any arguments of security or military utility or lack thereof. The preamble of the Protocol states that, "the use in war of asphyxiating, poisonous or other gases, and of all analogous liquids, materials or devices, has been justly condemned by the general opinion of the civilized world."[42]

With some exceptions, the ban on the use of chemical and biological weapons largely held during WWII. Nevertheless, a ban on the use of chemical and biological weapons was deemed inadequate without a more comprehensive prohibition of their development, production, possession, and transfer. In 1972, international negotiators completed the text of the Convention on the Prohibition of the Development, Production and Stockpiling of Bacteriological (Biological) and Toxin Weapons and on their Destruction. The drafters of the Convention once again referred to the inhumanity of biological and toxin weapons. The preamble to the Convention states that the parties to the treaty are "[d]etermined, for the sake of all mankind, to exclude completely the possibility of bacteriological (biological) agents and toxins being used as weapons" and "convinced that such use would be repugnant to the conscience of mankind."[43] This Convention was the first to outlaw the very possession of an entire class of weapons, but it was not the last. Notably, it does so without regard to whether possession of such weapons might deter other nations from obtaining or using such weapons, although there is evidence that the norm against the weapons has, so far, come to outweigh considerations of military utility. January 1993 marked the completion of the Convention on the Prohibition of the Development, Production, Stockpiling and Use of Chemical Weapons and on Their Destruction. Like the Biological Weapons Convention, this treaty sought to exclude completely the possibility of chemicals being used as weapons and referred to the 1925 Geneva Protocol, which had first singled out their inhumanity.[44]

The Ban Mines Treaty, completed in 1997, contained even more explicit language in its preamble that described the effects of antipersonnel land mines: "Determined to put an end to the suffering and casualties caused by anti-personnel mines, that kill or maim hundreds of people every week, mostly innocent and defenseless civilians and especially children."[45] The text of the 2008 Convention on Cluster Munitions expanded its humanitarian plea in its preamble. It contains three clauses related to the humanitarian concerns in its preamble, namely, "*Deeply concerned* that civilian populations and individual civilians continue to bear the brunt of armed conflict, *Determined* to put an end for all time to the suffering and casualties caused by cluster munitions at the time of their use, when they fail to function as intended or when they are abandoned, *Concerned* that cluster munition remnants kill or maim civilians, including women and children."[46]

Thus, international humanitarian law has had a major impact on arms control negotiations, the treaties that have resulted from these negotiations, and the implementation of those treaties. It is important to note here that the military effectiveness of biological and chemical weapons, land mines, and cluster munitions has not been questioned. All of these weapons have been significant components of military arsenals and all, except biological weapons, have been used on a wide scale. Their wholesale prohibition is a triumph of humanitarian considerations over military utility.

Arms Control in the United States

Although this volume presents points of view other than those of the United States, the author is most familiar with the arms control strategy of the United States. Each sovereign state that engages in arms control negotiations and makes decisions to sign, ratify, or accede to arms control agreements undergoes an internal process and has developed internal strategies to enhance its security through arms control. The following description of arms control in the United States is presented as an example, not as a model.

Throughout the Cold War, U.S. foreign policy objectives were relatively consistent and had wide bipartisan support, as hard as that may be to imagine today. U.S. priorities in arms control were first and foremost to maintain supremacy over, or parity with, the Soviet Union, regarding nuclear weapons and delivery vehicles and second, to the extent possible, contain the proliferation of nuclear weapons to other states. Successive U.S. governments sought to protect U.S. national security through deterrence. Negotiations that took place during the Cold War and agreements that were finalized were debated with an eye toward the U.S.–Soviet rivalry. The two nonnuclear treaties that were negotiated during the Cold War, the Biological and Toxin Weapons Convention of 1972 (BWC) and the Chemical Weapons Convention of 1993 (CWC) were also products of Cold War strategy on the part of the two superpowers. These multilateral conventions were completed only after the United States and the Soviet Union agreed on all relevant provisions. Other negotiating parties were influential, to be sure, but neither the United States nor the Soviet Union/Russia would have become a party to the treaty without the participation of the other.

The United States has participated in a host of arms control negotiations on nuclear weapons and other armaments. Many of these negotiations led to new treaties and obligations, such as the BWC, the CWC, and the 1990 Treaty on Conventional Armed Forces in Europe. Other negotiations have led to treaties that the United States has signed but not ratified, most notably the Comprehensive Test Ban Treaty (CTBT). Neither the United States nor the Russian Federation is party to the Ban Mines Treaty and the Cluster Munitions Treaty. Yet, close allies of the United States—the United Kingdom, Canada, and Australia—are parties to all three. Finally, some negotiations, such as the Fissile Materials Cutoff Treaty, are much discussed, but have not as yet entered into formal negotiations.

The negotiating of the three post–Cold War multilateral treaties, the Ban Mines Treaty, the CTBT, and the Cluster Munitions Treaty, differed greatly from the Cold War treaties that preceded them. The Ban Mines Treaty negotiations and the Cluster Munitions Treaty advocates abandoned the CD altogether as a negotiating forum. Moreover, the rationales for these treaties did not rely on standard security-based arguments. Rather, proponents of the agreements emphasized human rights and humanitarian benefits of outlawing these indiscriminate weapons.

The Executive Branch

The U.S. president, through the executive branch of government, directs arms control policy. Article II Section 2 of the Constitution of the United States grants the president the power "by and with the Advice and Consent of the Senate, to make Treaties." The Executive branch of government negotiates and signs treaties, and the Senate ratifies them.

Throughout the latter half of the 20th century, arms control had strong and sustained bi-partisan support. All U.S. presidents from Kennedy to Clinton negotiated and signed significant arms control agreements. Arguably, the administration of President George W. Bush reversed that trend. Bush withdrew the United States from the Anti-Ballistic Missile Treaty, opposed ratification of the CTBT, and did not negotiate any major treaties. The one treaty that Bush did negotiate, SORT, also known as the Moscow Treaty, did not eliminate or reduce any actual weapons; it merely promised to remove them from operational deployment. The agreement did not require the destruction of any weapons. The weapons removed from deployment could be returned to stockpiles. The Obama administration has returned the United States to the arms control fold. President Obama negotiated and signed the New Start Treaty, secured its ratification in the U.S. Senate, and has pledged to submit the CTBT to the Senate for ratification.

After the Soviet Union detonated its first nuclear weapon in 1949, arms control became a much higher priority in the United States than it had been before. While the U.S. nuclear arsenal was superior to that of the Soviet Union in the early years of the nuclear age, that superiority eventually waned. Arms control policy was directed from the White House during the Eisenhower administration. President Kennedy, however, established an independent agency, the Arms Control and Disarmament Agency (ACDA), to provide research and advice to the president on all arms control issues, to advocate for and negotiate arms control agreements, and to monitor compliance with treaties. ACDA's director reported directly to the president. Throughout the next roughly 35 years, ACDA operated independently, advocating for the Nuclear NPT when the State department opposed it, for example.[47] ACDA took the lead in negotiating a series of nuclear and nonnuclear treaties including bilateral nuclear treaties with the Soviet Union, the multilateral Nuclear NPT, and the multilateral treaties banning the possession and production of biological and chemical weapons. Yet, the ratification of the CWC led to the demise of ACDA as a strong independent voice for arms control.

One of the last actions of President George H. W. Bush was to sign the CWC on January 13, 1993. Despite support by President Bush and members of his administration, President Clinton faced considerable opposition within the Senate to ratification of the Convention. In particular, Senator Jesse Helms, as chairman of the Senate Foreign Relations Committee, was able to use bureaucratic maneuvering to keep the ratifying legislation in committee and delay a Senate vote on ratification. In negotiations with the Clinton administration, Helms agreed to allow the bill out of committee only if ACDA would be incorporated into the State Department. Since the deal was made in 1997, arms control policy in the executive branch is under the purview of the Under Secretary of State for Arms Control and International Security. To the extent that arms control is a tool of international diplomacy, it makes sense to have arms control policy developed within the State Department. On the other hand, the loss of an independent voice for arms control without direct access to the president indicates a lower political priority for arms control.

Congress

Although the Senate has the most direct Congressional role in arms control policy, nearly all arms control treaties submitted to the Senate in the second half of the 20th century have been ratified by strong, if not overwhelming, majorities.[48] There are important exceptions to this trend, however. President Carter was unable to secure ratification of the SALT II nuclear weapons treaty in 1979 after the Soviet Union invaded Afghanistan, and withdrew the treaty from consideration before a vote was taken. In 1999, the Senate, on a strongly partisan vote—48 in favor, and 51 opposed—rejected ratification of the CTBT. The Senate rejection of the CTBT was a sharp break from the past in which it had approved every previous security-related agreement since 1925 when the Senate did not ratify the 1925 Geneva Protocol banning the first use of chemical and biological weapons. The Senate did not ratify the Protocol until 50 years later, in 1975.

The advice and consent language of the section of the Constitution quoted previously has sometimes been interpreted by members of the Senate to mean that the president is obligated to inform and seek the advice of members of the Senate while treaties are under negotiation. Various presidents have done so to a greater or lesser degree. The Senate Foreign Relations Committee has principal responsibility for arms control. The Committee chair and the ranking minority member are typically quite instrumental in commenting on and, at times, shaping arms control policy and agreements. In addition, most arms control measures require implementing legislation that embeds treaties in domestic law. Such legislation requires passage by both houses of Congress.[49]

Other Arms Control Policy Actors

The military and intelligence communities are two additional influential voices in developing arms control policy within the U.S. government. Arms control policy has a direct effect on the military and therefore the military has a direct interest in influencing policy. The Department of Defense (DOD) often has supporters within it that are invested in particular weapons programs that arms control policy makers elsewhere in government may seek to limit or eliminate. Arms control has the potential to decrease DOD budgets and staffing. At the same time, DOD civilian and military leadership have understood the importance of halting the nuclear arms race and restraining the proliferation of nuclear and other weapons of mass destruction. Thus, while influencing the shape of arms control agreements, they have usually not adamantly opposed their negotiation or sought to block Senate passage.[50] Both the military and the intelligence communities have responsibilities to monitor compliance with arms control agreements. Members of each group advise the administration and testify before the Senate on the capabilities of their organizations to effectively monitor compliance with specific provisions of treaties.

As is appropriate in a functioning democracy, both the executive and legislative branches of government are influenced by other societal actors in developing arms control policy. Defense contractors and other industry representatives play a role. The Chemical Manufacturers Association, for example, was an important supporter of the CWC and frequently advised members of the U.S. negotiating team. Civil society organizations can also influence arms control policy through research and advocacy. The Nuclear Weapons Freeze Movement is an example of one such group. The Nuclear Freeze Movement swayed public opinion and candidates for office in the United States and around the world.[51] Staff members of research institutions such as the Brookings Institution or the Heritage Foundation often lend their voices in support of or opposition to specific arms control initiatives.

The making of U.S. arms control policy is a complicated endeavor involving numerous actors and institutions. The influence of all these actors as well as the press and the public help shape the U.S. arms control agenda and how that agenda is implemented through executive and legislative actions.[52]

The arms control policies of other states may be similar or quite different from that of the United States. States that are controlled by totalitarian governments may have much simpler internal policy-making apparatuses. Parliamentary democracies may face many fewer difficulties in treaty ratification. In Canada, for example, treaty ratification is controlled completely by the executive branch of government. In the United States, treaty ratification is laid down in the Constitution, while in other states, such as Israel, it has developed through custom rather than law.[53] Multiparty democracies may find it especially difficult to assemble a coalition to support various arms control proposals.

Overview

Chapter 2 of the volume explains the nuclear arms race between the United States and the Soviet Union and efforts to restrain it after the first use of nuclear weapons in Hiroshima in 1945. It describes the bilateral agreements between these two superpowers during the Cold War and moves on to explain treaties between the United States and the Russian Federation that further reduce their nuclear arsenals. The chapter describes how and why breakthroughs occurred and instances where other events blocked progress during negotiations. In addition to the series of treaties that constrained the size and make-up of nuclear forces, the chapter also looks at the Intermediate Range Nuclear Forces Treaty that eliminated an entire class of missiles carrying nuclear weapons. Finally, the chapter discusses the Anti-Ballistic Missiles Treaty that restricted defensive systems that would block in-coming missiles and the U.S. withdrawal from that agreement.

Chapter 3 focuses on efforts to eliminate the proliferation of nuclear weapons through the Nuclear NPT and the efforts to prevent nuclear testing. The NPT, the cornerstone of antiproliferation efforts, is an agreement between the five states that had exploded nuclear devices before January 1,

1967, and all other states, with three exceptions—India, Israel, and Pakistan. These three states, as well as North Korea, which withdrew from the treaty in 2003, exploded nuclear devices after 1967 and possess nuclear arsenals. The implementation of the NPT has encountered serious difficulties and major successes. Several review conferences of the agreement have failed to reach agreement or make any decisions. Nevertheless, the states parties to the treaty agreed to extend the treaty indefinitely in 1995, after it had been in operation for 25 years. Several states with nascent nuclear programs abandoned efforts to acquire nuclear weapons and joined the treaty as nonnuclear weapon states. Soviet republics that inherited nuclear weapons from the Soviet Union relinquished those nuclear weapons and also became treaty parties.

The chapter also discusses grave challenges to the NPT including compliance concerns, and the failure of the nuclear weapon states to disarm, as called for in Article VI of the treaty. While the United States argues that its reductions in nuclear weapons and delivery vehicles constitute a continuous and good faith effort to reduce its nuclear arsenal in concert with the Russian Federation, several nonnuclear weapons states do not interpret those actions as sufficient to comply with their NPT obligations.

Nuclear testing is considered to be an essential step in acquiring nuclear weapons and several treaties have addressed the restriction or abolition of nuclear testing—the Limited (or Partial) Test Ban Treaty of 1963 and the Comprehensive Test Ban Treaty (CTBT) of 1996. The first agreement banned what could be detected at the time—nuclear tests above ground and elsewhere, but allowed underground testing. In many instances, underground testing could not be distinguished from seismic activity. The Comprehensive Test Ban has been described as the longest sought and hardest fought for arms control treaty in history. Completing a test ban treaty was a condition that many nonnuclear weapon states imposed on the nuclear weapon states in order to secure indefinite extension of the NPT. Despite widespread support, Egypt, India, Indonesia, Iran, Israel, North Korea, Pakistan, and the United States have not ratified the CTBT and its terms require that each of these states ratify the agreement before it enters into force.

Chapter 4 moves on to the two treaties that ban the other weapons of potential mass destruction—chemical and biological weapons. The 1972 Biological Weapons Convention (BWC) was the first international treaty to ban the possession of an entire class of weapons. The chapter explains the negotiation and implementation of the Convention and efforts to address the absence of any significant verification provisions within it. The terms of the BWC contained obligations to negotiate a ban on CW. Though negotiations floundered for many years, the end of the Cold War and with it Soviet opposition to onsite inspection of chemical facilities paved the way for the 1993 Chemical Weapons Convention (CWC). Both treaties have confronted challenges to complete an effective implementation. The parties to the BWC have struggled with egregious violations of the treaty by the former Soviet Union and the absence of compliance and verification measures to detect and respond to violations. The negotiators of the CWC underestimated the time it would take to safely destroy chemical weapon stockpiles, and the United States and Russia have both exceeded the treaty deadlines, have been granted extensions, and have not met the new extended 2012 deadlines for stockpile destruction. Yet, the norms enshrined in the Conventions have taken deep root. There has been no confirmation that any state has used chemical or biological weapons against another state since the treaties went into effect and membership in both has grown over time.

Chapter 5 analyzes the processes that culminated in the treaties to ban land mines and cluster munitions. The negotiation procedures for these instruments were a sharp departure from previous arms control negotiations. Each negotiation limited participation to those countries that firmly supported the principle of an absolute ban on the production, acquisition, and use of their respective weapons. States that preferred less a restrictive covenant were not allowed to delay or block consensus. Active participation by NGOs in the negotiation process was another marked difference from previous negotiations. Furthermore, an independent foundation of experts is monitoring compliance with the Mine Ban Treaty and has met with considerable success. Similar mechanisms are in place for the Convention on Cluster Munitions (CCM). The CCM entered into force in 2010, and this alternative to elaborate international organizations responsible for monitoring compliance is worth continued attention.

Chapter 6, the conclusion, attempts to draw cross-cutting themes from the history and analysis presented in the earlier chapters. The chapter begins with the role of political opportunity in advancing and blocking arms control initiatives. It continues with a discussion of how distinct treaties influence the negotiation and implementation of other agreements. The role of verification in the various arms control regimes is discussed, as is the role of advances in science and technology. The chapter also addresses the enduring role of arms control in international relations and the expanding role of civil society and even business in the work of arms control. The chapter concludes with a discussion of the persistent challenges that several of the arms control agreements share, such as the quest for universal agreements.

Conclusion

Arms control treaties, their negotiation, and implementation are a central aspect of international security. Although nation states have sought to eliminate or outlaw the use of particular weapons for centuries, this book focuses on bilateral and multilateral efforts to achieve security through negotiated agreements between potential adversaries or among the community of nations since the dawn of the nuclear age. Having survived the end of the Cold War, arms control at the beginning of the 21st century has seen a new bilateral nuclear weapons agreement between the United States and Russia. The New START Treaty follows in the path of earlier bilateral agreements that have steadily diminished the size of U.S. and Russian nuclear stockpiles. At the same time, a new agreement banning the possession and use of cluster munitions has recently been completed and entered into force. The CCM, as well as the MBT, which preceded it at the close of the 20th century, has followed a new course in arms control. These agreements usher in a new era in the restriction or elimination of weapons not only because of their role in national security, but also because of the unacceptable harm that the weapons inflict on civilians.

The future of arms control, like the future of any phenomenon, is unpredictable. Yet, the momentum behind the practice is likely to continue to see innovation and progress. Nevertheless, each arms control regime, whether regarding nuclear, chemical, biological, or conventional weapons, faces serious challenges to its longevity and successful and complete implementation. The course of international politics will continue to have a profound effect on arms control and international conflict.

Notes

1. The number from 2010 is from *Landmine and Cluster Munition Monitor, 2011*, http://www.the-monitor.org/index.php/publications/display?url=lm/2011/es/Casualties_and_Victim_Assistance.html http://www.the-monitor.org/index.php/publications/display?url=lm/2011/es/Casualties_and_Victim_Assistance.html. The earlier statistic is taken from Maxwell A. Cameron, Robert J. Lawson, and Brian W. Tomlin (eds.), *To Walk without Fear, the Global Movement to Ban Landmines* (Toronto: Oxford University Press, 1998), 2.

2. See Daniel Barenblatt, *A Plague upon Humanity: The Hidden History of Japan's Biological Warfare Program* (New York: HarperCollins, 2004).

3. "Chemical Weapons," Global Security.org, last modified July 24, 2011, http://www.globalsecurity.org/wmd/world/iran/cw.htm.

4. For a comprehensive treatment of all 20th-century arms control agreements, see Jozef Goldblat, *Arms Control: The New Guide to Negotiations and Agreements* (Oslo: International Peace Research Institute, 2002).

5. Hedley Bull, *The Control of the Arms Race: Disarmament and Arms Control in the Missile Age* (New York: Frederick A. Praeger Publishers, 1961), 4–5.

6. Thomas C. Schelling and Morton H. Halperin, *Strategy and Arms Control* (New York: The Twentieth Century Fund, 1961), 2.

7. Jeffrey A. Larsen (ed.), *Arms Control: Cooperative Security in a Changing Environment* (Boulder, CO: Lynne Rienner Publishers, 2002), 2.

8. Stephen D. Krasner (ed.), *International Regimes* (Ithaca, NY: Cornell University Press, 1983).

9. "Entry into force" is the technical term that describes the date that the terms of a treaty take legal effect on the parties that have signed and ratified the treaty.

10. For a longer explanation, see The Acronym Institute for Disarmament Diplomacy, "Conference on Disarmament," 2004, http://www.acronym.org.uk/un/aboutcd.htm.

11. United Nations Institute for Disarmament Research and the Geneva Forum "The Conference on Disarmament and Negative Security Assurances," March 1, 2011, http://unidir.org/pdf/activites/pdf3-act593.pdf.

12. McGeorge Bundy, *Danger and Survival: Choices about the Bomb in the First Fifty Years* (New York: Random House, 1988), 517–42.

13. Schelling and Halperin, *Strategy and Arms Control*, 9.

14. Bull, *The Control of the Arms Race*.

15. Henry Kissinger, "NATO: The Next Thirty Years," *Survival*, November/December 1979, 265.

16. Ibid.

17. "U.S. Secretary of Defense Frank Carlucci on Nuclear Deterrence and Strategic Defenses January 17, 1989," http://nuclearfiles.org/menu/key-issues/nuclear-weapons/history/cold-war/strategy/report-carlucci-deterrence_1989–01–17.htm.

18. Christopher H. Achen and Duncan Snidal, "Rational Deterrence Theory and Comparative Case Studies," *World Politics* 41, no. 2 (1989): 161.

19. Alexander L. George and Richard Smoke, *Deterrence in American Foreign Policy: Theory and Practice* (New York: Columbia University Press, 1974).

20. Richard Ned Lebow and Janice Gross Stein, "Deterrence and the Cold War," *Political Science Quarterly* 110, no. 2 (1995): 162–63.

21. Ibid, 163.

22. Ibid, 180.

23. Ibid, 178.

24. Stephen I Schwartz (ed.), *Atomic Audit: The Costs and Consequences of U.S. Nuclear Weapons since 1940* (Washington, DC: Brookings Institution Press, 1998), 4.

25. Ibid, 433.

26. Ibid, xxii.

27. Bundy, *Danger and Survival*, 525–35.

28. Thomas C. Schelling, "An Astonishing 60 Years: The Legacy of Hiroshima," *Proceedings of the National Academy of Sciences of the United States of America* 103, no. 16 (2006): 6093, http://www.pnas.org/content/103/16/6089.full.pdf+html.

29. Ministry of Foreign Affairs, India, "Address by Foreign Secretary at NDC on 'Challenges in India's Foreign Policy,'" November 19, 2010, http://www.mea.gov.in/mystart.php?id=530116703.

30. "No First Use Policy of the Declared Nuclear Weapons States," April 5–6, 1995, http://www.nuclearfiles.org/menu/key-issues/nuclear-weapons/issues/policies/no-first-use_1995–04–05.htm.

31. Ali Ahmed, "Pakistan's 'First Use' in Prescriptive," last modified May 12, 2011, http://www.idsa.in/idsacomments/PakistansFirstUseinPerspective_aahmed_120511.

32. Associated Press, "North Korea Would Use Nuclear Weapons in a 'Merciless Offensive,'" *The Independent*, June 9, 2009, http://www.independent.co.uk/news/world/asia/north-korea-would-use-nuclear-weapons-in-a-merciless-offensive-1700590.html.

33. The United States used napalm extensively in Vietnam and the United States used firebombs with a different fuel mixture against Iraqi troops in 2003. Andrew Buncombe, "US admits it used napalm bombs in Iraq" *The Independent*, August 10, 2003. Global Security.org, http://www.globalsecurity.org/org/news/2003/030810-napalm-iraq01.htm.

34. Scott D. Sagan, *The Limits of Safety: Organization, Accidents, and Nuclear Weapons* (Princeton, NJ: Princeton University Press, 1993), 181.

35. See Geoffrey Fordan, "Reducing a Common Dange: Improving Russia's Early-Warning System," *Policy Analysis*, no. 399: 6–7, http://www.cato.org/pubs/pas/pa399.pdf and Public Broadcasting Service, "A Close Call: The Norwegian Rocket Incident," http://www.pbs.org/wgbh/pages/frontline/shows/russia/closecall/.

36. Sagan, *The Limits of Safety*, 264.

37. Brian Rappert, *Controlling the Weapons of War: Politics, Persuasion, and the Prohibition of Inhumanity* (London: Routledge, 2006), 5.

38. Frits Kalshoven and Liesbeth Zegveld, *Constraints on the Waging of War: An Introduction to International Humanitarian Law* (Geneva: International Committee on Red Cross, 2001), http://www.loc.gov/rr/frd/Military_Law/pdf/Constraints-waging-war.pdf.

39. The International Committee of the Red Cross, "Declaration Renouncing the Use, in Time of War, of Explosive Projectiles under 400 Grammes Weight," *International Humanitarian Law—Treaties & Documents*, http://www.icrc.org/ihl.nsf/FULL/130?OpenDocument.

40. Ibid.

41. The International Committee of the Red Cross, *International Humanitarian Law—Treaties & Documents, Declaration (IV, 2) Concerning Asphyxiating Gases*, The Hague, July 29, 1899, http://www.icrc.org/ihl.nsf/FULL/165?OpenDocument.

42. "Protocol for the Prohibition of the Use in War of Asphyxiating, Poisonous or Other Gases, and of Bacteriological Methods of Warfare," June 17, 1925, http://www.un.org/disarmament/WMD/Bio/pdf/Status_Protocol.pdf.

43. "Convention on the Prohibition of the Development, Production and Stockpiling of Bacteriological (Biological) and Toxin Weapons and on Their Destruction," April 10, 1972, http://www.un.org/disarmament/WMD/Bio.

44. Organization for the Prohibition of Chemical Weapons, "Convention on the Prohibition of the Development, Production, Stockpiling and the use of Chemical Weapons and on Their Destruction," http://www.opcw.org/index.php?eID=dam_frontend_push&docID=6357.

45. "Convention on the Prohibition of the Use, Stockpiling, Production and Transfer of Anti-Personnel Mines and on Their Destruction," September 18, 1997, http://www.un.org/Depts/mine/UNDocs/ban_trty.htm.

46. "Convention on Cluster Munitions," last modified May 30, 1998, http://www. clusterconvention.org/.

47. Ambassador Thomas Graham Jr., "A Return to Arms Control and Non-Proliferation Process," Testimony before the Subcommittee on Oversight of Government Management, the Federal Workforce, and the District of Columbia, Committee on Homeland Security and Government Organization, U.S. Senate, May 15, 2009, http://hsgac.senate.gov/public/_files/GrahamTestimony051508.pdf.

48. Of major arms control treaties ratified by the Senate from 1963 until 2000, only the Chemical Weapons Convention, although ratified by a comfortable 74–29 margin, received less than 80 percent support from the Senate.

49. For a longer discussion of Congress' role in arms control see Jennifer E. Sims, "The Arms Control Process: The U.S. Domestic Context," in *Arms Control: Toward the 21st Century*, ed. Jeffrey A. Larsen and Gregory J. Rattray (Boulder, CO: Lynne Rienner Publishers, 1996), 65–67.

50. An exception to this general rule was opposition to a Comprehensive Test Ban by the Joint Chiefs of Staff, see Sims, "The Arms Control Process," 65.

51. David Adams, *The American Peace Movements* (New Haven, CT: Advocate Press, 2002).

52. For a more in-depth discussion of the role of the intelligence community, the military, the press, industry, and nongovernmental agencies in influencing arms control policy, see Sims, "The Arms Control Process."

53. See "The Role of the Parliament in the Ratification of International Treaties and Agreements," The Knesset—Research and Information Center, July 10, 2003, .http://www.knesset.gov.il/mmm/data/pdf/me00647.pdf.

CHAPTER 2

Controlling the Growth of Nuclear Weapons and Delivery Systems: Nuclear Arms Control between the United States and the Soviet Union/Russian Federation

On August 6 and August 9, 1945, the United States dropped nuclear weapons on Hiroshima and Nagasaki, immediately killing 170,000 people, compelling Japan to surrender unconditionally, and inaugurating the nuclear age. The scale of destruction caused by the nuclear weapons was more than 1,000 times that of the largest single explosive bomb ever used before. Nuclear weapons kill not only through the force of the blast that they produce and the fires that they ignite, but also through the radiation disseminated in the blast. The effects of radiation can cause death in the weeks and months following exposure, lead to deadly cancers in the years to come, and cause birth defects in subsequent generations.

Despite the devastating magnitude of the first nuclear weapons, the bombing of Hiroshima and Nagasaki represented a continuation of the policy of strategic bombing. Air power, with its ability to attack targets far distant from battles on the ground, became a dominant force in WWII. Beginning in WWI, the intent of strategic bombing was to destroy military and industrial targets that supported the ground troops. Nevertheless, two factors meant that bombs dropped from airplanes took a very heavy toll on civilians. First, targets that limited the ability of states to supply troops in the field were frequently located in densely populated cities. Therefore, bombs that targeted arms depots, factories, and transportation hubs killed civilians living or working nearby. Second, the ability to precisely deliver bombs to the intended targets was woefully inadequate and many, if not most, bombs missed their military targets and landed on areas of cities with dense civilian populations.

The unintended civilian casualties were certainly foreseeable and known to war planners. Yet, strategic bombing in WWII continued and high civilian deaths and injuries were often considered a bonus of strategic bombing that was thought to lead to diminished civilian support for the war effort. Eventually, the bombing of cities culminated in bombing cities with few military assets simply for revenge.[1] The British, for example, changed their strategic bombing policy following the destruction of the city of Coventry by German bombs. Prior to the attack on Coventry, British planes identified and aimed at specific targets and "indiscriminate bombing was forbidden."[2] Following Coventry, "indiscriminate bombing was now required, and by early 1942 aiming at military or industrial targets within cities was barred. . . . The purpose of the raids was explicitly declared to be the destruction of civilian morale."[3]

Both the Axis and the Allies engaged in extensive bombing of cities in WWII, causing hundreds of thousands of civilian deaths and injuries. Indeed, the firebombing of Tokyo in March 1945 caused approximately 100,000 deaths, more than either of the atomic bombs dropped on Hiroshima or Nagasaki. However, the raid on Tokyo involved more than 300 planes and several hundred thousand pounds of bombs.[4] The nuclear weapons dropped on Hiroshima and Nagasaki demonstrated that a single plane dropping a single bomb could produce comparable damage.

The power of nuclear weapons gave the United States a temporary monopoly on the ability to rapidly destroy cities. At the same time, it presented a temptation to the rest of the world's countries: they, too, could acquire devastating force. The knowledge that enemies possessing nuclear weapons could turn into a threat against the United States posed a policy challenge that divided the Truman administration. Some advisors argued that the United States would be more secure if it prevented all other countries from acquiring nuclear weapons of their own. Others maintained that U.S. security could only be guaranteed by keeping nuclear weapons as a threat of retaliation and as a way to deter other countries from using nuclear warheads against the United States. The most immediate fear, of course, was that the Soviet Union would develop nuclear weapons. And in 1949, it did.

Nuclear Proliferation and the U.S.–Soviet Arms Race

The United Kingdom followed the United States and the Soviet Union with a nuclear test in 1952, France followed in 1960, and China in 1964, but the nuclear arms race was principally a competition between the United States and the Soviet Union.[5] Each of these Cold War adversaries quickly increased its nuclear arsenal and each feared the power and intentions of the other.[6] The arms race between the United States and the Soviet Union was not a single race, however, but several races occurring simultaneously. The arms

race had three principle dimensions: (1) a race to make more and more nuclear weapons, (2) a race to make more powerful strategic nuclear weapons
and less powerful or tactical nuclear weapons, and (3) a race to make more
reliable and more sophisticated ways of delivering warheads to their intended
targets. Moreover, unlike automobile, bicycle, or foot races, the nuclear arms
races had no finish line. The buildup of arms in an attempt to maintain superiority (stay ahead in the race), achieve parity (pull even in the race), or gain
superiority (overtake the other racer) was never-ending. Thus, the so-called
arms race was not so much a race as a Sisyphean task.

In 1957, the Soviet Union launched Sputnik, the first artificial satellite to
circle the earth from outer space—and an unmistakable signal that the Soviets had pulled ahead in the intercontinental ballistic missile (ICBM) race.
However, the United States was still far ahead of the Soviet Union in stockpiled warheads and bombers, and the race for submarine-launched missiles,
also known as sea-launched ballistic missiles (SLBMs),[7] had barely begun.

The largest buildup in U.S. nuclear weapons occurred between 1956 and
1966. In 1956, the U.S. nuclear weapons stockpile included slightly more
than 4,500 warheads; a decade later, the stockpile had peaked at nearly
32,000 warheads. The Soviet nuclear weapons stockpile, however, continued
to expand. In 1966, it had just over 7,000 warheads; by 1976, the stockpile
had grown to more than 21,000 warheads, and by 1986, it peaked at well over
40,000.[8]

A consequence of the successful test of a Soviet atomic bomb in 1949
was that it led the Truman administration to pursue the development of
much more powerful weapons using a different process from that of the fission bombs that destroyed the Japanese cities. The new hydrogen bombs, also
called thermonuclear bombs or fusion bombs, used a combined process of
fission and fusion to produce warheads with increased destructive capability.
The United States successfully exploded its first H-bomb in 1953.

Although some fusion bombs, notably the Soviet bomb that was tested in
1962, are several thousand times more powerful than the Hiroshima bomb,
most hydrogen bombs that became part of the arsenals of the nuclear powers
were much smaller. The average size of H-bombs in the U.S. arsenal is 24
times larger than that used in Hiroshima. In contrast, the gravity H-bomb,
also known as a free fall bomb because it does not have a guidance system,
was more than 700 times more powerful than the Hiroshima bomb. The
gravity H-bomb, however, has been retired by the United States. The largest
H-bomb produced was more than 3,000 times as powerful as the first atomic
weapons.[9]

Warheads, however, are not the only significant component of nuclear
warfare or nuclear arms control. Methods of delivering nuclear weapons, including different types of ballistic missiles, bombers, and submarines are also

Table 1. U.S. and Soviet Nuclear Warheads and Delivery Systems in 1969

	ICBM	SLBM	Bombers	Total	Total Stockpiled
US	1,096	4,452	6,421	11,969	26,910
USSR	1,338	204	596	2,138	10,538

Table 2. U.S. and Soviet Nuclear Warheads and Delivery Systems in 1975

	ICBM	SLBM	Bombers	Total	Total Stockpiled
US	2,251	6,586	6,911	15,748	27,052
USSR	2,277	896	596	3,743	19,443

Source: Natural Resources Defense Council, Table of U.S. Nuclear Warheads, *Archive of Nuclear Data*, http://www.nrdc.org/nuclear/nudb/datab9.asp.

essential components of a strategic weapons system. The nuclear weapons used at Hiroshima and Nagasaki were dropped from manned bombers. Prompted in part by bombers' vulnerability to being shot down before reaching their targets and in part by Germany's success with unmanned ballistic missile development, the United States and the Soviet Union both embarked on programs to develop ballistic missiles with ranges that would enable them to hit targets in each other's territory. At the same time, the two Cold War enemies developed programs to deliver nuclear warheads on missiles shot from submarines.

During the nuclear arms buildup and following the implementation of the first Strategic Arms Limitation Treaty (SALT I), in 1975, the United States had 15,748 strategic warheads: 6,911 for delivery by bombers, 6,586 for delivery by SLBMs, and 2,251 for delivery by ICBMs. In contrast, the Soviet Union in 1975 had just 3,743 strategic warheads. A larger percentage of the Soviet warheads, however, were for delivery by the more reliable ICBMs. Each side stockpiled additional warheads. Table 1 compares the U.S. and Soviet stockpiles in 1969; Table 2 shows the same comparison in 1975. The numbers are critical to understanding the context of the first strategic offensive arms control agreement between the United States and the Soviet Union, SALT I.

U.S. Nuclear Strategy

In the early years of the Cold War, the relatively small number of nuclear weapons possessed by the United States and the Soviet Union made it possible to believe that the United States could survive a nuclear exchange with the Soviet Union. Bernard Brodie, one of the architects of U.S. nuclear weapons strategy, argued that "even a total war which began with the enemy's surprise strategic assault upon [the United States] need not result . . . in the political extinction of the nation."[10] The origins of nuclear weapons policy thus envisioned fighting and presumably winning a nuclear war. Nevertheless, the advent of nuclear weapons and their proliferation to the Soviet Union, an archenemy, required a new strategy to address this perceived threat.

The strategy underpinning the U.S.–Soviet arms race was based on the widespread recognition that the country launching the first barrage would have a distinct advantage in any nuclear exchange. Secondly, that the United States would not launch a preventive war—a first strike against the Soviet Union.[11] While the United States perceived its own intentions of starting a war with the Soviet Union to be nonexistent, the United States could not be sure that the Soviet Union would not deliberately (or perhaps accidentally) launch a first strike against the United States. Consequently, the strategy required that the United States build a large enough nuclear arsenal that sufficient nuclear weapons would survive a first strike attack by the Soviets. Hence, the United States could retaliate with a devastating force against the Soviet Union. The weapons that survived a first strike would deter the Soviet Union from launching a first strike. The foregoing line of reasoning gave birth to the bedrock deterrence theory that dominated U.S.–Soviet relations for decades.

The origins of this nuclear strategy and the concomitant build up of U.S. military power, including nuclear forces, appears in National Security Council Report 68 (NSC 68).[12] The 1950 report was drafted shortly after the Soviet Union had tested its first nuclear weapon and after North Korea had invaded South Korea apparently with Stalin's approval. The report asserted that to contain the Soviet Union, the United States and its allies needed to possess "superior overall power."[13] The report also articulated two other pillars of Cold War strategy; first, that the United States would not have a declaratory policy of no first use of nuclear weapons and second, that the United States would not initiate a preventive war—a surprise attack on the Soviet Union without prior attack, or imminent provocation.

The report rejected arguments in favor of a no first use policy, contending that "[i]n our present situation of relative unpreparedness in conventional weapons, such a declaration would be interpreted by the USSR as an admission of great weakness and by our allies as a clear indication that we intended to abandon them." The subtext of this statement is that the conventional forces of the Soviet Union, particularly its standing army, were stronger than those of the United States and its allies. If the Soviet Union considered invading Western Europe with conventional forces, the United States could prevent that attack only by threatening to use nuclear weapons against Soviet cities, the invading conventional troops, and military capabilities of the Soviet Union and its allies in the Warsaw Pact.

In setting forth its arguments in favor of a large buildup in military power, NSC 68 outlined and rejected the alternatives of staying the existing course, isolation, and preventive war. The report asserted that preventive war is "generally unacceptable to Americans." The strategy document presented pragmatic arguments that it was questionable whether the United States could achieve its objectives through preventive war. Moreover, the report argued against preventive war on moral grounds. While acknowledging that the American people, "would probably rally in support of the war effort, the shock of responsibility for a surprise attack would be morally corrosive. . . . Many would doubt that it was a 'just war' and that all reasonable possibilities for a peaceful settlement had been explored in good faith."[14] The report went on to look at the aftermath of a preventive war started by the United States. It concluded that even if the United States achieved military objectives, establishing a new international order would be exceedingly difficult. Consequently, a preventive war would have long-term negative consequences that would outweigh a military victory over the Soviet Union.

NSC 68 also acknowledged the imperative of negotiation. While the report was not optimistic about the ability of the United States to achieve grand objectives through negotiations with the Soviet Union, the efforts might occasionally be worthwhile. The very process of engaging in negotiations would reassure a democratic nation and its allies that it was pursuing peaceful means of resolving the Cold War. The report considered that the pursuit of a peaceful end of the Cold War was "an essential element in the ideological conflict" between dictatorial communism and democratic capitalism.[15]

Some experts criticized this report of the National Security Council on the basis of its assumptions and its recommendation. Although NSC 68 was a classified report, it nevertheless became the foundation for U.S. foreign and arms control policy throughout the Cold War. The military buildup envisioned as necessary by the authors of NSC 68, however, was never fully implemented. Before such a buildup could be put into effect, President Truman was succeeded by President Eisenhower, who opposed the levels of military spending that would be necessary should the recommendations of NSC be made fully operational.[16]

Bilateral nuclear arms control negotiations between the United States and the Soviet Union and subsequently the Russian Federation have taken place over the last 50 years and resulted in a series of agreements addressing different aspects of nuclear warheads and delivery vehicles. The arms control record has been marked by remarkable achievements as well as setbacks. Both the United States and the Soviet Union initiated talks and terminated them. The two sides completed many agreements, the Strategic Arms Limitation Treaties I and II, the Anti-Ballistic Missile Treaty, the Intermediate-Range Nuclear Forces Treaty, the Strategic Arms Reductions Treaties I and II, the Strategic Offensive Reduction Treaty, and the New START Treaty. Yet, signing treaties did not always ensure their ratification and entry into force for unlimited duration. Political events unrelated to arms control often exercised a chilling effect on progress in the talks. Yet, the trajectory of nuclear arms control between the two former arch enemies is one that reveals that both sides were unwilling to continue to engage in continuous, expensive, and threatening arms buildups.

Strategic Arms Limitation Treaty (SALT) Talks

President Lyndon Johnson first approached the Soviets to determine their interest in limitations on strategic arms in late 1966. Moreover, the multilateral Nuclear NPT, completed in 1968, provided an impetus for the United States and the Soviet Union to take up the issue bilaterally. The NPT obligated those states that possessed nuclear weapons, to "pursue negotiations in good faith on effective measures relating to cessation of the nuclear arms race at an early date and to nuclear disarmament." The production of nuclear weapons and their means of delivery were beginning to take a toll on the U.S. and Soviet economies. Each country seemed to realize that any superiority in any element of its weapons systems was likely to be temporary as the other country shifted resources in order to keep up or race ahead. Thus, the United States and the Soviet Union entered into the historically important talks.

Delayed by the Soviet invasion of Czechoslovakia in 1968, the talks commenced in November 1969 under President Nixon and alternated between Helsinki and Vienna. The SALT talks took place over a span of more than two years and the delegations discussed many possible options for limitations and reductions of both offensive and defensive strategic arms. At the same time, U.S. national security advisor Henry Kissinger and Soviet ambassador to the United States Anatoly Dobrynin engaged in regular, secret talks on the topics under discussion in SALT. Meanwhile, the U.S. negotiators in the official, or Track I, negotiations were unaware of these Kissinger–Dobrynin talks.

Limits or reductions to ICBMs, SLBMs, strategic bombers, missiles with multiple nuclear warheads, and anti-ballistic missiles (ABM) were all on the table. Although the talks considered a comprehensive agreement covering both offensive and defensive arms, the delegations ultimately completed two separate agreements—an interim executive agreement on strategic arms (SALT I), and the ABM treaty.

SALT I Interim Agreement

SALT I was a five-year bargain between the two states. At its signing in May 1972, the agreement placed limits on fixed, land-based ICBMs, freezing them to the number already deployed or in construction. At the time of signing, the United States had 1,054 deployed ICBMs and the Soviet Union had 1,483.[17] The agreement also placed limits on submarines and SLBMs. The Soviet Union was allowed to have 950 SLBMs, the United States 710. The Soviet Union insisted that lower limits be placed on U.S. intercontinental and submarine-launched ballistic missiles than its own missiles, and the United States accepted those limits for a number of reasons. First, U.S. allies, namely Britain and France, also possessed SLBMs, which were threatening to the Soviet Union. Moreover, in 1970, the United States deployed the first Minuteman ICBM with the ability to deliver three nuclear weapons at a time, with the individual warheads aimed at a distinct targets within a larger footprint. Called "multiple, independently-targeted reentry vehicles" (MIRVs), such missiles were designed to overcome the ABM system that the Soviets had put in place. Although MIRVs were discussed in SALT, neither side thought it was in its interest to limit MIRVs at that time.[18]

The verification process for SALT I depended on national technical means. Both parties relied on satellite information to transmit information about nuclear installations. Clearly, the verification of SALT I was possible only because the Soviet Union had launched Sputnik and subsequently, the United States launched satellites into space. In addition, both parties agreed not to interfere with national technical means of verification and not to use deliberate concealment measures. Nevertheless, SALT I did not involve any cooperative measures for verification nor did it contain any provisions for onsite monitoring or inspection. Ultimately, each side had to accept some level of uncertainty about its ability to verify compliance by the other side. Each nation tried to be as accurately confident as possible that the other was in compliance with the treaty's provisions.

Criticism of the SALT I agreement came from many quarters. Hard-line Cold Warriors focused on the fact that the Soviet Union was allowed to have a greater number of ICBMs than the United States. They claimed that SALT I would perpetuate a disparity that favored the Soviet Union. Disarmament advocates were alarmed that the limitations of the SALT I agreement did not involve dismantling any of the existing warheads and did not reduce the number of deployed ICBMs or SLBMs. Indeed, during more than two years of talks, both the United States and the Soviet Union rapidly increased their nuclear stockpiles and the ballistic missiles needed to launch them. Similarly, the nonnuclear armed states who were parties to the NPT did not think that the agreement fulfilled the obligations of Article VI of the NPT, requiring the nuclear powers to negotiate in good faith to end the arms race and pursue nuclear disarmament.

The Anti-Ballistic Missile Treaty

The SALT talks included discussions between the U.S. and Soviet delegations limiting defensive weapons, as well as offensive weapons. ABMs, as the name implies, are methods of intercepting and destroying ballistic missiles in flight so that the nuclear (or conventional) warheads that they carry do not reach their intended targets. Ballistic missiles are one of the three principal methods of delivering nuclear weapons. The rocket carrying the warhead leaves the earth's atmosphere before reentering to strike its intended target. Germany developed the first ballistic missiles during WWII, with a range of around 200 miles. Following WWII, both the United States and the Soviet Union recruited German scientists to assist in the development of their own missile programs. The two superpowers developed both short- and long-range missiles. The United States and the Soviet Union sought missiles that could be launched from their own homelands and be able to reach the other nation. The range of the missiles needed to strike the territory of the other had to be in several thousands of miles, or an intercontinental range. The Soviet Union successfully tested the first ICBM in 1957. The United States did not test its own ICBM until 1959. The United States and the Soviet Union were now both in the position to attack the other through space. This ability, at least theoretically, increased the advantage of initiating a nuclear attack. Not surprisingly, both nations sought to develop interceptors— anti-ballistic missiles—that would destroy incoming ICBMs before they reached their targets.

The Soviets were initially publicly cool to an ABM treaty. After all, the Soviet Union argued, AMBs are a defensive weapon. They do not kill people or destroy infrastructure. They protect against incoming nuclear weapons carried on ballistic missiles. When the Soviet Union built its first AMB system, it was designed to protect the city of Leningrad. A second installation protected Moscow. In contrast, the United States did not build installations to protect its cities. The U.S. nuclear strategy of massive retaliation, or Mutual Assured Destruction (MAD), relied on the survivability of its ICBMs and thus built its AMB system to protect its nuclear weapons.

The preamble to the ABM treaty states that "effective measures to limit anti-ballistic missile systems would be a substantial factor in curbing the race in strategic offensive arms and would lead to a decrease in the risk of outbreak of war involving nuclear weapons."[19] This statement might seem counterintuitive on its face. If ballistic missiles armed with nuclear weapons could be shot down, if nations could defend their populations and territory against nuclear attack, wouldn't that be a good thing? To understand the importance of the ABM treaty and controversies over the decision of the George W. Bush administration to withdraw from the ABM treaty, one must understand why the United States and the Soviet Union thought it was in their interest to limit ABMs.

The destructive power of nuclear weapons can be directed against cities, factories, and populations, as Hiroshima and Nagasaki demonstrated. During the Cold War arms race, however, the U.S. strategy dictated that it must have the ability to retaliate with nuclear weapons. The United States feared that the Soviet Union would have an advantage if the Soviet Union used its first-strike weapons to destroy U.S. nuclear weapons. To the extent that nuclear weapons were vulnerable to a first strike, that vulnerability created an incentive to initiate nuclear war. For that reason, the United States deployed its first ABM system to protect its nuclear weapons and ICBM launchers.[20]

The purpose of limits on ABM systems was to create a balance between the nuclear forces of the two Cold War enemies so that neither would achieve an advantage in a first strike and, therefore, neither would have an incentive to initiate war. If each side had sufficient nuclear weapons to retaliate after a first strike and wreak overwhelming destruction on its opponent, both would be deterred from striking first. Thus, the theory of deterrence and the doctrine of Massive Retaliation or MAD were the intellectual foundation for the ABM Treaty.[21] In short, each side would be deterred from initiating nuclear war if its cities remained vulnerable to retaliatory forces from its adversary. The MAD doctrine recognized that each side had the capability to effectively destroy the other's state irrespective of which side initiated the use of nuclear weapons.

The ABM treaty would slow down or stop the offensive arms race through a similar mechanism. With robust ballistic missile defenses the Soviet Union and the United States would believe that they needed more offensive weapons to break through the defenses of each other, leading to a continuing upward spiral of more defenses and more offensive weapons. If, however, offensive weapons were invulnerable to a first strike and if the cities of each side were vulnerable to retaliatory strikes, an upper useful limit on offensive weapons was conceivable. Each superpower could have some confidence that it could successfully deter the other from initiating a nuclear strike.

Signed on the same day as the SALT I interim agreement, May 26, 1972, the ABM treaty permitted the United States and the Soviet Union to deploy only two ABM systems each. Each system was limited to 100 missile interceptors and coverage of an area with a radius of 150 kilometers. One system was allowed to defend the capital of the nation; the other was allowed to protect an offensive ICBM site. The treaty defined the components of an AMB system. The two countries agreed to prohibit developing, testing, and deploying any ABM system or its components in the sea, the air, or space. Additionally, the prohibition included land-based mobile ABM systems and components. The treaty placed limits on the number of intercept launchers at the allowed ABM sites and limited those launchers to one intercept each.

Like the SALT I interim agreement, verification of the ABM treaty was to be conducted through national technical means (NTM) without interference or deliberate concealment. The ABM treaty went further than the

SALT I agreement, however, by establishing a Standing Consultative Commission (SCC). The role of the Commission was to discuss and resolve any ambiguities or questions that might arise with the implementation of the treaty, provide a forum to exchange information between the two parties, and discuss any relevant changes in the strategic situation that might warrant amendments or other changes to the treaty. The treaty would have a formal review in five years, but by establishing the SCC, it provided a way for the United States and the Soviet Union to have discussions and resolve concerns about compliance in a timely fashion. Finally, Article XV of the treaty gave each nation the right to withdraw from the treaty in the event that the nation "decides that extraordinary events related to the subject matter of this Treaty have jeopardized its supreme interests."

The implementation of the ABM treaty began in a promising fashion. The U.S. Senate ratified the treaty on a vote of 88 to 2 just months after its signing. The SCC was established through a memorandum of understanding and a protocol by May 1973. In the 1974 Protocol to the treaty, the permitted ABM installations were further pared to just one each for the United States and the Soviet Union. The Soviet Union maintained its Moscow system and the United States maintained the system protecting its ICBM launchers. The Protocol also reduced the number of ICBM intercept launchers for each side from 200 to 100. The first two review conferences of the treaty, in 1977 and 1982, were unremarkable.

In 1983, however, several events sounded a more ominous tone. In March 1983, President Ronald Reagan announced that the United States would undertake a Strategic Defense Initiative (SDI). The program would entail research and development of an antimissile strategic defense system that included space-based interceptors. Although Reagan was careful to note that the program would be consistent with U.S. obligations under the ABM treaty, critics of SDI countered that SDI would be a violation of the treaty. Indeed, the Soviet Union charged that SDI violated the ABM treaty. Also, in 1983, the United States discovered an early warning radar installation at Krasnoyarsk in the Soviet Union that violated the treaty. According to the ABM treaty, the United States and the Soviet Union were "not to deploy in the future radars for early warning of strategic ballistic missile attack except at locations along the periphery of its national territory and oriented outward."[22] The radars at Krasnoyarsk were located in central Soviet territory, 800 kilometers from the nearest border, not at the periphery.

The United States and the Soviet Union each made claims accusing the other of treaty violations. The Soviet Union argued that "the United States was developing both a mobile and space-based ABM system, was working on multiple warheads for ABM interceptors, was building and upgrading new large phased-array radars . . . that . . . cover large areas of the United States and could serve as battle management radars for a future US ABM system and was incorporating ABM capabilities in the intelligence radar on Shemya Island, [Alaska]."[23] The United States charged that the Krasnoyarsk radar array "almost certainly constitutes a violation of legal obligations under the ABM Treaty of 1972 in that its associated siting, orientation, and capability is prohibited by the Treaty."[24]

The breakup of the Soviet Union into 15 successor states in 1991 further complicated the status of the ABM treaty. Three of the non-Russian states, Belarus, Kazakhstan, and Ukraine, had nuclear weapons and ABM assets on their territories. Each of the three transferred the nuclear weapons to the Russian Federation. In 1997, the ABM treaty was extended to these three states, making it a multilateral treaty. At the same time, the AMB treaty parties signed two accords with provisions regarding theatre missile defense (TMD). The accords permitted TMD with certain restrictions on deployment, velocity, and testing.[25] The treaty parties also agreed to a yearly exchange of information on nonstrategic missile defense plans and programs.[26]

While the U.S. Congress appropriated funds for SDI, Reagan's grand plan to eliminate the threat of ballistic missiles, there were technical and economic barriers to developing a missile shield. The plan was scaled down and renamed several times during successive presidential administration. In May 2001, however, President George W. Bush announced a plan to revive the moribund missile defense system and move beyond the constraints of the ABM treaty. By the end of 2001, he gave formal notice to Russia that the United States would withdraw from the treaty in six months and the United States did so in 2002. At the time, the U.S. Senate had not ratified the 1997 agreements, which, therefore, never entered into force. Although the United States withdrew from the ABM treaty, critics have argued that grounds for withdrawal—"extraordinary events related to the subject matter of this Treaty have jeopardized its supreme interests"—had not been met.

SALT II

The United States and the Soviet Union continued talks on a long-term comprehensive agreement that would replace the SALT I interim agreement scheduled to last only five years. SALT II negotiations, which started six months after the signing of SALT I and the ABM treaty, lasted seven years and spanned three U.S. administrations. The treaty that was produced was submitted to the U.S. Senate for ratification but then withdrawn from consideration when the Soviets invaded Afghanistan in December 1979. There were many issues on the negotiation table early in the SALT talks and several of them—including MIRVed missiles, cruise missiles, and bombers—were left unresolved by the interim agreement. The definition of strategic weapons is yet another example. The Soviets considered any U.S. nuclear weapons that could reach the Soviet homeland as strategic. Many ballistic missiles of relatively short range that were based in Europe were within this definition. In contrast, the United States considered these weapons to be tactical. Moreover, there were important differences between the U.S. and Soviet weapons, such as destructive power, or throw weight, that made them difficult to compare.

In 1974, U.S. president Gerald Ford and Soviet leader Leonid Brezhnev issued a joint statement agreeing to a formula for a 10-year SALT II agreement that would limit each side to a ceiling of 2,400 weapon launchers. Each side could distribute its ceiling among ICBMs, SLBMs, heavy bombers and long-range air-to-surface missiles as it wished. In addition, the number of launchers with MIRVs was limited to no more than 1,300. U.S. missiles based in Europe were not included in the ceilings. Despite this formula, negotiators were unable to reach an agreement and the negotiations dragged on for another five years. Among the thorny disputes were how to consider cruise missiles, MIRV verification provisions, throw-weight limits, and whether certain Soviet aircraft would be considered heavy bombers.

The Carter administration sought much lower limits than Ford and Brezhnev had agreed to, but the Soviets insisted on negotiating within the formula already agreed on. Ultimately, the 1974 formula was incorporated into the SALT II agreement along with many other provisions including:

- a ban on construction of additional fixed ICBM launchers,
- a ban on air-to-surface ballistic missiles,
- a limit of 10 warheads on a new type of permitted ICBM,
- limits on the number of cruise missiles per heavy bomber,
- bans on new weapons systems such as long-range ballistic missiles on surface ships and ballistic missiles and cruise missiles on the seabed, and
- limits to the throw-weight of strategic ballistic missiles.

The treaty was completed in June 1979, and President Carter submitted it to the U.S. Senate for ratification. However, he withdrew it after the Soviets invaded Afghanistan, and the treaty was never ratified.

International law requires states to abstain from any activities that would defeat the object and purpose of any treaty that they sign, even in the absence of ratification or its political equivalent. Presidents Carter and Reagan agreed that the United States would abide by the provisions of SALT II if the Soviet Union reciprocated. However, after alleging that the Soviet Union had not complied with all of the terms of SALT II and had violated the ABM treaty, Reagan announced that decisions on U.S. strategic forces would be based on assessments of the threat to the United States, rather than on the limits contained in SALT II. Nevertheless, both the United States and the

Soviet Union found it to be in their interest not to exceed the SALT II limits, particularly during the Intermediate-Range Nuclear Forces (INF) talks that had been ongoing since 1980 and the Strategic Arms Reduction Talks (START) that began in 1982.

Intermediate-Range Nuclear Forces (INF) Treaty

The INF treaty marked the first nuclear disarmament treaty, in contrast to arms limitation treaties. The status of nuclear weapons in Europe had long been an area of disagreement between the United States and the Soviet Union. The United States had deployed nuclear warheads in Europe beginning in 1954, but they were to be delivered with bombers, not missiles. In the late 1950s, the Soviet Union began to deploy ballistic missiles in the western, European, territory of the Soviet Union armed with nuclear warheads. These missiles had ranges of 2,500 and 4,000 kilometers. The United States responded by stationing missiles with a 2,500-kilometer range in Europe but removed them as part of the resolution of the Cuban Missile crisis in 1962. After the Soviet Union began to replace its first, relatively vulnerable missiles, with more modern, mobile versions, NATO countered the Soviet move by announcing in late 1979 that it would deploy more than 500 U.S. intermediate-range nuclear-tipped missiles in Europe.[27] Brezhnev called for a moratorium on nuclear missile deployment in Europe and called for negotiations. The United States rejected the moratorium; it would have frozen the status quo with Soviet nuclear missiles remaining on European soil and U.S. missiles not yet deployed there. The United States did agree, however, to enter into talks concerning the matter.

However, shortly after taking office in 1981, President Reagan publicly proposed that all ballistic and cruise missiles in Europe be eliminated. This zero option had its origins in the antinuclear movement in Europe. Numerous demonstrations took place throughout Western Europe opposing the U.S. deployment of nuclear missiles and opposition to the recognition that nuclear war, if initiated by either the Soviet Union or the United States, might be limited to the European theater. The United States did not yet have any ballistic missiles deployed in Europe when Reagan made the proposal, but it had plans to deploy both ballistic and cruise missiles beginning in 1983. In contrast, the Soviet Union would have had to remove already deployed missiles if it accepted Reagan's proposal. To the surprise of no one, the Soviet Union repeatedly rejected the U.S. proposal.

The first round of negotiations in Geneva revealed clear differences in the positions of the two parties. The Soviet Union was unwilling to accept the U.S. zero option and eliminate the missiles that were on its own soil. The Soviet Union wanted to include French and British intermediate-range missiles whereas the United States focused only on U.S. and Soviet missiles. Consistent with its zero-option position, the United States wanted to eliminate all U.S. and Soviet intermediate-range missiles, including those of the Soviet Union that were deployed in the Asian portion of the Soviet Union and targeted on Asia. The two sides also differed on issues of destruction of missiles versus withdrawal of Soviet missiles beyond where they could reach Western Europe. Over the next several years, the United States and the Soviet Union tabled and rejected various proposals to limit the existing intermediate-range missiles in Europe and halt the proposed U.S. deployment of missiles.

As the talks continued, the United States and the Soviet Union were unable to reconcile their positions. In response, the United States proceeded with its planned deployment of ballistic and cruise missiles in Europe. The U.S. deployment, in turn, prompted the Soviets to refuse to resume the INF talks.[28] The U.S. intermediate-range missiles that were deployed in Europe would have been able to arrive at their targets in western portions of the Soviet Union in 10 minutes. The short time between firing the missiles and their reaching their targets meant that Soviet leaders would have a disturbingly short interval to make a decision to counterattack if they received warning that an intermediate-range missile had been launched.

After the political upheavals in the Soviet Union that followed Brezhnev's death and the short rule of Soviet Premiers Yuri Andropov and Konstantin Chernenko, Mikhail Gorbachev consolidated his power in the Soviet Union in 1985 and the talks recommenced. A number of factors continued to complicate the negotiations. West Germany possessed missiles that carried U.S. nuclear warheads, for example. At last, the Soviet Union accepted the zero option. Advances occurred at various settings, and ultimately the Soviet Union agreed to the zero option in a bilateral agreement with the United States.

The new INF treaty eliminated all U.S. and Soviet ballistic and cruise missiles in Europe but allowed the United Kingdom and France to retain their nuclear-armed ballistic missiles. In an attempt to outlaw Reagan's proposed SDI, Gorbachev's government originally proposed that space weapons (another name for anti-ballistic missiles based in space) also be part of the agreement. Eventually, in 1987, the two sides reached an agreement requiring both nations to remove and dismantle ballistic and cruise missiles armed with nuclear weapons that had already been deployed and to cancel all plans for further deployments of such missiles.[29]

When the treaty was signed, the Soviet Union had 857 intermediate and shorter range deployed missiles; the United States had 429 deployed missiles. Among the Soviet intermediate-range missiles were 405 missiles that carried three nuclear warheads each. The rest of the Soviet missiles and all of the

U.S. missiles were of the single warhead type. Consequently, the treaty called for removing 1,667 Soviet and 429 U.S. warheads. The treaty required that the missiles be removed from European soil, that the nuclear warheads be removed from the missiles, and that the missiles' guidance systems be destroyed. The treaty did not, however, require that the nuclear warheads themselves be destroyed, and according to the terms of the treaty, the warheads could either be returned to the respective country's stockpile or placed in other missiles, including ICBMs. The INF treaty also prohibited the production and testing of missiles in the relevant range (500–5,500 kilometers) and any stages of such launchers.

The INF treaty was combined with a Memorandum of Understanding (MOU), a Protocol on Inspection, and a Protocol on Elimination. The MOU between the two nations dealt with some definitions, categories of data relevant to the treaty that could be updated over time. Under the treaty and the terms of the MOU, the United States and the Soviet Union would provide precise data, including photographs and site diagrams of deployed and produced missiles. In an important breakthrough the Soviet Union agreed that onsite inspections would augment NTM of verification and the procedures for the inspections were outlined in the Protocol. Each side was allowed to inspect certain sites for 13 years after the treaty took effect and both were allowed to continuously monitor the portals of missile production and assembly plants.

The Elimination Protocol sets rules and procedures for destroying relevant missiles. Several other documents of clarification were subsequently made part of the package of documents that comprise the INF Treaty. The treaty also contained an agreement that it would be implemented in phases. The elaborate structure for inspections and verification of compliance marked a significant departure from previous bilateral treaties.

Similar to the SALT I agreement, the INF Treaty established a forum to resolve questions related to compliance with the obligations under the agreement. In the case of the INF, the forum, called the Special Verification Commission, was to meet at the request of either of the two parties to the treaty.

The treaty entered into force June 1, 1988. Three years later, the United States had destroyed its final ground-launched missiles and the Soviet Union had destroyed its last SS-20, as called for in the agreement. A total of 2,296 missiles were destroyed including all U.S. and Soviet missiles that had been deployed in Europe and more than 1,400 missiles that had not yet been deployed. After the Soviet Union disintegrated into separate sovereign republics in late 1991, the United States concluded agreements with the relevant successor states to the Soviet Union—Belarus, Kazakhstan, Russia, Turkmenistan, Ukraine, and Uzbekistan. On May 31, 2001, all states concluded their inspection and monitoring activity.

Strategic Arms Reduction Treaty (START)

START I Agreement

The START talks were a series of negotiations between the United States and the Soviet Union to move beyond limiting nuclear weapons launchers and grapple with reducing the aggregate number of nuclear warheads and the aggregate number of strategic nuclear delivery vehicles (SNDVs). The START negotiations began in 1982, were stalled by the U.S. deployment of ballistic missiles in Europe, and subsequently revived in 1985, after Gorbachev took power in the Soviet Union. The START I treaty was completed and signed in July 1991, just weeks before Communist hardliners attempted a coup to regain power in the Soviet Union. By the end of 1991, the Soviet Union had fractured into the Commonwealth of Independent States.

The treaty required each country to reduce its aggregate number of deployed ICBMs, SLBMS, and heavy bombers to 1,600 and to reduce the number of warheads associated with those delivery vehicles to 6,000. The number of U.S. nuclear warheads associated with its SNDVs peaked in 1987 at 13,685; Soviet warheads peaked at 11,529. Recalling that the SALT II limits were 2,400 for each side, START I obligated each side to reduce its delivery capabilities by one-third and its warheads by roughly one half. While the U.S. Senate quickly ratified START I, the breakup of the Soviet Union delayed its entry into force. When the Soviet Union disintegrated, Belarus, Kazakhstan, and Ukraine all had nuclear weapons inside their territories, as did Russia. Subsequently, the three independent republics transferred their nuclear weapons to Russia and all of them became parties to the Nuclear Non-Proliferation Treaty.

START II

In 1992, the United States and the Russian Federation—successor to the Soviet Union—quickly concluded a follow-on treaty to START I that further reduced strategic forces. START II required the two parties to reduce their total deployed nuclear warheads from 6,000 to no more than 3,500 and established limits within the overall maximum for warheads deployed on ICBMs and SLBMs. These reductions were to be phased in with an initial reduction to 4,200 and completed by January 2003.

START I and START II also required reducing and ultimately eliminating Soviet era heavy ICBMs, and established an upper limit of 3,600 metric tons on missile throw-weight. START II also prohibited all MIRVs on ICBMs. In addition, the United States and the Russian Federation completed an extension protocol to START II, pushing the deadline for reductions to the end of 2007. An additional MOU between the United States, the Russian

Federation, and the other Soviet Union successor states—Kazakhstan, Ukraine, and Belarus—clarified that each of the successor states were bound by the obligations of the ABM treaty.[30]

The U.S. Senate approved the START II treaty in January 1996 and the Russian Duma ratified it and its extension protocol in April 2000. The Duma had postponed ratification on two earlier occasions to protest U.S. and British air strikes against Iraq and the NATO bombing of the former Yugoslavia.[31]

Following the completion of the START II protocol and the MOU, U.S. president Bill Clinton and Russian president Boris Yeltsin released a joint statement announcing their intention to reduce nuclear forces to between 2,000 and 2,500 in a START III treaty. START III would also have included transparency measures of warhead inventories and destruction of warheads to promote the goal of making the treaties irreversible and of unlimited duration.[32]

The negotiations for START III were never completed, however. The treaty fell victim to other foreign policy issues, underscoring that arms control negotiations do not take place within a vacuum. While the United States was still a party to the ABM treaty, its research on missile defense continued to rankle Russia. Additionally, Russia opposed NATO expansion that included members of the former Warsaw Pact alliance and the U.S. Joint Chiefs of Staff opposed the 1,500 weapons limit that Russia asked for.

Strategic Offensive Reduction Treaty (SORT)

During a U.S.–Russia summit in May 2002, U.S. president George W. Bush and Russian president Vladimir Putin signed the Strategic Offensive Reduction Treaty (SORT). The treaty text is extremely concise, consisting of a preamble and five articles. Article I states the obligations of the parties; each side is to reduce the aggregate number of deployed nuclear warheads in its arsenal to 1,700–2,000. However, although the two countries reduced the number of deployed nuclear weapons, the agreement did not limit the number of delivery vehicles for the warheads, and both nations would be permitted to store warheads that were not deployed, according to the terms of the agreement.

The United States and Russia were unable to agree on a new verification system for the treaty. And ironically, the treaty was to expire at the end of December 2012—on the same day that its limits would have been put into effect. Both countries ratified the SORT agreement, but it has been superseded by the New START Treaty.

New START Treaty

U.S. president Barack Obama and Russian president Dmitry Medvedev signed the New Strategic Arms Reduction Treaty (New START) on April 8,

2010, in Prague. New START limits each side to no more than 700 deployed strategic nuclear delivery vehicles—ICBMs, SLBMs, and heavy bombers—and 1,550 deployed strategic warheads, which can be distributed among the delivery vehicles as each of the parties sees fit.[33] Each party is allowed an additional 100 nondeployed delivery vehicles. The treaty restricts where the deployed and nondeployed delivery vehicles may be located and tested.

The treaty has a verification regime that combines elements of START I with new elements tailored to New START. In addition to national technical means to verify compliance, the treaty establishes the rights of each party to conduct inspections to confirm the accuracy of data declarations that each side is obligated to provide to the other. To increase confidence and transparency, the treaty provides for the exchange of telemetry (missile flight test data) and does not limit missile defenses or long-range conventional strike capabilities. The inspections can take place at ICBM bases, submarine bases, and air bases. In December 2010, the U.S. Senate ratified the treaty by a vote of 71 in favor and 26 opposed and the Russian Duma did the same in January 2011. The agreement entered into force in February 2011 and it will last for 10 years. The parties must implement the limits set by the treaty by 2018.

Discussion

The Cold War was the central political and military phenomenon of the two most powerful countries on earth in the latter half of the 20th century. Bilateral, nuclear arms control formed just one element, albeit an important and enduring element, of a complex relationship between the two superpowers. In addition to nuclear arms control described in this chapter, the United States and the Soviet Union were also the principal participants in other multilateral arms control negotiations described elsewhere in this volume. Nevertheless, the arms race and the efforts of these two nations to cap and then scale back weapons programs that had the potential to destroy each other's very existence, and perhaps all life on earth, are essential to understand that relationship and its legacy in the 21st century.

In examining arms control in the last 50 years, a striking theme is the persistence of the United States and the Soviet Union to pursue means to restrain the nuclear arms race. Every U.S. president from John F. Kennedy to George H. W. Bush pursued an agenda with the Soviet Union that included the control of nuclear weapons and their delivery systems. Similarly, Soviet leaders Khrushchev, Brezhnev, and Gorbachev all sought arms control agreements with the United States.[34] Nevertheless, nuclear arms control was rarely, if ever, the top priority of any U.S. or Soviet administration. Consequently, the pace of arms control negotiations during the Cold War was frequently slow and the participation of one side or the other was halted during periods of high tension or disagreement. The United States pulled out of SALT talks in 1968 to protest the Soviet invasion of Czechoslovakia and, after the Soviet invasion of Afghanistan, the U.S. Senate never ratified SALT II. Similarly, the Soviets refused to resume INF talks after the United States deployed ballistic and cruise missiles in Europe. Each side was willing to sacrifice progress in arms control to protest military actions by the other.

Numerous NGOs sought to reduce or eliminate U.S. and Soviet nuclear weapons as an objective per se in order to reduce the ability each nation had to destroy the other either deliberately or accidentally. The Nuclear Freeze movement in the 1980s sought to end the growth in nuclear arsenals. Demonstrations across Europe fought the planned deployment of U.S. nuclear armed missiles in Europe. In contrast, the governments of both nations saw arms control as a means to several ends. Schelling and Halperin identified the goals of arms control as "reducing the likelihood of war, its scope and violence if it occurs, and the political and economic costs of being prepared for it."[35] In the United States, each administration faced domestic political pressure to reduce or eliminate nuclear weapons but simultaneously faced opposition to arms control and even to negotiating with the Soviet Union. Many perceived the Soviet Union was an unreliable foe with a penchant for secrecy, and feared that arms control agreements with the Soviets would weaken the United States. Remarkably, both liberal and conservative U.S. governments have been able to balance these competing domestic pressures and make progress in their arms control agenda.

Some U.S. proposals for reductions in nuclear weapons and delivery systems were often fodder for domestic political support rather than serious negotiating proposals. Many, if not most, of the proposals, particularly on the U.S. side, were initially greeted with considerable pessimism about the likelihood that the Soviet Union would agree to them. Analysts believed the Soviet Union would emphatically reject the early INF proposals, for example, and it did. Nevertheless, early pessimism about the likelihood of reaching agreement ultimately gave way to surprise when it became apparent that agreements could be reached. And despite early pessimism, strategic offensive arms control often exceeded the expectations of analysts and critics. This pattern—declaring a desire for an agreement on certain aspects of arms control, followed by pessimism, rejection of terms, prolonged negotiating, and ultimate agreement—is a pattern evident in other multilateral arms control negotiations, too. Thus, we see that the very process of meeting face to face with a team of negotiators from another government often leads to agreements that are beneficial to both sides. Despite suspicion, distrust, and enmity, the United States and the Soviet Union established a cooperative relationship on some issues of how to limit, control, and reduce nuclear weapons.

Leaders matter. In both the United States and the Soviet Union, leaders at the highest levels were able to achieve breakthroughs in arms control negotiations despite bureaucratic politics impeding substantive advances.[36] In the United States, each American president was instrumental in some phase of achieving arms control success. With the exception of Yuri Andropov and Konstantin Cherenkov, who served very short terms, Soviet leaders were also able to advance arms control. In the same vein, however, leaders of the superpowers could also single-handedly pull out from negotiations, or, as in the case of the ABM treaty, withdraw from a treaty that had been in force for decades.

Notes

1. For details of the development of strategic bombing, see Richard R. Muller, "The Origins of MAD: A Short History of City-Busting," in *Getting MAD: Nuclear Mutual Assured Destruction Its Origins and Practice*, ed. Henry D. Sokolski, The Strategic Studies Institute, November 2004, http://www.strategicstudiesinstitute.army.mil/pdffiles/pub585.pdf.

2. Michael Walzer, "World War II: Why Was This War Different?," *Philosophy & Public Affairs* 1, no. 1 (1971), http://www.jstor.org/stable/pdfplus/2265089.pdf.

3. Ibid, 12.

4. Joseph Coleman, "1945 Tokyo Firebombing Left Legacy of Terror, Pain," Published on Thursday, March 10, 2005, by the Associated Press. Posted on "Common Dreams" http://www.commondreams.org/headlines05/0310-08.htm.

5. National-Archives, *Operation Hurricane: The Explosion of the first British Bomb*, 2008, http://www.nationalarchives.gov.uk/films/1951to1964/filmpage_oper_hurr.htm.

6. Atomic-Archive, *Nuclear Testing Chronology*, http://www.atomicarchive.com/Almanac/TestingChronology.shtml.

7. Also called sea-launched ballistic missiles.

8. National Resources Defense Council, Archive of Nuclear Data Table of USSR/Russian Nuclear Warheads1949–75, 1976–2002, http://www.nrdc.org/nuclear/nudb/datab10.asp.

9. Ward Wilson, "A-Bomb v. H-bomb," 2011, http://wardhayeswilson.squarespace.com/a-bomb-v-h-bomb/.

10. Bernard Brodie, *Strategy in the Missile Age* (Princeton, NJ: Princeton University Press, 1959, 1965), 392.

11. Ibid.

12. National Security Council Report 68, "A Report to the National Security Council—NSC 68," President's Secretary's File, Truman Papers, April 12, 1950, http://www.trumanlibrary.org/whistlestop/study_collections/coldwar/documents/pdf/10-1.pdf.

13. National Security Report 68, VI A, 1.

14. National Security Report 68, IX C.

15. National Security Report 68, IX.

16. Mark Trachtenberg, "Making Grand Strategy: The Early Cold War Experience in Retrospect," *SAIS Review* 9, no. 1 (1999): 33–40, http://www.sscnet.ucla.edu/polisci/faculty/trachtenberg/cv/grandstrat%28sais%29.html.

17. Natural Resources Defense Council, *Archive of Nuclear Data*, http://www.nrdc.org/nuclear/nudb/datainx.asp.

18. See Kissinger (1979, 534–31) for his explanation of the Dobrynin talks and the internal discussions on Congressional and administration politics shaping the U.S. position in SALT.

19. "Treaty between the United States of America and the Union of Soviet Socialist Republics on the Limitation of Anti-Ballistic Missile Systems," signed in Moscow, May 26, 1972, http://www.state.gov/t/isn/trty/16332.htm.

20. United States Senate. Committee on Appropriations. Soviet Strategic Force Development: Joint Hearing before the Subcommittee on Strategic and Theater Nuclear Forces of the Committee on Armed Forces and the Subcommittee on Defense, 99th Cong., 1st sess., June 26, 1985, http://www.loc.gov/law/find/nominations/gates/00100766905.pdf.

21. Shelling and Halperin (1961) explained it in this way: "since the advantage in striking first is largely in rescuing or precluding a punitive return attack, measures to defend the homeland against incoming punitive weapons are complementary to offensive weapons of surprise attack. Thus abstention from active defense of cities . . . might increase the potency of each side's retaliatory forces in a manner analogous to the protection of the retaliatory forces themselves."

22. "Treaty between the United States of America and the Union of Soviet Socialist Republics on the Limitation of Anti-Ballistic Missile Systems."

23. National Academy of Sciences, *Nuclear Arms Control and Background Issues* (Washington, DC: National Academy Press, 1985), 158.

24. Ibid.s

25. "Nuclear Successor States of the Soviet Union," The Monterey Institute for International Studies and the Carnegie Endowment for International Peace (Monterey, CA; Washington, DC, and Moscow), March 1998, http://cns.miis.edu/reports/pdfs/statrep.pdf.

26. "Anti-Ballistic Missile Treaty," Nuclear/Strategic Treaties and Agreements, Naval Treaty Implementation Program, http://www.ntip.navy.mil/abm_treaty.shtml.

27. Committee on National Security and Arms Control, National Academy of Sciences, *Nuclear Arms Control: Background and Issues* (Washington, DC: National Academy Press, 1995), 109, http://www.nap.edu/openbook.php?record_id=11&page=109.

28. Ibid, 107–35.

29. "Treaty Texts & Fact Sheets: Intermediate-Range Nuclear Forces (INF) Treaty," Defense Treaty Inspection Readiness Program, http://dtirp.dtra.mil/tic/treatyinfo/inf.aspx.

30. Federation of American Scientists, "Memorandum of Understanding," FAS, http://www.fas.org/sgp/othergov/mou-infoshare.pdf.

31. "Brief Chronology of START II," Arms Control Association, http://www.armscontrol.org/factsheets/start2chron.

32. "1997 Helsinki Joint Statement," Nuclear Threat Initiative, http://www.nti.org/db/nisprofs/fulltext/treaties/abm/abm_heje.htm.

33. U.S. Department of State, "Treaty between the United States of America and the Russian Federation on Measures For the Further Reduction and Limitation of Strategic Offensive Arms," April 8, 2010, http://www.state.gov/documents/organiza tion/140035.pdf.

34. Soviet leaders Yuri Andropov and Konstantin Chernenko held office for short periods of time and did not take on any arms control initiatives.

35. Schelling and Halperin, *Strategy and Arms Control*, 2.

36. Steve Weber, *Cooperation and Discord in US–Soviet Arms Control* (Princeton, NJ: Princeton University Press, 2006), 280.

CHAPTER 3

Multilateral Nuclear Arms Control: Controlling the Spread and Testing of Nuclear Weapons

As nuclear weapons proliferated rapidly in the decades following WWII— first to the Soviet Union in 1949, then to the United Kingdom in 1952, to France in 1960, and to China in 1964—governments worldwide struggled to devise a system to halt or limit the trend. On January 24, 1946, the newly created UN General Assembly passed a resolution establishing the UN Atomic Energy Commission to address the ominous problem that the discovery of atomic energy had created. The commission's most important task: eliminating atomic weapons from national arsenals.

Origins of the Nuclear Non-Proliferation Treaty

In June that year, Bernard Baruch, the U.S. ambassador to the UN, presented a plan to give "managerial control or ownership of all atomic energy activities potentially dangerous to world security" to an international authority. The authority was to be given power to control, inspect, and license all atomic activities that were not undertaken by the international authority. Nations that violated the plan by developing atomic weapons would be subject to serious penalties, which could not be vetoed by any permanent member of the Security Council.[1] The Soviet Union promptly refused to consider the Baruch proposal. Before it would agree to implement the plan, the Soviets insisted that the United States destroy its own nuclear weapons stockpile. The United States firmly rejected the Soviet proposal. The United States and the Soviet Union were at a stalemate, the Baruch Plan languished, and the Soviet Union continued to develop a nuclear arsenal. In 1949, it detonated its first atomic weapon.

Four years later, in 1953, U.S. president Dwight Eisenhower sowed the seeds of the NPT. In a speech to the UN, Eisenhower recommended that an international atomic energy agency be established under the aegis of the UN. Nations would contribute fissionable materials to the agency, which would be responsible for them. The agency would also be responsible for devising ways for those fissionable materials to be used for peaceful purposes, including research on the effects of nuclear radiation or the provision of nuclear energy.[2] The program came to be known as Atoms for Peace, but was ultimately unable to halt the spread of nuclear weapons. Then, in 1956, the International Atomic Energy Agency (IAEA) was established by 81 countries, by statute.[3]

The statute establishing the IAEA envisioned that the Agency would be instrumental in halting the spread of nuclear weapons while enabling states to obtain nuclear materials for energy and other peaceful purposes. Unfortunately, the early years of the agency saw both China and France develop and test nuclear weapons. Concurrent with the establishment of the IAEA, the six European countries forming the European Common Market set up an organization that would rival the IAEA in certain respects—EURATOM. The United States curtailed the power of the IAEA in its early years by transferring nuclear material to requesting states through bilateral agreements rather than through IAEA and applying EURATOM rather than IAEA safeguards.[4] Confidence in the IAEA grew over time, however, and it became an instrumental component of the NPT. Yet, because the IAEA predated the NPT, participation in IAEA by states that are not parties to the NPT continues. In December 1961, the UN General Assembly passed several resolutions on arms control and disarmament. One of them laid out a set of responsibilities for all nations—whether or not they possessed nuclear weapons—that became the foundation for the NPT. The resolution put forth a double set of obligations—one for nations that possessed nuclear weapons, and a second for nations that did not. Distilled to the simplest terms, the resolution called on countries with nuclear weapons to agree to neither sell nor provide such weapons to other countries, nor provide other countries with information on how to manufacture them. The resolution called on countries without nuclear weapons to agree not to acquire, accept, or manufacture them.[5]

Heightened tensions in the Cold War, particularly the Cuban Missile Crisis in 1962, added pressure on the nuclear powers, particularly the United States and the Soviet Union, to find a means to address the issue of proliferation. A 1963 U.S. Department of Defense estimate of nuclear proliferation led President Kennedy to announce at a press conference that 15 to 25 states might acquire the capability to produce nuclear weapons by the 1970s.[6] Not until the Johnson administration, however, did negotiations on a treaty to staunch nuclear weapons proliferation become a political priority. Cold War tensions stalled the completion of the NPT. The United States wanted to cement its superiority while the Soviet Union wanted to make sure it had parity with the United States.[7] Moreover, U.S. guarantees of nuclear protection for its NATO allies, including the deployment of U.S. nuclear weapons on European soil, clouded the issue of proliferation.[8]

Provisions of the NPT[9]

The NPT created separate obligations for nuclear weapon states (NWS) and nonnuclear weapon states (NNWS).

NWS were defined as states that had manufactured and exploded a nuclear weapon or other nuclear device as of January 1, 1967. Under the provisions of the treaty, these states agreed not to transfer or give control of nuclear weapons to any recipient, or help nonnuclear weapon states acquire the weapons. NWS also agreed to pursue nuclear disarmament and negotiations to end the nuclear arms race.

NNWS agreed not to manufacture, acquire, or receive nuclear weapons. They were also obliged to accept safeguards on their nuclear energy facilities. The safeguards were to be negotiated with the IAEA, which would verify that the facilities complied with the NPT obligations.

Additionally, the agreement also provides benefits to NNWS as an incentive to join the treaty. The treaty formally acknowledges the right of nonnuclear weapon states to produce and use nuclear energy for peaceful purposes and requires all states parties ensure that the benefits of peaceful uses of nuclear explosions be available to all other states parties.

The obligations contained in Article VI of the treaty have frequently been a topic of intense disagreement between NWS and NNWS. The Article requires all parties to negotiate in good faith to end the arms race and to achieve nuclear, as well as general, disarmament.

The threaty called for a conference to review the treaty's operation five years after it had entered into force. It also provided a process for the parties to the treaty to call subsequent review conferences. Finally, the agreement called for a conference to be held 25 years after the treaty's entry into force to determine whether it should continue indefinitely, or for one or more set periods beyond the initial 25 years. The agreement specified that this decision would be made by majority vote.

In conjunction with the completion of the NPT, the UN Security Council passed a resolution that provided additional incentives to nonnuclear states to become party to the agreement. Resolution 255 provided what are known as positive security assurances. The resolution states that if a nuclear weapon state used or threatened to use nuclear weapons against a nonnuclear weapon state, the Security Council "would have to act immediately." The United Kingdom, the United States, and the Soviet Union agreed to come to the assistance of any nonnuclear weapon state that was threatened with nuclear weapons or was the target of a nuclear weapon. The resolution also recognized that some states had expressed the intention to provide assistance to nonnuclear weapon states in that situation.[10] Nevertheless, some nonnuclear weapon states believed that Resolution 255 was too weak. For one thing, the resolution did not contain negative security assurances—pledges by the nuclear powers not to threaten or use nuclear weapons against nonnuclear weapon states. Finally, prior to the 1995 conference that would determine the future of the NPT, the Security Council passed Resolution 984 that strengthened the positive security assurances and contained some weakly worded negative security assurances. All five NPT nuclear weapon states agreed to come to the aid of a country threatened with or the target of nuclear weapons. China agreed not to use nuclear weapons under any circumstances against a nonnuclear weapon state that was a party to the NPT. The other four states stated some conditions under which they would use nuclear weapons against a nonnuclear weapons member state.

Operation of the Treaty

The NPT entered into force in March 1970, with three NWS—the United States, the Soviet Union, and the United Kingdom—and 43 NNWS. The number of states parties to the treaty grew slowly to its current membership of 189 states parties, the largest number of any arms control agreement. Only India, Israel, and Pakistan have never been members of the NPT. North Korea was a member, but withdrew from the treaty in 2003.

Figure 1 Growth in NPT Membership over Time

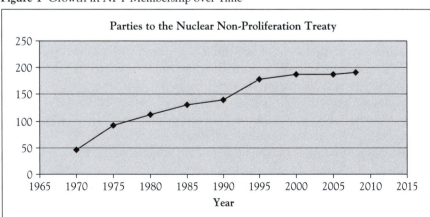

But the raw numbers do not tell the whole story. The growth of NPT states parties reveals some unexpected and significant details. Many states with substantial technical capabilities were not original signatories. Australia and Japan, for example, were missing from the list. When the treaty entered into force in 1970, only 11 European countries were among the original parties. All the Scandinavian states were original parties, but most other Western European states were not. Among European members of NATO, only Denmark, Iceland, Ireland, and the United Kingdom were original NPT member states. Belgium, The Netherlands, Italy, Spain, Portugal, Turkey, and what was then West Germany were notably absent. France, a nuclear weapon state, was also absent; it did not join the NPT until 1992, more than 20 years after the treaty entered into force.[11]

Membership among the Warsaw Pact European states was also spotty. East Germany, Hungary, Poland, and Romania were original members, but Albania, Bulgaria, and Czechoslovakia were not. Nonaligned Austria and Yugoslavia were original parties, but neutral Switzerland was not.

South America's original membership was similarly patchwork. Only four states—Bolivia, Ecuador, Paraguay, and Peru—were original parties to the treaty. They were joined by Mexico and Costa Rica in Central America. In the Caribbean, only Haiti and Jamaica were original parties. In Africa, 12 states were original members: Burkina Faso, Botswana, Cameroon,

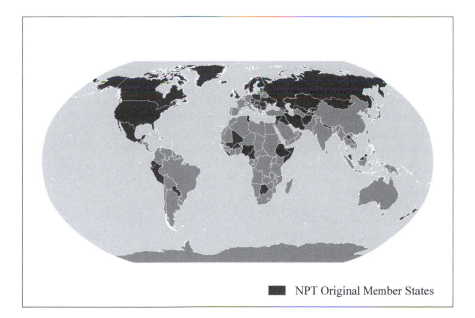

■ NPT Original Member States

Ethiopia, Liberia, Mali, Mauritius, Nigeria, Somalia, Swaziland, Togo, and Tunisia. In the Middle East, Iraq, Iran, Jordan, and Syria were all original members.

Asia had sparse early membership. Besides the Soviet Union, only Afghanistan, Malaysia, Mongolia, Nepal, and Taiwan were original members. China, which had exploded its first nuclear weapon in 1964, did not accede to the treaty until 1992.

1975 Review Conference

By the time the first Review Conference (RevCon) on the NPT was held in 1975, 91 states were NPT members, nearly double the number of original members. There were new members from every geographic area. But membership was far from universal, and significant states withheld their membership. Three main issues elicited significant concern and discussion—not just during the RevCon in 1975, but at later RevCons, as well. The issues were: (1) safeguards for fissionable material in NNWS; (2) the security of NNWS; and (3) the obligation, in particular of the NWS, to end the arms race and work toward nuclear disarmament. The Final Declaration of the 1975 RevCon emphasized that it was necessary for all states that had not yet concluded safeguard agreements with the IAEA to do so.[12]

The declaration also recommended improvements in safeguards. In addressing the topic of NNWS' security, the Final Declaration referred to UNSC Resolution 225, discussed the importance of nuclear weapons-free zones, urged all states to refrain from the threat or use of force, and stressed the obligation of NWS to strengthen the security of NNWS.

Referring to Article VI of the NPT agreement, which deals with the obligation of NWS to end the nuclear arms race, the Final Declaration declared "serious concern that . . . the nuclear arms race is continuing unabated." The declaration outlined several steps to improve the situation, including tackling the technical and political difficulties in reaching a conclusion to a treaty banning all nuclear weapons tests, and negotiating follow-on agreements to the SALT I treaty.

1980 Review Conference

By 1980, membership in the NPT had climbed to 112 states.

Primarily because of disagreements about NWS' obligation to stop the nuclear arms race, delegations to the second NPT RevCon in 1980 did not reach consensus on a Final Declaration. Disagreements about language on full-scope safeguards for nuclear material in nonnuclear weapon states also remained unresolved. Participating delegates did reach an agreement on language about the importance of safeguards, and the importance of consultation before implementing export controls on nuclear materials and technology—but they failed to agree on other controversial topics. As a result, even where agreement existed, the absence of a Final Declaration meant that those provisions were not implemented.[13]

1985 Review Conference

The delegations to the Third RevCon of the NPT in 1985 avoided the outcome of the 1980 RevCon and produced an extensive Final Declaration. With more than a hundred paragraphs, the declaration covered all aspects of the NPT's operation. Several issues were particularly noteworthy. One serious concern was the nuclear capabilities of Israel and South Africa, neither of which was a party to the treaty. Despite the several successes of the NPT, the RevCon dealt with the specter of nuclear proliferation. It called on all states to completely ban transferring to Israel and South Africa any materials relevant to nuclear weapons. It also urged all nonnuclear weapon states that were not parties to the treaty to make a legally binding commitment not to acquire nuclear weapons and to put their peaceful nuclear activities under IAEA safeguards. Four of the five NWS had concluded safeguard agreements with IAEA covering their peaceful nuclear activities, and the Final Declaration urged China to do the same. There were disagreements about the extent to which the NWS fulfilled their obligation to end the arms race and work toward disarmament, but the conference acknowledged that progress was evident and made recommendations for future work.

The recommendations of the conference included completion of the Comprehensive Test Ban Treaty (CTBT), a halt to the production of fissile material, and a phased program for balanced reductions of nuclear stockpiles. The Declaration noted that there were many proposals for ending the arms race, but also noted, with regret, that the negotiations had not produced any results and nuclear weapons systems were still being developed and deployed.

1990 Review Conference

Disagreements among delegations at the 1990 RevCon stymied efforts to complete a Final Declaration, just as had happened at the RevCon 10 years earlier. Member states acknowledged some progress on the Article VI obligation of NWS to end the nuclear arms race. In 1987, the United States and the Soviet Union completed the Intermediate Range Nuclear Forces Treaty, which removed all of the U.S. and Soviet missiles with a target range of 500 to 5,500 kilometers from Europe and Asia. Nevertheless, disagreements about the Article VI obligations of NWS prevented consensus. Neither France nor the United Kingdom for instance got rid of its shorter range missiles. Delegations from the NNWS were particularly distressed by the lack of progress in the CTBT negotiations. They reiterated the importance of a CTBT in every review conference, and indicated that their patience was wearing thin.

One hundred forty states were party to the NPT in 1990, more than a threefold increase in 20 years. Nevertheless, implementation issues continued to plague the treaty. As of 1990, 51 treaty parties, all of them NNWS, had still not completed safeguard agreements with IAEA, required under Article III of the Treaty to be completed within 180 days after the treaty entered into force for a state party.

1995 Review Conference

Between 1990 and 1995, as a result of a push to make the NPT universal, 38 new states acceded to the treaty, and by the time of the 1995 RevCon, the NPT had 178 parties. New members included France and China, both NWS. The increase in membership was the biggest since the five-year interval between when the treaty was entered into force in 1970 and the first RevCon in 1975. Many of the new parties were former republics of the Soviet Union. Remarkably, in an important development, Belarus, Kazakhstan, and Ukraine all joined the NPT as NNWS after they transferred to Russia the nuclear weapons that each of them had inherited from the Soviet Union. South Africa also joined the NPT as a nonnuclear weapon state in 1991; before turning over the reins of government to the majority black South Africans, the country's apartheid government had dismantled its secretive, sophisticated nuclear weapons program.[14]

The four prior RevCons set a pattern leading up to the critical RevCon in 1995. According to Article X of the Treaty, in 1995, the parties were to decide whether to extend the treaty indefinitely or for a fixed period of time. The decision was to be made by a majority vote. In the years and months preceding the 1995 RevCon, there had been a flurry of diplomatic activity.[15] The United States, for example, placed a very high priority on extending the treaty indefinitely and administration personnel traveled the globe to urge allies and other states to support a permanent extension.

To increase incentives to accede to the NPT, the UN Security Council passed Resolution 984, which dealt with assistance if a state were the recipient of a nuclear attack or under threat of a nuclear attack.[16]

Themes from the earlier NPT RevCons were on the agenda again in 1995. The most important of those themes was the nuclear arms race and obligations of the NWS to disarm. Early in the three-week conference, the states favoring an indefinite extension appeared to be in the majority. But many states did not want a state-by-state vote on the treaty extension. Reasons varied. Some states did not want to go on record as opposing or supporting an indefinite extension. Other states, which firmly opposed an indefinite extension, wanted a greater commitment from the NWS.

The RevCon chairman, Jayantha Dhanapla of Sri Lanka, crafted a package of agreements that included something desirable for all parties, even if it did not address top priorities of all delegations. Conference delegates made three decisions: first, they strengthened the treaty's review process; second, they established a set of principles and objectives for nuclear nonproliferation and disarmament; and third, they decided to extend the NPT indefinitely. In a separate measure they adopted a Resolution on the Middle East.

The first decision, to strengthen the NPT's review process, had several important features. Preparatory meetings for the RevCons, which previously had been held only in the year preceding a RevCon, would now be held annually. The purpose of the preparatory meetings was to include ways to promote full implementation and universality of the treaty. The RevCons were also instructed to look to the future as well as to the past: in addition to reviewing the treaty's implementation during the relevant time period in the past, they also were to consider ways in which "further progress should be sought in the future."[17]

The second decision—the most extensive of the three—contained a preamble and 20 paragraphs of principles and objections organized into seven categories: universality, nonproliferation, nuclear disarmament, nuclear weapons–free zones, security assurances, safeguards, and peaceful uses of nuclear energy. The objectives on nuclear disarmament called for a CTBT, to be completed no later than 1996, and immediate negotiations to ban production of fissile material for nuclear weapons. The decision also called for a legally binding international agreement to embody the security assurances contained in the UN Security Council Resolution 984 and elsewhere. The final section of the decision, on the peaceful uses of nuclear energy, called for transparency in export controls.[18]

The third decision addressed the question of whether or not to extend the treaty. States parties decided there would be no state-by-state vote on an indefinite extension. Instead, the delegates agreed by consensus that a majority of them favored an indefinite extension, and so the NPT would be extended indefinitely.[19]

The Conference delegates also passed a resolution on the Middle East. Without mentioning any state by name, the resolution called on all states in the region to accede to the NPT. It also called for a Middle East zone that would be free of all weapons of mass destruction—nuclear, chemical, and biological—and the delivery systems for such weapons. The resolution noted that there were nuclear facilities in the Middle East not under IAEA safeguards. It also made a pointed reference to Israel's nuclear weapons facilities and to the nascent nuclear program in Iraq that had been halted and destroyed by the UN Special Commission on Iraq after the 1991 Gulf War. Despite their consensus agreement on the decisions taken at the 1995 RevCon and the Middle East Resolution, the Conference delegates were again unable to reach agreement on a Final Declaration. And, as before, the failure was due primarily to disagreements about nuclear disarmament by the NWS.[20]

2000 Review Conference

Despite deadlocks during yearly interim reviews in 1997, 1998, and 1999, the 2000 RevCon completed a consensus Final Document—the first RevCon since 1985 to do so. By 2000, the CTBT had been completed, as called for in Decision 2 of the 1995 RevCon. However, there had been little progress on a treaty to ban the production of fissile material (also called a fissile material cutoff treaty). Although completed, the CTBT has still not entered into force.

The 2000 Final Document consists of three volumes. The first deals extensively with the substantive review of the treaty. Because of the history of animosity among member states about the disarmament obligations of the NWS, the Final Document's review of the pertinent Article VI specifies 13 practical steps for the "systematic and progressive efforts to implement Article VI."[21] A summary of these 13 steps covered familiar ground:

1. early entry into force of the CTBT;
2. a moratorium on nuclear weapons tests and any other nuclear explosions;
3. negotiations on a treaty banning the production of fissile material;
4. establishing a body within the Conference on Disarmament to deal with nuclear disarmament;
5. applying the principle of irreversibility to nuclear disarmament;
6. total elimination of the nuclear arsenals of the NWS;
7. early entry into force of START II and the conclusion of START III while preserving and strengthening the AMB Treaty;
8. completion of the Trilateral Initiative between the United States, Russia, and the IAEA;
9. nuclear disarmament in a way that promotes international stability and undiminished security:
   - unilateral efforts to reduce nuclear arsenals,
   - increased transparency with regard to nuclear capabilities and promotion of confidence building measures,
   - further reduction of nonstrategic nuclear weapons,
   - measures to reduce the operational status of nuclear weapons systems,
   - a diminishing role for nuclear weapons in security policies,
   - engagement of all NWS in the process of nuclear disarmament;

10. placing fissile material no longer needed for military purposes under the IAEA;
11. reaffirmation of the ultimate objective of general and complete disarmament under effective international control;
12. regular reports on the implementation of Article VI of the NPT and the Principles and Objectives Decision of the 1995 RevCon; and
13. further development of verification capabilities to provide assurance of compliance with nuclear disarmament agreements.

Despite the 2000 RevCon's accomplishments, serious disagreements remained. One commentator noted: "The final document was achieved only because deep differences between states on several crucial matters were papered over—issues such as missile defense, nuclear doctrines, and treaty compliance."[22]

2005 Review Conference

Those papered-over differences were intensified further by several subsequent events and came into sharp focus at the 2005 RevCon. In 2003, North Korea withdrew from the NPT. Also, in 2003, an IAEA report charged Iran with conducting secret nuclear activities that violated its NPT obligations.[23] The Bush administration in the United States made no secret of its dislike of the CTBT and withdrew from the ABM treaty. And very little progress was made on the 13 practical steps established in 2000. After wrangling over the agenda for weeks, none of the main committees of the conference were able to finish reports, and the RevCon was widely viewed as a complete failure.

2010 Review Conference

The 2010 NPT RevCon was a sharp contrast to the one five years earlier. Meeting throughout May, conference participants completed a lengthy Final Document that described 64 steps for the future. The steps are organized around six main themes: first, nuclear disarmament; second, assurances that NWS will not use those weapons against NNWS; third, an end to nuclear testing; fourth, negotiating a treaty banning the production of fissile material; fifth, preventing the proliferation of nuclear weapons; and sixth, the peaceful uses of nuclear energy. Each theme includes many specific steps to take to achieve these broad goals.

However, delegations to the conference did not agree on the Final Document easily. There was a serious disagreement between the United States and Iran and, to a lesser extent, between the United States and other Middle East nations. The disagreement centered on the language in the Final Document relating to implementation of the Middle East Resolution, which had been

created during the 1995 RevCon. The resolution called for a conference in the Middle East on weapons of mass destruction to discuss establishing a zone free of weapons of mass destruction. Fifteen years later, there had still been no progress.

The heart of the dispute was a disagreement about whether Israel and Iran should be identified by name in the portion of the Final Document that called for implementing the 1995 Middle East Resolution. Because decisions at RevCons are made by consensus, the disagreement could make it impossible to move forward. Without consensus, the 2010 RevCon would end in failure. The United States opposed naming Israel as the only Middle East state with nuclear facilities not under IAEA safeguards, but Iran refused to agree to the Final Document unless it identified Israel by name. Because Israel is not a member of the NPT, it cannot vote and, consequently, does not have the power to block a decision.

Meanwhile, Iran refused to agree to the Final Document if it included any mention that Iran was not in compliance with the NPT. In the end, the United States agreed that Israel could be named in the document if Iran agreed to the Final Document in its entirety. The document does not identify Iran as not in compliance; if it did Iran, of course, would have refused to sign. In essence, Iran had less to lose than the United States if the conference was unable to agree on a Final Document.

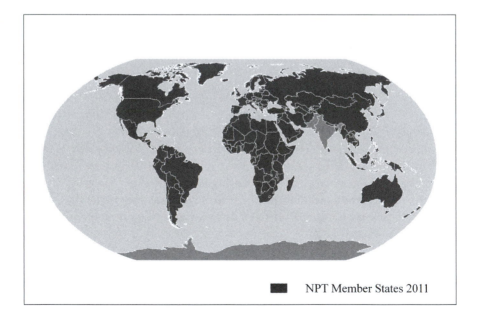

NPT Member States 2011

Nuclear Weapon States Outside the NPT: Israel, India, Pakistan

Since the NPT's inception, Israel, India, and Pakistan have each steadfastly refused to become a party to the NPT. Instead, each has produced and stockpiled nuclear weapons. The three countries have also resisted other measures for arm controls such as the CTBT.

Israel

Since Israel declared its independence from British rule in 1948, its security has been of utmost importance. Israel has fought wars, suffered numerous attacks on its people, and occupied territories that it took possession of after the 1967 Arab–Israeli war. As early as 1955, Israeli prime minister David Ben Gurion alluded to the importance of developing nuclear weapons to ensure Israel's security, "Our security problem could have two answers: if possible, political guarantees, but this is not up to us. But what depends on us, we must invest all our power, because we must have superiority in weapons, because we will never achieve superiority in manpower."[24] Unlike NWS that ostensibly developed nuclear weapons in response to nuclear weapons acquisition in hostile states, Israel did not have enemies who possessed nuclear weapons. Israel acquired nuclear weapons to deter conventional war from hostile neighboring states.

Israel had a nuclear weapons program at the time the NPT was completed in 1968,[25] but it was cloaked in deepest secrecy and hidden from the country's own population and closest allies. Israel had been developing the components for nuclear weapons since the 1950s, when there were no international norms or constraints on the activity. It could not sign the NPT as a NWS, however, because it had not tested or exploded a nuclear weapon by the date the NPT had designated as the qualifying deadline. But, even if Israel had qualified for the status of a NWS, it would almost certainly have been detrimental to NPT membership among Arab states in the Middle East and North Africa, as well as Iran. It has always been considered extremely desirable for Middle Eastern and North African states to participate in the NPT, but if Israel had been included as a NWS, its antagonistic neighbors would have likely refused to sign and ratify the NPT.

There is little, if any, doubt that Israel possesses a nuclear weapons stockpile, but its government still officially maintains a policy of ambiguity, neither admitting nor denying that it has nuclear weapons. Nor has Israel ever openly tested its weapons.[26] Publicly, Israel has stated that it will never be the country to introduce nuclear weapons into the Middle East.[27] However, Israel's definition of "introduce" does not imply that the weapons are not already present on Israeli soil. Israel argues that to introduce means to test and publicly announce that it possesses nuclear weapons, and perhaps deploy these weapons. Because of this qualified definition, Israel continues to maintain that it has kept its word regarding nuclear weapons and the Middle East. Estimates of the size of Israel's nuclear weapons stockpile vary from a low of about 70 warheads to a high of 400; the larger number would make the stockpile approximately the size of stockpiles in the United Kingdom and China.[28]

As the open secret of Israel's nuclear weapons became more open and less secret, NNWS within the NPT explored strategies to compel Israel to get rid of its weapons. The most frequently suggested strategy was to seek an agreement to establish a nuclear weapons–free zone in the Middle East similar to the nuclear weapons–free zone in Latin America and the Caribbean that had been created by the Treaty of Tlatelolco.[29] The Middle East Resolution, which called for a nuclear weapons–free zone in that region, passed by consensus at the 1995 RevCon of the NPT, but it is highly unlikely that Israel will accede to the NPT as long as it feels that it is under threat from hostile and aggressive neighbors who refuse to recognize Israel's right to exist.

India

Like Israel, India refused to sign the NPT in 1968 and has consistently maintained that stance ever since. Also, like Israel, India began work on its nuclear program long before the NPT came into existence.[30] India has been explicit about why it won't join: it objects to the very structure of the NPT, with its two categories of nuclear haves and nuclear have-nots. India has repeatedly described the treaty as discriminatory and declared that it will never accede to the NPT as either a nuclear weapon state or a nonnuclear weapon state. India also points out that it shares borders with China and Pakistan, both of whom have nuclear weapons.[31] Although India has hostile relations with both countries, its public rationale for acquiring nuclear weapons has pointed to a nuclear threat from China, not Pakistan.

In 1974, India conducted what it refers to as a "peaceful nuclear explosion." Although not a true weapons test, it demonstrated India's ability to produce nuclear weapons. It did not conduct any further nuclear tests until 1998 in response to Pakistan's first nuclear tests.[32] Nevertheless, with its 1998 tests, India demonstrated conclusively that it possessed nuclear weapons. The size of India's nuclear weapon stockpile is unknown but estimated to include 70–110 warheads.[33]

Pakistan

Among many states with a nuclear weapons arsenal, the rationale for the buildup is, at least partly, a response to an adversary's nuclear capabilities. So the Soviet Union acquired nuclear weapons in response to the United States, China acquired them in response to the Soviet Union, India in response to China, and Pakistan in response to India. In a similar manner, Pakistan did not join the NPT initially and remains outside the treaty in large part because of India's refusal to join.

In 1971, East Pakistan—now Bangladesh—fought successfully, with assistance from India's military, for independence from West Pakistan. Pakistan initiated its nuclear weapons program following its defeat, and then accelerated its program after India's peaceful nuclear explosion in 1974. In 1987, Pakistan crossed a nuclear threshold and acquired the ability to test a nuclear weapon. However, it did not actually conduct a test until 1998. At the upper end, the estimated size of Pakistan's stockpile is believed to be the same as India's—110 weapons—and at the lower end, somewhat smaller.[34]

Withdrawal from the NPT: North Korea

North Korea's nuclear weapons program, undertaken in violation of its NPT obligations, was shrouded in secrecy. North Korea, which was not an initial signatory of the NPT, initiated a nuclear energy research program in the mid-1960s and did not accede to the NPT until 1985, under international pressure to do so. Like all parties to the NPT, North Korea was required to declare its nuclear materials and facilities to the IAEA and complete an agreement to put them under IAEA safeguards. However, North Korea refused to sign the IAEA agreement. It would not do so until 1992 after the United States had removed nuclear weapons from South Korea. IAEA then began inspections of North Korea's declared nuclear facilities, but in 1993, North Korea refused to give IAEA permission to inspect a facility that it had not declared and that was suspected of containing nuclear waste.

In 1993, North Korea announced its intention to withdraw from the NPT; it subsequently suspended the notice and began talks with the United States on its suspected nuclear weapons program.[35] Those talks culminated in 1994 with the Agreed Framework. North Korea agreed to come into full compliance with its NPT obligations and to halt operations and construction of nuclear reactors suspected of producing fuel for the country's clandestine weapons program. In exchange, the United States agreed to supply North Korea with light water reactors for nuclear power (which are less able to convert nuclear fuel into weapons) and energy assistance—heavy fuel oil—until the new reactors could provide North Korea with energy.

But the task of implementing the many phases of the Agreed Framework (which is not a formal treaty) was anything but smooth. Construction of the light water reactors was delayed. Deliveries of heavy fuel oil were unpredictable. There were also indications that North Korea diverted some of the fuel to North Korea's military, a violation of the agreement. North Korea asked to be compensated for the oil delivery delays and threatened to resume its nuclear program.[36] All the while, the IAEA and North Korea continued to have disputes about inspections of facilities. Finally, in January 2003, the IAEA's Board of Governors issued a strongly worded resolution insisting that North Korea come into full compliance with its Safeguards Agreement and give IAEA inspectors access to facilities. North Korea reacted swiftly, announced that it would withdraw from the NPT, and then did just that.[37] North Korea's efforts to construct and test ballistic missiles further complicated the issue of its nuclear weapons program. Throughout the 1990s, North Korea built, tested, and shared missile technology with other states and the United States imposed sanctions in response.

Between 2003 and 2007, North Korea—no longer a member of the NPT—entered into another series of negotiations, known as the six party talks. The countries involved were North Korea, the United States, Russia, Japan, China, and South Korea. The talks were complex, with each of the parties pursuing its own national interest. Then, in October 2006, in the midst of the talks, North Korea conducted a successful nuclear weapons test and announced it to the world, confirming that the country had crossed the nuclear threshold. Nevertheless, in 2005, the six party talks produced a Statement of Principles and in 2007, an agreement, the North Korea Denuclearization Action Plan. Under the terms of the plan, North Korea agreed to dismantle its nuclear weapons program in exchange for energy, economic and humanitarian aid, and other monetary incentives.[38] In a dramatic move, in June 2008, North Korea blew up the cooling tower at its most famous, and most worrisome, nuclear reactor at Yongbyon.

However, by January 2009, North Korea had still not agreed to a verification plan for its denuclearization efforts, and throughout the year, it continued to defy the other five members of the talks. Most dramatically, in May 2009, North Korea conducted its second underground nuclear weapons test. The explosion was preceded by a failed rocket test that, if it had been successful, could have launched nuclear-armed missiles. Then, on July 4, 2009—a date apparently selected to signal its contempt for the United States—North Korea conducted a test of its short-range missiles. This was the second time the country had chosen to test missiles on the day that the United States celebrates its independence. North Korea had also tested missiles on July 4, 2006 and it tested missiles again in 2010.

The UN Security Council responded to the 2009 underground nuclear weapons test with yet another resolution condemning the test. But North Korea has ignored Security Council Resolutions in the past and is likely to continue doing so. In November 2010, North Korea announced that it had constructed a 2,000-centrifuge uranium enrichment facility.[39] Following the announcement, Pyongyang escalated tensions by firing artillery rounds at South Korea.

North Korea's actions prompted China to call for emergency six party talks. However, Japan, South Korea, and the United States refused.

In February 2011, South Korea and the United States conducted joint military exercises, further escalating tensions. North Korea threatened South Korea with attacks but no further attacks ensued. In April 2011, renewed efforts to negotiate were put forward when former U.S. president Jimmy Carter visited Pyongyang. Minimal progress has been made since that time.

Over the more than two decades that North Korea has pursued nuclear weapons and ballistic missiles, it has shown little or no interest in complying with UN Security Council Resolutions, responding to the IAEA, nor fully meeting the terms of agreements negotiated with the United States. The United States is not without fault in the failure of the Agreed Framework to halt North Korea's nuclear ambitions. Although the United States and North Korea once again began talks in late 2011, not much optimism is expressed on either side.

A closed and isolated nation, North Korea's actions are frequently puzzling to observers. It continues to seek monetary compensation for each and every concession that it makes regarding its missile and nuclear weapons programs. A revolutionary change in North Korea's leadership and governing structure may be necessary before real progress can occur. The recent death of Kim Jong Il and doubts about the ability of his 27-year-old son, Kim Jong Un, to consolidate and wield the same power that his father held have introduced new uncertainties into the North Korean nuclear weapons and missile programs and the international response to it.[40]

Suspicious Activity—Iran

Iran joined the NPT in 1970 and since 1992 has given the IAEA permission to inspect Iran's nuclear energy facilities. Since 2003, however, IAEA personnel and Iran have had several disputes about Iran's nuclear activities over the last 20 years. A 2007 report issued by the IAEA frames the problem this way:

> Given the existence in Iran of activities undeclared to the Agency for 20 years, it is necessary for Iran to enable the Agency, through maximum cooperation and transparency, to fully reconstruct the history of Iran's nuclear programme. Without such cooperation and transparency, the Agency will not be able to provide assurances about the absence of undeclared nuclear material and activities in Iran or about the exclusively peaceful nature of that programme.[41]

The crux of the dispute with Iran involves the enrichment of uranium. Iran has numerous centrifuges that take naturally occurring uranium and increase the concentration of fissionable uranium. Highly enriched uranium is needed to produce nuclear weapons; Iran claims that its enrichment program produces only low-enriched uranium, for fuel use. The IAEA has verified that Iran's enrichment activities and materials are consistent with Iran's declarations. But the question remains: does Iran plan to further enrich some, or all, of its low-enriched uranium, thereby making it a weapons-grade material? The IAEA and the UN Security Council have requested that Iran provide information that would answer the question; Iran has not complied.

During 2010 and 2011, Iran took part in talks with six other states: the United States, Britain, France, Russia, China, and Germany. All but Germany are NWS in the NPT, and members of the UN Security Council. Dubbed the Iran Six, the group met in Istanbul, Turkey, in January 2011 to take up once again the issue of Iran's nuclear program, and sanctions that the United States has imposed on Iran. According to Catherine Ashton, the head of EU foreign policy who chaired the meetings, the talks ended with no progress.[42] The Iran Six called on Iran to freeze its uranium enrichment program, but Iran refused to do so. Although in May 2011 Iran sought to reopen the talks, the response from the EU and the United States was not positive.[43]

In August 2011, after a push from Russia to move the six party talks forward, IAEA deputy director general Herman Nackaerts was given access to Iran's five nuclear facilities, in an effort to show "Tehran's 100 percent transparency and openness."[44] The visits did not curb concerns however. Iran began moving centrifuges in August 2011 from the Natanz enrichment plant to the fortified Fordow facility.[45] In September 2011, the IAEA Board of Governors met in Vienna. During the five-day meeting, the board examined the possible threat of Iran's nuclear ambitions. September also marked the launch of Iran's Bushehr nuclear power station.[46]

In November 2011, the IAEA director general issued the harshest report to date on Iran's nuclear weapons program. Contrasting the language of the 2011 report with that of 2007 quoted earlier in this section, the IAEA states it "is unable to provide credible assurance about the absence of undeclared nuclear material and activities in Iran, and therefore to conclude that all nuclear material in Iran is in peaceful activities." The IAEA also stated that it "has serious concerns regarding possible military dimensions to Iran's nuclear programme. After assessing carefully and critically the extensive information available to it, the Agency finds the information to be, overall, credible. The information indicates that Iran has carried out activities relevant to the development of a nuclear explosive device."[47] In response to the report of the director general, the IAEA Board of Governors adopted a resolution expressing "deep and increasing concern about the unresolved issues re-garding Iran's nuclear program."[48] In response, the EU announced that it would impose new sanctions on Iran and ban the import of Iranian oil by July 2012. The move by the EU underscores the seriousness with which it views the Iranian nuclear program, showing a willingness to suffer a rise in oil prices at a time of economic crisis. The price of oil rose following the EU announcement. The EU had been purchasing 450,000 barrels of Iranian oil a day—at more than a $100 a barrel, which amounts to more than $16 tril-lion a year.[49] The announced sanctions may already be having some effect on Iran. The director general of the IAEA announced in May, 2012, Iran was prepared to sign an agreement granting IAEA inspectors access to dis-puted facilities and the right to conduct an investigation into Iran's uranium enrichment program.[50]

Iran's uranium enrichment program and its sporadic willingness to cooper-ate with the IAEA continue to worry the agency, other governments, and arms control advocates. If Iran continues to enrich its existing stocks of ura-nium, the country would have enough weapons-grade uranium to make one or two nuclear weapons. How soon that could occur is a subject of debate.

Controlling Nuclear Weapons Tests

Testing nuclear weapons, or acquiring data from nuclear weapons tests, has been an integral component of most successful nuclear weapons programs. Detection of a successful nuclear weapons test is typically the manner through which states confirm that others have developed, acquired, or produced nu-clear weapons. Moreover, testing nuclear weapons creates radioactive fallout that is dangerous to human and animal health and to the environment. Con-sequently, limiting or eliminating nuclear weapons tests has long been a goal of arms control advocates and the nonnuclear weapon states, particularly the nonnuclear weapon states that are parties to the Nuclear NPT.

The Early History of Nuclear Weapons Tests

The United States conducted the first nuclear weapons test in the New Mexico desert near Alamogordo on July 16, 1945, in order to test the pluto-nium nuclear device, "Fat Man." The purpose of the first test, named Trinity, was to establish that the design of the weapons would function successfully. The nuclear device was hoisted to the top of a 100-foot tower and detonated. Following this successful test, the United States dropped a nuclear weapon of the Fat Man design on Nagasaki, Japan, on August 9th, 1945. The simpler enriched uranium device used in the first atomic weapons attack on Hiro-shima on August 6 was not tested prior to its use.

In the summer of 1946, the United States continued testing nuclear weapons despite the unconditional surrender of Japan that ended WWII. The United States conducted a series of nuclear weapons tests in the Marshall Islands near the Bikini Atoll. The purpose of Operation Crossroads, as these tests were named, was to gather data about the effects of the weapons, rather than to test their design. The design of the weapons used in these tests was of the same Fat Man type used at Nagasaki. The first test in Operation Crossroads was a bomb that was dropped from an aircraft, while the second weapon was detonated approximately 90 feet underwater.[51]

The United States tested three more nuclear weapons during April and May 1948. These tests, which also took place in the Marshall Islands, at Enewetak Atoll, were undertaken to test new weapons designs. Following the 1948 tests, the United States built its nuclear weapons stockpile with the new design. The Soviet Union conducted its first nuclear test in 1949 with a weapon whose design was identical to that used by the United States on Nagasaki in 1945. The Soviet Union acquired the design through espionage. The test was conducted in a remote area of the Soviet Republic of Kazakhstan, at the Semipalatinsk Test Site.[52] Only days following the first Soviet atomic weapon test, the United States announced plans to develop a hydrogen nuclear weapon, a much more powerful weapon than those used in Japan in the final days of WWII. The nuclear arms race was on. The United Kingdom was the next state to test an atomic weapon. In October 1952, the United Kingdom tested its first nuclear weapon, once again based on the design of Fat Man. The weapon was contained in the hull of a ship. The test was conducted at the Monte Bello Islands off Western Australia. The site was chosen, as were other sites, because of its remoteness and sparse population.[53]

The United States, the Soviet Union, and the United Kingdom continued to test nuclear weapons in the atmosphere throughout the 1950s. The United States conducted 119 tests at its Nevada test site, which had been established in 1950. As in earlier tests, these were conducted to test the design of weapons and their effects. The tests were conducted on the surface of the earth and underground, as well as aboveground. The United States continued to test nuclear weapons and by the time of the Partial Test Ban Treaty (PTBT) had completed more than 300 weapons tests. Following its initial successful test, the Soviet Union also continued nuclear testing, completing more than 200 tests by the time it signed the PTBT.

In 1958, U.S. president Eisenhower announced a unilateral moratorium on nuclear weapons testing, which was honored by the United Kingdom and, for a short time, by the Soviet Union. The Soviet Union, however, continued secret plans for testing and resumed with the largest nuclear weapons test to date in 1961. The United States quickly resumed its own tests. The United Kingdom ceased its independent nuclear weapons tests in 1958, following an agreement whereby the U.S. government agreed to share its nuclear weapons designs with the United Kingdom. Thereafter, the United States and the United Kingdom conducted a number of joint nuclear weapons tests starting in 1962 and continuing until 1991.

Concern over fallout from nuclear weapons tests had existed since the effects of radiation became known after the U.S. weapons attacks on Hiroshima and Nagasaki. However, the U.S. test of a thermonuclear or hydrogen bomb in early 1954 in the Marshall Islands mobilized international opposition to nuclear testing. The bomb test, known as "Castle Bravo," demonstrated that the device was even more powerful than its designers had estimated; moreover, weather patterns were not sufficiently analyzed and the test was not postponed when the weather changed. Consequently, the amount of fallout from the test blast was greater than anticipated and was deposited in an area not planned for by those conducting the test. Residents of the Marshall Islands, U.S. servicemen, and Japanese fishermen, whose craft, the Fifth Lucky Dragon, was in the path of the fallout plume, all were exposed to dangerous radiation. The 23-member crew of the Fifth Lucky Dragon was exposed to the largest amount of radiation and one of them died following exposure.[54]

Indian prime minister Jawaharlal Nehru was the first world leader to call for a standstill agreement among the NWS on nuclear testing a month following the radiation exposure in the Pacific occasioned by the Castle Bravo nuclear test. The Soviet Union proposed a halt of nuclear weapons tests at the UN Disarmament Commission in 1955. The Commission had been created by the UN General Assembly to address general disarmament questions.

The early test ban negotiations were marked by a number of disagreements among the five nation subcommittee of the Commission, the United States, the United Kingdom, the Soviet Union, Canada, and France. All of the nations except the Soviet Union argued that a cessation of nuclear weapons tests should be linked to other arms control issues, including a ban on the production of fissionable material. Another point of contention was whether a ban on nuclear testing could be effectively verified in the absence of on-site inspections, which the Soviets steadfastly opposed. In 1959, the United States and the United Kingdom dropped their insistence on linkages to other arms control agreements, but France did not. Furthermore, the Soviets then switched their position and sought linkages.[55] Little progress was apparent in the negotiations over the next few years.

The Limited Test Ban Treaty

The Cuban Missile Crisis ended the stagnation in the negotiations, as both the United States and the Soviet Union sought to improve their relationship. The crisis had a sobering effect throughout the world. The subcommittee of the Disarmament Commission began to tackle whether a partial or limited test ban could circumvent the verification problems associated with a total ban on nuclear testing.

By the early 1960s, the nuclear powers had begun to conduct nuclear tests underground. In contrast to atmospheric testing, which could easily be detected, some underground nuclear explosions could not be distinguished from naturally occurring seismic events.

In 1963, the United States, the Soviet Union, and the United Kingdom agreed to ban nuclear explosions of any kind in the earth's atmosphere, in outer space, and underwater. Ultimately signed by more than 100 states, the Partial (or Limited) Test Ban Treaty (PTBT) restricted where nuclear explosions could take place but did not constrain the number or size of nuclear tests as long as they took place underground. Indeed, more than 2,000 nuclear weapons tests have taken place since the first was conducted in 1945; the United States has conducted the most nuclear tests, more than 1,000.

The preamble to the agreement underscores that the disagreement that the original parties to the PTBT—the United States, the Soviet Union, and the United Kingdom—were unable to resolve would be taken up at a later date. Thus, the continuing controversy over how to detect underground nuclear tests without onsite inspections was postponed, for more than 30 years as it turned out. Greater secrecy regarding the outcome of nuclear weapons tests was one of the consequences of the cessation of tests in the atmosphere.

The Comprehensive Test Ban Treaty

Developing reliable nuclear weapons, or reliable new nuclear weapons, is difficult without testing them. Therefore, eliminating nuclear weapons tests has been integral to arms control and nonproliferation policy. Following the PTBT, multilateral negotiations to end all nuclear tests commenced but dragged on for decades.

Initially, India was a supporter of CTBT. As early as 1954, Indian prime minister Nehru called for the prohibition of nuclear testing. India was also a sponsor of the UN General Assembly Resolution 48/70 that established a mandate for the CTBT to be negotiated and was a full participant in the talks.[56]

The negotiations moved slowly in 1994, but specific dividing lines between the NWS, which included China, France, Russia, United Kingdom, and the United States, and nonnuclear, nonaligned states, referred to as the Group of 21 (G-21), soon emerged. Posturing began as various proposals were put forward and states acknowledged their positions. Significant differences were evident in terms of the scope of CTBT in regards to testing. The United States, Russia, France, and the United Kingdom sought provisions that would allow them to carry out low-yield tests for safety and reliability. China argued that the treaty should not limit testing for peaceful purposes. On the other hand, Sweden and Germany, and the G-21 sought a true zero-yield test ban, including a ban on test simulations. Positions on entry into force (EIF) were also important in setting the stage for future negotiations. Initial proposals called for a flexible signatory process, a position supported by the United States. The United Kingdom and Russia noted that no treaty would be sustainable if this EIF did not require ratification from the so-called threshold states—India, Israel, and Pakistan.

India's initial primary concern was over establishing a zero-yield treaty.[57] On May 20, 1994, U.S. president Clinton and Indian prime minister Rao made a joint statement on their commitment to push for nuclear disarmament, the CTBT, and a ban on fissile materials.

The second year of negotiations opened amid the shadow of the 25-year NPT RevCon. Between January and April 1995, the NWS made concessions on testing. In the midst of its own internal political conflict, the United States changed its stance, committed to a zero-yield testing agreement, and continued to foster a relationship with India. Additionally, the United Kingdom and France dropped their demand for safety and reliability testing. In March, Australia tabled a proposal to expand the scope of the treaty to move beyond weapons testing explosions to include a ban on all nuclear explosions, an issue that would regain importance after the NPT RevCon.[58]

The CTBT negotiations in the CD were suspended for the Nuclear Non-Proliferation RevCon, which ran from April 17 to May 12, 1995. However, the threshold states of India, Pakistan, and Israel were not parties to NPT and therefore were not full participants in the pivotal NPT RevCon. India, long a vocal opponent of the discriminatory NPT, refused to attend even as an observer, although Israel and Pakistan did attend as observers.[59] As part of a package of measures, "Principles and Objectives for Nuclear Nonproliferation and Disarmament" introduced by South Africa were also adopted. The objectives included a call for the completion of the CTBT no later than 1996. Only three days after the NPT RevCon ended, China continued its nuclear testing. Shortly thereafter, newly elected French president Chirac announced that he would fulfill his campaign promise to conduct eight nuclear test explosions between September 1995 and May 1996, ending their tests just before the target date for completion of the CTBT. The United States, linking China's testing and France's announcement, also publicly declared that it might resume testing as well.[60]

The actions of the NWS ignited anger among the nonnuclear weapon states who felt that they had been deceived.[61] In response, India, Pakistan, and Indonesia moved toward the positions already established by Germany and Sweden to call for the complete end to weapons testing, even to computer simulations.

In response, each of the NWS put forward declarations reestablishing their commitment to a CTBT and true zero-yield testing. The United States agreed to aid France in speeding up its efforts to finalize their tests by providing France with new computer simulation technologies.[62]

However, given the concerns by the U.S. Congress, Pentagon, and the scientific community, President Clinton specified six conditions for the United States to support a true zero-yield CTBT including "stockpile stewardship; the maintenance of modern, well financed nuclear laboratories; the retention of a 'basic capacity' to resume nuclear testing; continuation of research and development programmes to improve treaty monitoring and operations; and continuing resources for and development of intelligence gathering" and, seen as most important, "the right under treaty article allowing for withdrawal on grounds of supreme national interest."[63]

With pressure from other CD member states following the commitment of the United States and France to a zero-yield treaty, Russia and the United Kingdom eventually followed suit. On September 14, 1995, the United Kingdom declared support for a zero yield CTBT. Initially furious about the decision to accept a zero yield, the Russians formally accepted that position on October 23.[64] China continued to advocate its position on exceptions for explosions conducted for peaceful purposes.

Despite progress on the issue of yield, serious divisions remained among the parties. The issue of EIF began to take on a more significant role in the negotiations, particularly when China joined Russia, France, and the United Kingdom in their call to require ratification from the threshold states as a condition of EIF.

In June 1995, the U.S. Congress overturned an existing ban on military aid to Pakistan, which cleared the way for a transfer of $658 million in military equipment to the South Asian state.[65] This move strained India's relationship with the United States. Additionally, elections were pending in India and its public became increasingly frustrated with the way it perceived India being treated in the CD. The opposition Bharatiya Janata Party (BJP) in India increasingly took a pronuclear stance and publicly pressured the government to demonstrate their resolve on issues, particularly disarmament. Accordingly, India took a strong stand on linking the success of the CTBT negotiations to a specific date for disarmament by the NWS. This issue would become the catalyst for India's ultimate refusal to sign CTBT. "In an October 1995 statement at the United Nations, New Delhi noted it could not ignore the unconditional extension of the NPT which, in its opinion, perpetuated and legitimized the division of the world into nuclear haves and have-nots."[66]

A crushing blow to the relationship between the United States and India came at the end of 1995 and catapulted India into taking a stringent stance in negotiations. On December 14, 1995, a *New York Times* article reported leaks from U.S. Intelligence on India's progress on what was thought to be "nuclear test preparations at the Pokhara test site in Rajasthan." According to Rebecca Johnson, executive director of the Acronym Institute, the "reports unleashed a turbulent debate in India about nuclear policy, national interests and the CTBT." She continued by stating that it "became clear that a large majority linked the retention of India's nuclear option with independence, status and future security."[67]

In January 1996 as the CD negotiations resumed, France conducted its sixth and final weapons test, two less than initially planned, and pledged to begin the dismantling of two of its test facilities.[68] In response to a U.S. Department of Energy statement that the United States would pursue subcritical testing, 13 of the G-21 states countered by calling for a commitment to end the qualitative improvement of nuclear stockpiles through such testing. The United Kingdom, France, and the United States, however, opposed the move.

Indicating the first sign that it would refuse to join CTBT despite its active participation in negotiations, India broke from the G-21 and tabled three proposals, all of which contained language that tied CTBT EIF with a timeline for nuclear disarmament.[69]

As the deadline for resolution neared, the chair of the CTBT talks, Dutch ambassador Jaap Ramaker, created a chair's draft treaty. The United States began to aggressively lobby other states in an attempt to reach a conclusion before the September deadline. While some states argued that Ramaker's draft moved too fast, it provided a single working draft when the spring session opened on May 28, 1996, to which he attached a list of outstanding issues.

By June, the majority of states expressed support for the draft treaty. When the chair sought consensus on the final treaty text, India blocked it. On August 20, Ramaker handed over the report to the CD and in doing so handed over the responsibility of the treaty. On August 22, the CD met in plenary session. Amidst a large crowd, many of those present gave impassioned speeches. Belgium surprised many when its ambassador requested that the chair's draft CTBT text become an official CD document.[70] This in effect gave the treaty official status, while bypassing consensus. The same day, the Australian ambassador to the UN called for the UN to take action on Resolution 50/60 (CTBT) and requested that the CD document containing the full treaty text be attached to Resolution 50/60.

The UN General Assembly adopted the CTBT with Resolution A/RES/ 50/245 on September 10, 1996, with a vote of 153–3; only Bhutan, India, and

Libya objected.[71] CTBT was opened for signatures on September 24, 1996. In May 1998, India conducted five nuclear weapons tests and Pakistan responded with five tests of its own. These 1998 tests broke the de facto moratorium on nuclear testing that was established after the adoption of the CTBT in September 1996.[72] Following the 1998 nuclear weapons tests, the United States and others, including the G-8 (Group of 8: Canada, France, Germany, Italy, Japan, Russia, the United Kingdom, and the United States), put pressure on both countries through nonhumanitarian economic sanctions.[73]

Provisions of the CTBT

The text of the CTBT with annexes runs to more than 190 pages. Its essential obligations, embodied in Article I, prohibit treaty parties from conducting nuclear weapons tests, or any other nuclear explosion, thereby producing a truly comprehensive, zero-yield treaty that also bans so-called peaceful nuclear explosions. The remaining articles of the treaty establish the CTBT Organization (CTBTO), a Conference of States Parties, an Executive Council, and a Technical Secretariat to implement and administer the treaty. The treaty specifies the composition, powers, functions, and duties of each of these bodies. The CTBTO is headquartered in Vienna, the site of the IAEA, and has been operating even though the agreement has yet to enter into force.

The treaty contains detailed verification provisions involving four complementary elements: an international monitoring system; procedures for bilateral or multilateral consultation and clarification procedures among or between states parties; onsite inspections; and confidence-building measures. The International Monitoring System is at the heart of the verification regime. Facilities for collecting seismic and other scientific data, located and operated by states parties, will provide data to the Informational Data Centre, which will facilitate a data exchange among parties. The treaty explicitly encourages parties to consult one another and seek and provide clarification if questions of possible noncompliance arise before engaging in more formal procedures. Bilateral consultation and clarification discussions are typically less contentious and less politically charged than procedures involving the Executive Council. If consultation and clarification measures do not resolve compliance questions, a state party may request an onsite inspection to determine whether or not another state party has conducted a prohibited weapons test. If approved by the CTBT Executive Council, any state party is obligated to permit an onsite inspection on its territory or any territory under its control, under strict and detailed procedures set forth in the treaty, its Protocol, and annexes.

The drafters anticipated that the treaty might remain in a legal limbo if the requisite states did not sign and ratify the CTBT in a timely fashion. It called for a Conference of the States that had ratified the treaty to take place three years after it opened for signature if it had not yet entered into force.

Status of the CTBT

The treaty requires that all states that formally participated in the concluding year of the negotiations—1996—and which possessed nuclear reactors as of 1995 ratify the treaty before it can enter into force. The total came to 44 states.[74] Of the 44 required signatures needed for the treaty to enter into force, only three states have yet to sign—India, Pakistan, and North Korea; six additional states have yet to ratify the agreement—China, Egypt, Indonesia, Iran, Israel, and the United States.[75]

The U.S. Senate voted against ratification of the CTBT when President Clinton submitted the treaty in 2000. Despite strong Senate Republican opposition to ratification, President Obama has pledged to resubmit the treaty for Senate approval. Former Secretaries of State Schultz and Kissinger's support for bringing the CTBT into force may be persuasive enough to some Senate Republicans to secure ratification.

As of mid-2012, 157 states had ratified the agreement and the CTBTO was functioning in Vienna with a total staff of 246 people. One of the missions of the CTBTO is to ensure that all preparations for verifying the CTBT are operational. The organization has installed 85 percent of the network that will comprise the International Monitoring System, including stations for monitoring all types of scientific data. Preparations for onsite inspections have been tried out in exercises, recently in Jordan. The CTBTO also assists state parties in developing their national capacities to fulfill their treaty obligations. The second part of the CTBTO's mission is to promote signature and ratification efforts so that the treaty may enter into force.

Because eight critical states have withheld their ratification of the CTBT, the Conferences on Facilitating the Entry into Force of the CTBT, authorized under Article XV of the Convention, have taken place every other year since 1995. The conferences have adopted Final Declarations, urging the signatories that have not yet ratified the agreement to do so, and urging the 13 states that did not sign the treaty to sign and become a member of it. The most recent conference was held in New York in 2011. Like previous conferences, the 2011 gathering agreed on a Final Declaration and adopted other measures to encourage the eight hold out states to ratify or accede to the treaty. India, Pakistan, and North Korea, whose membership is required for EIF, did not sign the CTBT and an additional 10 states have not signed.

Although in a protracted state of limbo, the CTBT is in some ways operating as though it were a functioning treaty that has entered into force. The work of the CTBTO is similar to that of organizations like the CWC organization and the IAEA that support treaties that are in force.[76] Member states undertake and refrain from many activities as required by the treaty provisions. How the CTBTO and the member states continue to operate in this state of limbo remains an open question. Will the states that have ratified the CTBT ever agree to implement the global verification regime that has been built up since 1997? Will they continue to support the activities and the budget of the CTBTO? The CTBTO is operating in uncharted territory, yet the profound commitment of the states that have ratified the CTBT augurs well for its future.

Prospects for the CTBT entering into force in the near future are not promising. Nevertheless, there have been more than 2,000 nuclear explosions and nuclear weapons tests since 1945, with an annual high of 178 tests in 1962. Yet, only North Korea has conducted nuclear weapons tests, one in 2006 and one in 2009, since the Indian and Pakistani tests in 1998. There is thus strong evidence that the norm against testing nuclear weapons is robust and perhaps becoming stronger. The norm, arising first from the nuclear weapons testing moratoriums of the 1990s and the emphasis put on the cessation of nuclear tests in the NPT review conferences has joined the norms against the use of nuclear, chemical, and biological weapons.

A Fissile Material Cutoff Treaty

Fissile material, highly enriched uranium or plutonium, is necessary for the construction of atomic and hydrogen weapons. Acquiring sufficient fissile material to construct a nuclear weapon is a significant barrier to weapons production. Hence, banning the production of fissile material would theoretically diminish the threat of nuclear proliferation and also limit growth in nuclear weapons stockpiles.

During the Cold War, the nuclear powers resisted the control of nuclear material. They did not want limits on the size of their weapons stockpiles or the material to produce weapons. The United States and the Soviet Union were not willing to accept a prohibition on the production of fissile material without parity of nuclear forces, in particular forces that would survive a first strike by the enemy. Bilateral nuclear arms control, SALT I, SALT II, the START and New START treaties, first limited the growth of nuclear weapons stockpiles, then limited nuclear weapons delivery vehicles, and ultimately reduced the number of nuclear weapons on each side. The stockpiles of the other NWS, China, France, the United Kingdom, Israel, India, North Korea, and Pakistan, were, and still are, much smaller than the U.S., and now Russian, stockpiles.

Following the end of the Cold War, the United States and Russia agreed that there should be a plan to reduce the amount of fissile material available for use for nuclear weapons in order to limit the slow but growing problem of nuclear proliferation. At his first speech to the UN General Assembly, on September 27, 1993, President Clinton announced a number of security initiatives including support of a treaty that would ban the production of plutonium and highly enriched uranium.[77] The following December, the UN General Assembly passed a resolution, by consensus, that called for "a non-discriminatory, multilateral and international and effectively verifiable treaty banning the production of fissile material for nuclear weapons or other nuclear explosive devices."[78] The NPT review conferences in 1995 and 2000 also called for further progress on the issue.[79]

While the United States has made a Fissile Material Cutoff Treaty (FMTC) a priority for years, other countries' insistence that the issue be negotiated alongside other nuclear control issues prevented the CD from taking up the issue. Because the CD operates on a consensus model, any country can block an item on the agenda.

The George W. Bush administration's refusal to negotiate issues of space security and its withdrawal from the ABM treaty kept the negotiation of an FMCT off the table at the CD.[80] In May 2000, the parties to the NPT stated a goal of having a negotiated FMCT by 2005, but that did not come about. The Bush administration, by refusing to support the CTBT's entry into force and withdrawing from the 1972 ABM treaty, took steps that prevented the negotiation of an FMCT.[81] Nevertheless, the Bush administration produced a draft text for an FMCT in 2006.

In the absence of an FMCT, the United States, the United Kingdom, France, and Russia have all declared that they are no longer producing fissile material for weapons purposes. The Soviet Union is believed to have halted production of HEU in the late 1980s and plutonium in 1994, and China, too, is assumed to have stopped production of fissile material for military or weapons purposes in the late 1980s. The United States ceased production of plutonium in 1990 and HEU in 1992.[82] The main goal of an FMCT now would be to limit the production of fissile material by India, Iran, Israel, North Korea, and Pakistan for weapons use.[83] Obligating NWS who have ceased producing nuclear fissile material to a permanent end to production would also be of value.

NNWS that are party to the NPT have already agreed not to produce fissile material for weapons. The NWS, if they became parties to the FMCT, would agree to cap their existing stockpiles. Countries not party to the NPT would also cap their stockpiles and agree not to produce additional fissile materials for weapons use. An attempt in 2003 to begin discussions on an FMCT during the Conference on Disarmament did not achieve consensus to proceed. The countries that are really needed to participate—namely India, Iran, Israel, North Korea, and Pakistan—are the ones least likely to want to negotiate a treaty to limit the production of fissile material.[84]

A major incentive for the declared NWS to negotiate an FMCT, given that all of them have ceased fissile material production, is for the undeclared states to commit themselves to the same. They also have an interest in making it more difficult, if not impossible, for substate actors and terrorists to acquire fissile material. China's participation is largely dependent on whether they perceive that their current stockpile will meet their present and future needs. The U.S. discussion of building a national missile defense system may lead China to believe that its current stockpile is insufficient. If they continue to be concerned about the adequacy of their weapons, they will not find it in their interest to negotiate an FMCT. Indeed, they have threatened to "hold FMCT talks hostage" unless the United States gives up its missile defense plan.[85] China, however, does have an interest in trying to curb the fissile material production of India, which has an infrastructure that could, eventually, outpace China's ability to keep up with its historical enemy.[86]

In 2006, the United States made more concerted efforts toward getting negotiations rolling. It tabled a draft FMCT treaty and called on the CD to establish an Ad Hoc Group to negotiate its terms. The brief, five-page draft treaty called for a cessation on the production of fissile material. It included no provisions for verification of the treaty, leaving questions of compliance with its provisions to consultations between parties, a meeting of all the treaty parties, or to the UN Security Council. Interestingly, the draft required only that the five declared NWS, China, France, Russia, the United Kingdom, and the United States, ratify the treaty in order for it to enter into force.[87] In addition to the U.S. draft treaty, two NGOs, Greenpeace and the International Panel on Fissile Materials (IPFM), have also proposed draft treaties that differ significantly from the draft introduced by the Bush administration. Because the IPFM draft goes beyond production, to a cutoff of production, it refers to its draft as "A Fissile Material (Cut-Off) Treaty" or FM(C)T.

One of the primary motives for the Bush administration was the need to get support from the U.S. Congress on the U.S.–India nuclear deal, whereby India may purchase nuclear materials for commercial purposes from the United States. If there was an FMCT, India's ability to stockpile fissile materials would be limited. India, however, while open to the prospect of an FMCT, viewed an FMTC as something far in the future, not an immediate goal.

In the FMCT talks, the United States and India differed on questions of verification and other issues that should be negotiated alongside the FMCT at the CD.[88] India was also concerned that the FMCT would be discriminatory; it would effectively freeze the number of nuclear weapons of the so-called threshold states while allowing countries that have preexisting stockpiles of fissile material to restart weapons production. In a cascading effect, China was worried about the asymmetry vis-à-vis the United States, especially given the U.S. push for ballistic missile defense. India was worried about asymmetry vis-à-vis China with whom it has fought several border wars. Pakistan was worried about asymmetry vis-à-vis India. Indeed, Pakistan agreed that it could support a ban on future production, as long as "this language does not preclude any delegation from raising the issue of the scope of the convention during the actual negotiations" and will reserve the right to ensure that "the question of asymmetric stockpiles" is considered.[89] Nevertheless, Pakistan took umbrage when the United States called for India to join the Nuclear Suppliers Group and in 2009 Pakistan once again blocked the CD from taking up the negotiation of an FMCT.[90]

Israel, too, is reluctant to support an FMCT because it does not want interference or verification activities at its plutonium reactor at Dimona, where production of tritium takes place.[91] If, however, the FMCT relied on mutual inspection—rather than on inspection by the IAEA or other international organization—and on freezing current production rather than looking at past activities or existing stockpiles, Israel might accept an agreement.[92] Mutual inspections with the United States or one of the other NWS might be acceptable to Israel.

Primary Issues

Even if all the relevant parties agreed to negotiation, significant issues divide them and make the likelihood of completing an FMCT any time soon questionable. The most contentious issues are: the definition of fissile materials, preexisting stockpiles, the production and use of fissile materials for civilian purposes, what, if any, manner of verification, the use of fissile material for military purposes other than weapons production, and the duration of the treaty.

Definition of Fissile Material

The 2006 U.S. draft included a definition similar to the IAEA definition for weapon-usable, direct-use material: uranium enriched to more than 20 percent in U-235 or U-233 and plutonium containing more than 80 percent Pu-238. Russia proposed an alternative, more lenient definition in 2005, to only ban production of weapons-grade plutonium and uranium, containing more than 90 percent Pu-239 and U-235, respectively. Other members of the CD do not support Russia's narrow definition. The IAEA also defines neptunium-237 and americium as "alternative nuclear materials."[93] The IPFM draft takes into account these alternative nuclear materials in its definition by including a broad clause in its definition: "any other fissile material suitable for the manufacture of nuclear weapons." In doing so, the IPFM draft also considers that in the future other materials could possibly be used in the manufacture of nuclear weapons and thus closes a potential loophole in the more narrow definitions.

Tritium, a heavy form of hydrogen with a 12-year half-life, is not a fissile material but is often used in nuclear weapons production to increase the power of the fusion triggers. Because of its short half-life, weapons-producing states have to produce it faster than the fissile materials used in weapons. An attempt to include tritium in a FMCT would face resistance from weapons states because nations have to produce it regularly, while plutonium and HEU do not degrade as rapidly.

Preexisting Stockpiles

The UN resolution calling for an FCMT does not make any reference to fissile material stockpiles existing before the treaty would go into force and most of the weapon states support this exclusion. The 2006 draft proposed by the United States explicitly excludes "activities involving fissile material produced prior to entry into force of the Treaty" (Article II.3).

Nonweapon states, however, want preexisting stocks to be included in the constraints placed on states parties to the treaty. When the CD considered FMCT negotiations in 1995, the "Shannon mandate" explicitly did "not preclude any delegation from raising for consideration . . . past production [or] the management of such material."[94] Preexisting fissile material used for civilian use, material from excess Cold War weapons, and highly enriched uranium being reserved for future naval reactor use may all be considered for constraints or banning, according to the CD.

Each of the NWS, including Israel, North Korea, India, and Pakistan, have different amounts of fissile material available for making nuclear weapons and different capacities to produce fissile material. The United States and Russia have the largest amount of fissile material, by far. The dismantlement of nuclear weapons that began to take place in the United States and Russia led to a large quantity of HEU and plutonium that came from the dismantled weapons. As of 2010, the International Panel on Fissile Material estimated that Russia, which has not declared its stockpile, had approximately 500–750 metric tons of HEU available for nuclear weapons. The United States has declared that it has 216 metric tons of HEU available for weapons use. By comparison, the estimated, combined stockpiles of the United Kingdom, France, China, India, Israel, and Pakistan amount to 52 metric tons.[95] The amount of plutonium available for weapons use is also held predominately by the United States and Russia. The United States has declared that it holds 38 metric tons of plutonium in its military stockpile; Russia is believed to have approximately 88 metric tons of plutonium in its military stockpile. Once again, the combined estimated total of the other NWS is approximately 10 metric tons.[96]

Both the Greenpeace and the IPFM draft treaties would require parties with existing stocks of fissile material to subject the stockpiles to somewhat different verification controls. The Bush administration concluded that existing stocks of fissile material could not be reliably verified without unacceptable intrusiveness and omitted the issue of existing stockpiles from its draft treaty.

Verification

The 1993 UN resolution called for an "effectively verifiable" FMCT. In 2004, however, the Bush administration said that verification was not possible without compromising national security interests. The U.S. draft treaty limited verification to "national means and methods" and submitted a proposal to revise the original 1993 mandate to take out the "effectively verifiable" part.[97] The Obama administration, however, has called for a verifiable treaty, signaling a change in the U.S. position.[98]

To the extent that international verification will be a viable option in the treaty at all, its scope is a contentious issue. Nonweapon states prefer a comprehensive approach in which the entire civilian fuel cycles in NWS would be put under the same safeguards required by the NPT in nonweapon states, making IAEA safeguards the same in weapons and nonweapon states, except inside nuclear weapons facilities. These obligations would counter India's argument that the treaty would discriminate between the NWS and the threshold states.[99]

Weapon states prefer a focused approach, in which safeguards are applied only to enrichment and reprocessing facilities. Inputs and outputs would be monitored to ensure that uranium-enrichment plants are not producing HEU, or, if they are, that it is going to approved uses. Natural uranium, or low-enriched uranium facilities, would not require safeguards under a focused approach. The primary argument for this approach is that it would be far less expensive and intrusive. In 1995, the IAEA estimated that the comprehensive approach would cost $140 million per year, in comparison to the total safeguards budget that year of $87 million. The IPFM however, suggests that this estimation may be too high, and that it would, in fact, cost less than $140 million per year to implement the comprehensive approach.[100]

Another goal of verification beyond making sure proper safeguards are in place at declared nuclear facilities is to ensure that there are no clandestine facilities involved in banned enrichment or reprocessing. All the states that are party to the NPT have signed on to the Additional Protocol, which gives IAEA inspectors greater rights of access if clandestine activities are suspected. Under an FMCT, the Additional Protocols would need to be amended to allow inspectors to look for enrichment or reprocessing plants in all weapons states, which they can already do in NNWS.

The issue of verification of preexisting stocks will be up for debate in the negotiation of an FMCT. The Greenpeace draft treaty would create an independent organization to implement the provisions of the treaty. The organization would be required to verify that no fissile material held in a stockpile could be diverted to weapons use. The IPFM draft would require all states to accept IAEA safeguards for all of their fissile material. Currently, nonnuclear weapon states that possess fissile material for commercial purposes, for the production of nuclear power for example, have already accepted IAEA safeguards. The verification provisions, therefore, would apply to the NWS and the threshold states.

Military Use of Fissile Material

The United States, United Kingdom, Russia, China, France, and India all have submarines in their fleets that are powered by nuclear reactors. An important verification challenge to an FMCT—and a current challenge with NPT verification—is detecting when highly enriched uranium that is used for naval fuel cycles is diverted to weapons use. Ideally, most countries with nuclear-powered naval ships will convert, as did France, to the use of low-enriched uranium.[101] The IPFM draft treaty would require IAEA safeguards on fissile material used to power submarines also.

Civilian Purposes

There have been attempts to ban the use of highly enriched uranium as a fuel source for nuclear reactors since the 1970s. Recent years have seen international efforts rising to curb its use out of the fear that terrorists may gain access to the HEU, enabling them to make explosive nuclear devices. Fissilematerials.org suggests that this general consensus could lead to a ban of the use and production of fissile materials for civilian use, in addition to banning weapons use.

Most of the fissile material used for civilian purposes is held in one of nine countries—Belgium, Canada, France, Germany, Japan, Russia, Switzerland, the United Kingdom, and the United States. All of them have declared that their fissile material is to be used solely for civilian applications. The European facilities are already subject to Euratom safeguards, and the advent of an FMCT would simplify the safeguard systems and cover additional preexisting plutonium. India has a stockpile of reactor-grade plutonium, and it is unclear whether they will want to make a declaration that it is solely for civilian purposes. In connection with the U.S.–India nuclear deal of 2005, India plans to exempt the plutonium from IAEA safeguards.[102]

Efforts to ban the separation of plutonium for use as civilian fuel would see resistance from France, India, Japan, and Russia, all of which are currently involved in civilian reprocessing. Once again, the IPFM draft treaty addressed this potentially thorny issue by requiring IAEA safeguards for all fissile material for civilian uses.

Entry into Force

While the U.S. draft treaty only required the declared NWS to ratify a FMCT in order for the agreement to enter into force, the IPFM draft would enter into force after 40 states, including at least four nuclear weapons or threshold states, ratified it. The Greenpeace draft would require only 30 ratifications and does not specify that any of them should be nuclear weapons or threshold states.

In a discussion of this provision in the IPFM draft, the panel acknowledges the influence of the status of the CTBT in their recommendation of only four NWS. The IPFM recognized the importance and benefits of having a FM(C)T begin to operate for those states—France, Russia, the United States, and the United Kingdom—that have already ceased production of fissile material.

Duration of FMCT

The U.S. draft of the treaty stated that it would be in force for 15 years after its entry into force, with extensions through consensus. This would likely be opposed by nonweapon states who support a permanent treaty.[103] Both the Greenpeace and the IPFM drafts would have treaties of unlimited duration.

Future of the FMCT

Negotiations toward an FMCT do not appear to be moving forward in the CD. Recognizing the current deadlock in the CD, a coalition of the willing could step up to discuss a voluntary moratorium on fissile material production for weapons use. Taking up a suggestion of the Arms Control Association, the United States has recently proposed that negotiations proceed with the five permanent Security Council members. India, Pakistan, and Israel could join with the already-declared United States, United Kingdom, France, and Russia to have discussions on how moratoriums could be enforced and verified in parallel to continuing discussions in the CD.[104]

Discussion

The NPT is a bulwark against the proliferation of nuclear weapons. The degree to which it has succeeded depends on one's point of view. Is the cup half empty or half full? Moreover, although NPT's three goals are entwined, each has different measures of success.

The first goal is to prevent nuclear weapons from proliferating beyond the five states—the United States, Russia, the United Kingdom, China, and France—that possessed such weapons when the treaty was first drafted. In the 1960s, many experts predicted that by the end of the 20th century, 20 states would have nuclear weapons. Using that as a measure, the treaty has had moderate success; it has helped to limit, but not altogether prevent, nuclear proliferation.

India, Pakistan, and Israel have shunned the NPT and developed nuclear weapons; and North Korea, which was a member of the NPT, developed nuclear weapons in defiance of its obligations, then withdrew from the agreement and tested them. Nevertheless, there have been successes too. Argentina and Brazil had once shown interest in developing nuclear weapons but changed course and joined the NPT in the 1990s. South Africa also joined the treaty and destroyed its nuclear weapons arsenal.

The consequences of Israeli, Indian, and Pakistani absence from the NPT are profound and enduring. A serious problem is that none of these states is bound by NPT obligations to refrain from assisting nonnuclear weapon states in acquiring or developing nuclear weapons. Pakistani scientist A.Q. Khan provided materials and expertise to North Korea, Libya, and Iran to help them develop nuclear weapons. And Israel allegedly helped the apartheid-era government of South Africa in its nascent nuclear weapons program. South Africa and Libya are now members of the NPT and their nuclear facilities are under IAEA oversight. Suspicions linger, also, that non-NPT states could assist nonstate actors in acquiring nuclear materials or weapons. None of them are members of the Nuclear Suppliers Group (NSG). The 46-member NSG established guidelines for nuclear exports in order to minimize the likelihood of contributing to nuclear weapons proliferation.[105]

A second problem relates to the relationship between the NPT and the CTBT. The NWS that are party to the NPT pledged to conclude a CTBT during the 1995 RevCon. Although the treaty was completed in 1996, prospects for its entry into force more than 15 years later seem bleak. Forty-four specific countries are required to ratify the treaty before it can enter into force. Nine of the 44 have not yet ratified the treaty and 3 of the 44 have not signed the agreement. An examination of the hold-outs is illuminating. Of the NWS, only France, the Russian Federation, and the United Kingdom have ratified the treaty. China, North Korea, India, Israel, Pakistan, and the United States show no signs of ratifying the agreement; India, Pakistan, and North Korea have not even signed it. The nonnuclear weapon states required for entry into force that have not yet ratified the treaty are Egypt and Iran. In spite of President Obama's recent commitment to send the CTBT to the U.S. Senate for ratification, a successful outcome of that effort is not assured. The Senate rejected the treaty in 1999 when President Clinton sought ratification.[106] The annual meetings of the NPT parties could continue to exert pressure on NPT member states to ratify the CTBT, but the non-NPT states, India, Israel, North Korea, and Pakistan, are not subject to the same kind of pressure. Hence, an agreement long sought by the nonnuclear member states to the NPT remains in limbo.

A third problem is the long-term endurance of the NPT itself. From 1970 until North Korea's withdrawal from the NPT, its membership grew steadily. Revelations about Iran's nuclear activities and its relationship with the IAEA have raised questions about whether Iran, too, will eventually withdraw from the NPT. And if Iran withdraws, will other states follow suit? No state has withdrawn from the NPT in response to North Korea's withdrawal. Neither South Korea nor Japan, possible targets of a North Korean nuclear weapon, has succumbed to the temptation to initiate their own weapons program. In doing so, they have broken the pattern of proliferation shown by the Soviet Union, China, India, and Pakistan. But the situation remains ominous nevertheless.

The second goal of the NPT, nuclear disarmament, could be deemed an abject failure. With the passage of time, it becomes increasingly implausible for nations with nuclear weapons to argue that they need the weapons while other nations do not; yet all five NWS still have and rely on nuclear weapons for security. Even so, there has been movement in the right direction: both the United States and Russia—the two largest NWS—have drastically cut, and continue to cut, their stockpiles. Both nations cite recent steps they have taken to reduce their stockpiles and diminish their reliance on nuclear weapons. Other nations, however, argue that the United States and Russia have not done enough. Additionally, after the breakup of the Soviet Union, three countries that had been part of the Soviet Union—Belarus, Kazakhstan, and Ukraine—transferred their nuclear weapons to Russia, and then joined the NPT as nonnuclear weapon states.

The third goal, distributing benefits of nuclear energy to states that have agreed to forego weapons, has been consistently successful, although it has drawn little media attention. The Final Document of the most recent (2010) RevCon includes 17 steps to promote this goal.

The implementation of the NPT encapsulates the weaknesses of large-scale international diplomacy. Consensus decision making often hamstrings efforts. Without consensus, progress halts. In an effort to reach consensus, agreements often become diluted, weak. Governments typically spin the accomplishments of what they like and criticize what they don't—always arguing that in order to achieve consensus they were forced to accept some things they disagreed with. It is little different for the NPT—although arguably more complicated. The challenges the NPT faces are similar to other multilateral agreements—how to achieve its goals without universal membership and how to react to alleged violations of its terms.

The CTBT presents different challenges. A voluntary moratorium on nuclear testing among the NWS is an obviously more fragile arrangement than an international treaty prohibiting nuclear testing. The linkages between the CTBT and the NPT, as noted previously, also point to increasing tensions in the NPT, particularly between the nonnuclear weapon states and the United States and China. Yet, even if the NPT issues were resolved through U.S. and Chinese ratification of the CTBT, the NWS outside the NPT, Israel, India, North Korea, and Pakistan, show limited willingness to formally forego nuclear testing. Indeed, among those states, Israel is the only nation that has signed the CTBT. Moreover, prospects for U.S. and Chinese ratification appear to be remote, despite support from U.S. president Obama and Chinese president Hu Jintao.

Interested parties continue to press for a FMCT. Amendments and refinements on draft proposals elicit attention among NGOs and some governments. Nevertheless, steady progress and ultimately a completed FMCT will require action outside the CD unless the current logjam in the CD suddenly dissolves.

Multilateral nuclear arms control is a messy and complex process. The increase in the number of states that possess nuclear weapons since the conclusion of the NPT in 1968 leads to more protracted and complicated negotiations on multilateral nuclear issues. Yet, the nuclear taboo discussed in the introductory chapter and the aversion that nuclear weapons evoke continue to be a strong force for continued progress despite the difficulties inherent in the process. The consequences of a widespread breakout from the NPT, with its attendant increase in the likelihood of a deliberate or accidental nuclear exchange, continue to be a sobering reminder of the importance of the topic and a call to an ongoing dedication to the field.

Notes

1. The Baruch Plan, Presented to the United Nations Atomic Energy Commission, June 14, 1946. The Atomic Archive, http://www.atomicarchive.com/Docs/Deterrence/BaruchPlan.shtml.

2. Dwight D. Eisenhower, Address by Mr. Dwight D. Eisenhower, president of the United States, to the 470th Plenary Meeting of the United Nations General Assembly, 1953, http://www.iaea.org/About/history_speech.html.

3. Statute of the IAEA, 1956, www.iaea.org.

4. David Fischer, *History of the International Atomic Energy Agency: The First Forty Years* (Vienna: The International Atomic Energy Agency, 1997), 60–61, 76–77.

5. United Nations General Assembly Resolution, "Prevention of the Wider Dissemination of Nuclear Weapons," A/RES/1665/XVI, 1961.

6. Public Papers of the presidents of the United States: John F. Kennedy, 1963, 1964 (Washington, DC: U.S. Government Printing Office), 280.

7. Peter R. Lavoy, "Predicting Nuclear Proliferation: A Declassified Documentary Record," *Strategic Insights* 3, no. 1 (2004), http://www.fas.org/man/eprint/lavoy.pdf.

8. Joseph Nye, "The Superpowers and the Non-Proliferation Treaty," in *Superpower Arms Control: Setting the Record Straight,* ed. Albert Carnesale and Richard N. Haass (Cambridge, MA: Ballinger Publishing Company, 1987), 165–190.

9. Full test of the treaty can be found at: http://www.un.org/disarmament/WMD/Nuclear/pdf/NPTEnglish_Text.pdf.

10. United Nations Security Council, Resolution 255 (1968), "Question Relating to Measures to Safeguard Non-Nuclear-Weapon States Parties to the Treaty on the Non-Proliferation of Nuclear Weapons," June 19, http://daccess-dds-ny.un.org/doc/RESOLUTION/GEN/NR0/248/36/IMG/NR024836.pdf?OpenElement.

11. While France did not become a member of the NPT, it stated that it would comply with its provisions as if it were a member state. Greece was not an original state party but joined a mere week later.

12. "Review Conference of the Parties to the Treaty on the Non-Proliferation of Nuclear Weapons Final Document, NPT/CONF /35/1," http://www.un.org/disarmament/WMD/Nuclear/pdf/finaldocs/1975%20-%20Geneva%20-%20NPT%20Review%20Conference%20-%20Final%20Document%20Part%20I.pdf.

13. Carlton Stoiber, "The Evolution of NPT Review Conference Final Documents, 1975–2000," *The Nonproliferation Review* 10, no. 3 (2003): 126–66, http://cns.miis.edu/npr/pdfs/103stoi.pdf.

14. See Helen Purkitt and Stephen Burgess, *South Africa's Weapons of Mass Destruction* (Indianapolis, IN: Indiana University Press, 1995), 1–84 for a detailed description of South Africa's nuclear weapons program.

15. Stephen W. Young and British American information Council *U.S. Policy Leading into the NPT Conference* (London: British American Security Information Centre, 1995).

16. United Nations Security Council Resolution 284 S/RES/984 (1995), http://daccess-dds-ny.un.org/doc/UNDOC/GEN/N95/106/06/PDF/N9510606.pdf?OpenElement.

17. Decision 1: Strengthening the Review Process for the Treaty, Npt/Conf.1995/32 (Part I), Annex (1995), http://www.un.org/disarmament/WMD/Nuclear/1995-NPT/pdf/NPT_CONF199532.pdf.

18. Decision 2: Principles and Objectives for Nuclear Non-Proliferation and Disarmament (1995), http://www.un.org/disarmament/WMD/Nuclear/1995-NPT/pdf/NPT_CONF199501.pdf.

19. Decision 3: Extension of the Treaty on the Non-Proliferation of Nuclear Weapons (1995), http://www.un.org/disarmament/WMD/Nuclear/1995-NPT/pdf/NPT_CONF199503.pdf.

20. In September 1995, France conducted a series of nuclear weapons tests. Some states were outraged by France's test; however, France defended the tests, arguing that it would be unable to sign the CTBT, which it did in 1996, without data from these tests.

21. "The Final Document of the 2000 Review Conference of the Parties to the Treaty of the Non-Proliferation of Nuclear Weapons," Arms Control Association, www.armscontrol.org/act/2000_06/docjun.

22. Tariq Rauf, "An Unequivocal Success? Implications of the NPT Review Conference," *Arms Control Today* 30 (2000), http://www.armscontrol.org/act/2000_07–08/raufjulaug.

23. Paul Kerr, "The IAEA's Report on Iran: An Analysis," *Arms Control Today* 33 (2003), http://www.armscontrol.org/act/2003_12/IAEAreport.

24. Munya M. Mardor, *Rafael* (Tel Aviv: Misrad Habithaon, 1981), 120–21, as quoted in Avner Cohen, *Israel and the Bomb* (New York: Columbia University Press, 1998), 43.

25. Cohen, *Israel and the Bomb*, 470.

26. Some analysts have speculated that a 1979 explosion in the Indian Ocean was a joint South African–Israeli nuclear test.

27. Avner Cohen and William Burr, "Israel Crosses the Threshold," *Bulletin of the Atomic Scientists* 62, no. 3 (2006): 22–30.

28. Federation of American Scientists, *Israel Special Weapons Guide: Nuclear Weapons*, 2007, www.fas.org/nuke/guide/israel/index.html.

29. All 33 states in the region are parties to the treaty, which has been in operation for more than 40 years.

30. "India Profile," Nuclear Threat Initiative, 2003, http://www.nti.org/e_research/profiles/India/Nuclear/.

31. "The Secret History of the ABM Treaty, 1969–1972," in National Security Archive, Electronic Briefing Book No. 60, last updated November 8, 2001, www.gwu.edu~nsarchiv/NSAEBB/NSAEBB60.

32. Michael Krepon, "LOOKING BACK: The 1998 Indian and Pakistani Nuclear Tests," *Arms Control Today* 38 (2008) http://www.armscontrol.org/act/2008_05/lookingback.

33. Nuclear Weapon Stockpile Chart, July 2005, Carnegie Endowment for International Peace, http://www.carnegieendowment.org/publications/?fa=view&id=19238.

34. Karen deYoung, "Pakistan Doubles Its Nuclear Stockpile," *The Washington Post*, January 31, 2011, http://www.washingtonpost.com/wp-dyn/content/article/2011/01/30/AR2011013004682.html.

35. Jean du Preez and William Potter, "North Korea's Withdrawal from the NPT: A Reality Check," in *Research Story of the Week*, Center for Nonproliferation Studies (Monterey Institute of International Studies, 2003), http://cns.miis.edu/stories/030409.htm.

36. D. A. Pinkston, "Implementing the Agreed Framework and Potential Obstacles," in 12th Pacific Basin Nuclear Conference 2000, Center for Nonproliferation Studies (Monterey Institute of International Studies: Seoul, South Korea), http://cns.miis.edu/reports/kaeri.htm.

37. Ibid.

38. "North Korea—Denuclearization Action Plan, February 13, 2007," The Acronym Institute, Disarmament Documentation, http://www.acronym.org.uk/docs/0702/doc01.htm.

39. Arms Control Association, http://www.armscontrol.org/factsheets/dprkchron.

40. Max Fisher, "What If Kim Jong Il's Successor Isn't Ready?" *The Atlantic*, December 19, 2011, http://www.theatlantic.com/international/archive/2011/12/what-if-kim-jong-ils-successor-isnt-ready/250169/.

41. Board of Governors, International Atomic Energy Agency, Implementation of the NPT Safeguards Agreement and Relevant Provisions of Security Council Resolution 1737 (2006) in the Islamic Republic of Iran, 2007, http://www.iaea.org/Publications/Documents/Board/2010/gov2010–62.pdf.

42. Valentin Flauraud, "Iran Six 'disappointed' by nuclear talks in Istanbul". RIA Novosti, January 22, 2011. http://en.rian.ru/world/20110122/162251094.html?id=.

43. "EU Says Iran Offer on Nuclear Talks Not New", Voice of America. May 10, 2011. http://www.voanews.com/content/eu-says-irans-offer-on-nuclear-talks-not-new-121632749/172936.html.

44. Fredrik Dahl, "Iran Shows U.N. Official All Nuclear Sites: Envoy," Reuters, August 23, 2011, http://www.reuters.com/article/2011/08/23/us-iran-nuclear-idUS-TRE77M6ZW20110823.

45. "Iran Moving Centrifuges to Fordow," ISIS Iran in Brief, last modified August 24, 2011, http://www.isisnucleariran.org/brief/detail/iran-moving-centrifuges-to-fordow/.

46. "IAEA Chief 'Concerned' about Iran's Nuclear Ambitions," *VOA News*, last modified September 12, 2011, http://www.voanews.com/english/news/middle-east/UN-Nuclear-Chief-Concerned-About-Irans-Nuclear-Ambitions—129648218.html.

47. International Atomic Energy Agency Board of Governors, Report by the director general, "Implementation of the NPT Safeguards Agreement and Relevant Provisions of Security Council Resolutions in the Islamic Republic of Iran" GOV/2011/65, November 8, 2011, 10, http://www.iaea.org/Publications/Documents/Board/2011/gov2011–65.pdf.

48. International Atomic Energy Agency Board of Governors, "Implementation of the NPT Safeguards Agreement and Relevant Provisions of United Nations Security Council Resolutions in the Islamic Republic of Iran," Resolution adopted by the Board of Governors on November 18, 2011, GOV /2011/69, http://www.iaea.org/Publications/Documents/Board/2011/gov2011–69.pdf.

49. Grant Smith, "Oil Climbs as European Union Agrees on Sanctions against Iran," *Bloomberg Businessweek*, January 31, 2012, http://www.businessweek.com/news/2012–01–23/oil-climbs-as-european-union-agrees-on-sanctions-against-iran.html.

50. Stephen Erlanger, "Iran Nears Deal on Inspecting Atomic Site, U.N. Chief Says," *New York Times*, May 23, 2012, http://www.nytimes.com/2012/05/23/world/middleeast/un-nuclear-monitor-strikes-deal-with-iran-reports-say.html?_r=1&ref=todayspaper.

51. Atomic-Archive, *Operation Sandstone 1948*, July 10, 1997, cited 2008, http://nuclearweaponarchive.org/Usa/Tests/Sandston.html.

52. International Atomic Energy Agency, *The Semipalatinsk Test Site, Kazakhstan*, August 30, 2008, http://www-ns.iaea.org/appraisals/semipalatinsk.htm.

53. Grabosky, P.N., "A Toxic Legacy: British Nuclear Weapons Testing in Australia," in *Wayward Governance: Illegality and Its Control in the Public Sector* (Canberra: Australian Institute of Criminology, 1989).

54. Atomic-Archive, *Operation Castle: 1954 Pacific Proving Ground*, May 2006, http://nuclearweaponarchive.org/Usa/Tests/Castle.html.

55. United States Department of State, *Treaty Banning Nuclear Weapon Tests in the Atmosphere, in Outer Space and Under Water*, http://www.state.gov/t/ac/trt/4797.htm.

56. UN Document, 48/70 Comprehensive Test Ban Treaty, http://daccess-dds-ny.un.org/doc/RESOLUTION/GEN/NR0/711/54/IMG/NR071154.pdf?OpenElement.

57. Dinshaw Mistry, "India and the Comprehensive Test Ban Treaty," *ACDIS Research Reports* (1998), http://acdis.illinois.edu/publications/207/publication-IndiaandtheComprehensiveTestBanTreaty.html.

58. Rebecca Johnson, *Unfinished Business: The Negotiation of the CTBT and the End of Nuclear Testing* (New York: United Nations Publications, 2009), 87.

59. Mistry, "India and the Comprehensive Test Ban Treaty," 12; see also Rebecca Johnson, *Unfinished Business*, 73–76 for additional discussion on the NPT conference and its impact on CTBT relations.

60. Johnson, *Unfinished Business*, 78.

61. Ibid, 78–79.

62. Mistry, "India and the Comprehensive Test Ban Treaty,"16.

63. Johnson, *Unfinished Business*, 88.

64. Ibid, 84–90.

65. CRS Issue Brief, "Pakistan–U.S. Relations," http://www.fas.org/spp/starwars/crs/94–041.htm.

66. Mistry, "India and the Comprehensive Test Ban Treaty," 17.

67. Johnson, *Unfinished Business*, 96.

68. Ibid, 95.

69. Ibid, 96. The Indian proposals specifically called for a 10-year timetable and offered "explicit language on preventing qualitative developments of new weapons." See also Mistry, "India and the Comprehensive Test Ban Treaty,"17.

70. Johnson, *Unfinished Business*, 140.

71. UN Document, A/RES/50/ 245 Comprehensive Test Ban Treaty, http://www.un.org/documents/ga/res/50/a50r245.htm. See also vote summary at http://www.un.org/depts/dhl/resguide/r50.htm.

72. CTBTO, "Timeline of CTBT," http://ctbto.org/the-treaty/.

73. CTBTO, "Timeline of CTBT."

74. Algeria, Argentina, Australia, Austria, Bangladesh, Belgium, Brazil, Bulgaria, Canada, Chile, China, Colombia, Democratic People's Republic of Korea, Egypt, Finland, France, Germany, Hungary, India, Indonesia, Iran (Islamic Republic of), Israel, Italy, Japan, Mexico, Netherlands, Norway, Pakistan, Peru, Poland, Romania, Republic of Korea, Russian Federation, Slovakia, South Africa, Spain, Sweden, Switzerland, Turkey, Ukraine, United Kingdom of Great Britain and Northern Ireland, United States of America, Vietnam, and Zaire.

75. Center for Nonproliferation Studies, "Comprehensive Nuclear Test Ban Treaty," http://nti.org/e_research/official_docs/inventory/pdfs/ctbt.pdf.

76. CTBTO Preparatory Commission www.ctbto.org.

77. President Bill Clinton, "Confronting the Challenges of a Broader World," Address to the UN General Assembly, September 27, 1993, *Dispatch Magazine* (Georgetown, TX: United States Bureau of Public Affairs, 1993), http://dosfan.lib.uic.edu/ERC/briefing/dispatch/1993/html/Dispatchv4no39.html.

78. United Nations General Assembly Resolution 48/75L, "Prohibition of the Production of Fissile Material for Nuclear Weapons or Other Nuclear Explosive Devices," December 16, 1993, http://daccess-dds-ny.un.org/doc/RESOLUTION/GEN/NR0/711/59/IMG/NR071159.pdf?OpenElement

79. "A Fissile Material Cutoff Treaty," The International Panel on Fissile Materials, http://www.fissilematerials.org/ipfm/pages_us_en/fmct/fmct/fmct.php.

80. Michael Krepon, "The Conference on Disarmament: Means of Rejuvenation," *Arms Control Today* 36 (2006), http://www.armscontrol.org/act/2006_12/Krepon.

81. "US Reviewing FMCT Policy," *Arms Control Today* 33 (2003), http://www.armscontrol.org/node/3247.

82. "Global Fissile Material Report 2010," International Panel on Fissile Materials, http://www.fissilematerials.org/ipfm/site_down/gfmr10.pdf.

83. "US Reviewing FMCT Policy."

84. Krepon, "The Conference on Disarmament."

85. Ibid, 30.

86. Ibid.

87. "Treaty on the Cessation of Production of Fissile Material for Use in Nuclear Weapons or Other Nuclear Explosive Devices," http://www.reachingcriticalwill.org/political/cd/speeches06/18MayDraftTreaty.pdf.

88. Daryl G. Kimball, "Impact of the US–Indian Nuclear Deal on India's Fissile Production Capacity for Weapons," Press Release, Arms Control Association, 2006, http://www.armscontrol.org/pressroom/2006/20061115_Indian_Fissile.

89. Guy B. Roberts, "This Arms Control Dog Won't Hunt: The Proposed Fissile Material Cut-Off Treaty at the Conference on Disarmament," Institute for National Security Studies US Air Force Academy, Occasional Paper 36, January 2001, 31, http://www.dtic.mil/cgi-bin/GetTRDoc?Location=U2&doc=GetTRDoc.pdf&AD=ADA435059.

90. Peter Crail, "Pakistan's Nuclear Buildup Vexes FMTC Talks," *Arms Control Today* (2011), http://www.armscontrol.org/act/2011_03/Pakistan.

91. "A Fissile Material Cutoff Treaty."

92. Roberts, "This Arms Control Dog Won't Hunt," 33.

93. "A Fissile Material Cutoff Treaty."

94. Ibid.

95. "Global Fissile Material Report 2010," 9.

96. "Global Fissile Material Report 2010," 12.

97. Jackie W. Sanders, Remarks to the Conference on Disarmament, The Acronym Institute for Disarmament Diplomacy, 2004, http://www.acronym.org.uk/docs/0407/doc08.htm.

98. Arend Meerburg and Frank N. Von Hippel, "Complete Cutoff: Designing a Comprehensive Fissile Material Treaty," Arms Control Today 39 (2009), http://www.armscontrol.org/print/3546.

99. "A Fissile Material Cutoff Treaty."

100. Ibid.

101. Meerburg and Von Hippel, "Complete Cutoff."

102. Ibid.

103. "A Fissile Material Cutoff Treaty."

104. Krepon, "The Conference on Disarmament."

105. Nuclear Suppliers Group, "What Is the NSG," April 25, 2011, http://www.nuclearsuppliersgroup.org/Leng/default.htm.

106. Susan Cornwell, "Obama Administration to Push for Test Ban Treaty," Reuters, May 10, 2011, http://www.reuters.com/article/2011/05/10/us-nuclear-usa-testing-idUSTRE7496M020110510.

CHAPTER 4

Controlling Biological and Chemical Weapons

Prior to the 20th century, biological, chemical, and toxin weapons were not distinguished from one another and were lumped together under the category of poisons. A number of earlier agreements, including the 1874 Brussels Convention on the Law and Customs of War and the Hague Convention of 1899,[1] attempted to restrict or ban the use of poisons in war. Following the extensive use of chemical weapons during WWI, the international community began a prolonged effort to outlaw CW; biological and toxin weapons were subsequently added to the campaign. These efforts produced the 1925 Geneva Protocol (GP), the 1972 Biological and Toxin Weapons Convention (BWC), and the 1993 Chemical Weapons Convention (CWC). The GP prohibited the use in war of chemical and biological weapons while the BWC and CWC outlawed the possession of biological and chemical weapons.

This chapter describes how states have used chemical and biological weapons and those that have been part of states' arsenals. It goes on to describe the 1925 GP in greater detail, and discusses the negotiations and implementation of the treaties that have prohibited the production and possession of these nonconventional weapons. It closes with a discussion of the problems facing international negotiators as they cope with trying to make these treaties universal and comprehensive.

Chemical Weapons

Germany launched the first major attack of CW, using chlorine gas in WWI in April 1915. Thereafter, both the Allies and the Central Powers used CW extensively. The belligerents mainly used three different agents: chlorine, phosgene, and mustard gases. Chlorine gas causes violent coughing and choking. If enough chlorine is inhaled, death occurs within 2–24 hours from suffocation. Phosgene is a gas that is more potent than chlorine. It also causes coughing, frothing at the mouth and leads to death from respiratory failure or heart failure. In contrast to chlorine and phosgene, mustard gas is an agent that causes severe blistering of the skin and mucous membranes, the eyes, and lungs when it is inhaled.[2] While phosgene caused most of the deaths due to CW in WWI, mustard gas caused 80 percent of the chemical casualties. Although the fatality rate from mustard was quite low, soldiers exposed to mustard gas often spent weeks or months in hospital, recovering from the attack. After the initial gas attacks, protective gear in the form of increasingly sophisticated gas masks greatly reduced the number of fatalities from gas. Nevertheless, gas attacks continued to cause numerous casualties; soldiers inhaled some of the gas before they were able to don their masks. Victims exposed to gas attacks often had lifelong disabilities. It is estimated that more than 1,240,000 men were casualties of gas attacks and more than 90,000 died from the effects of the gas.

CW in WWI and thereafter were most effective when used against unprotected troops or civilians, either downwind of the battle area or the direct target of chemical munitions. Soldiers quickly realized that even crude barriers would provide some protection against CW. Military planners quickly developed more and better gas masks to protect against inhalation of poisonous chemicals and ultimately full body gear to insulate the skin from skin-penetrating agents.

The first major use of CW after WWI occurred following Italy's invasion of Ethiopia in 1935. The Italian army sprayed mustard gas from airplanes, devastating the largely unprotected Ethiopians. The Emperor Haile Salassie described the effects of the attacks in this way:

> Special sprayers were installed on board aircraft so they could vaporize over vast areas of territory a fine, death-dealing rain. Groups of 9, 15, or 18 aircraft followed one another so that the fog issuing from them formed a continuous sheet. It was thus that, as from the end of January 1936, soldiers, women, children, cattle, rivers, lakes, and pastures were drenched continually with this deadly rain. In order more surely to poison the waters and pastures, the Italian command made its aircraft pass over and over again. These fearful tactics succeeded. Men and animals succumbed. The deadly rain that fell from the aircraft made all those whom it touched fly shrieking with pain. All those who drank poisoned water or ate infected food also succumbed in dreadful suffering. In tens of thousands the victims of Italian mustard gas fell.[3]

The Japanese army also used CW, including mustard gas, after invading China in 1935.

During WWII, the major belligerents did not use CW against each other, but WWII brought the development of deadly nerve agents that kill by interfering with the central nervous system.

Exposure to nerve agent affects many bodily systems. Victims of nerve gas typically experience respiratory distress, gasp for air, vomit, have convulsions and seizures prior to death. Extremely toxic, nerve agents can cause death within minutes if inhaled. If absorbed through the skin, death occurs more slowly. Germany developed the first nerve agent, tabun, and continued to work on agents that were odorless, persistent, and deadly. Lack of odor meant that soldiers exposed to the highly toxic agents would not be able to detect their presence in the air in time to don effective defensive gas masks. Skin exposure, although slower acting, led to the development of full body defensive chemical suits.

The use of nerve agents in war has been infrequent, but significant. Egypt reportedly used nerve agents in support of Yemeni rebels during the Yemen Civil war in 1963.[4] There is ample evidence that Iraq used CW, including mustard and nerve agents, against Iran after Iraq's 1980 invasion of Iran became a stalemate. Moreover, Saddam Hussein used nerve agents against his own civilian Kurdish population, most notably in the city of Halabja in 1988.

During the Vietnam War, the United States used massive quantities of defoliants and herbicides to strip the jungles bare of plant cover that provided ample means for North Vietnamese soldiers and sympathizers to simply melt into the morass. The United States also used tear gas, a nonlethal chemical agent that causes weeping, irritation, and pain in Vietnam. Widely criticized for initiating chemical warfare and violating the norms embodied in the 1925 Geneva Protocol, the U.S. government staunchly denied that the use of these agents constituted chemical warfare. It argued that herbicides and defoliants were not harmful to humans and consequently were not chemical warfare agents. Similarly, because tear gas was a harassing, not a lethal, agent and used in domestic police action, it was not chemical warfare. Subsequently, however, it has been shown that dioxin, one of the components of Agent Orange, a widely used defoliant in Vietnam, is a powerful mutagen and carcinogen. Mutagens cause mutations in the DNA that lead to birth defects and other genetic abnormalities while carcinogens are a leading cause of cancer.[5] Many Vietnamese people as well as US Vietnam veterans have suffered the effects.

During the 1990s, several sources alleged that the Yugoslav army and its successor, the Serbian Army, may have used chemical weapons in Bosnia and Kosovo.[6] The United States used white phosphorus shells in its attack on Fallujah, Iraq, in November 2004. The U.S. government claimed that the army used white phosphorus for illumination purposes, and as an incendiary weapon, not a CW.

CBW Arms Control: The Geneva Protocol

Prior to WWI, nations sought to prohibit poisons in warfare, but the instruments that they devised were either circumvented or ignored in the Great War. The massive casualties and suffering caused by chemical agents in WWI, including blindness and other persistent debilitating respiratory effects, garnered great interest in reviving restrictions on CW. In May 1925, under the auspices of the League of Nations, the Conference for the Supervision of the International Trade in Arms and Ammunition and in Implements of War considered provisions prohibiting international trade in poisonous or asphyxiating gases. However, banning trade without baning production and use was controversial, and ultimately the delegates to the Convention prohibited use, without baning production or trade, and concluded the Protocol for the Prohibition of the Use of Asphyxiating, Poisonous or Other Gases, and of Bacteriological Methods of Warfare on June 17, 1925. The Protocol first acknowledged that "the use in war of asphyxiating, poisonous or other gases, and of all analogous liquids materials or devices, has been justly condemned by the general opinion of the civilized world." The signatories of the Protocol agreed to be bound by this prohibition against the use of such arms in war and extended the prohibition to the use of bacteriological methods of warfare. Moreover, the Protocol goes on to establish that the prohibition "shall be universally accepted as part of International Law."[7] The inclusion of the prohibition as part of international law is significant, binding even those states that are not parties to the treaty, creating a universal standard against the first use of chemical and biological weapons.[8]

Nevertheless, the Protocol had major weaknesses as well. It did not ban the use of CW against states that were not contracting parties to the Protocol. Many states reserved a right to retaliate against the use of CW if a contracting party used them first. The Protocol banned use in warfare, but not domestic use, to quell rebellions or attempted coups, for example. Because the Protocol did not ban the development, production, and stockpiling of chemical weapons, many states continued these activities and made CW a part of war plans.

Prior to the conclusion of the BWC and the 1993 Chemical Weapons Convention, 35 states reserved the right to retaliate with the prohibited weapons if another state used the weapons first. Nevertheless, the vast majority of states parties did not have reservations to the Protocol, and the Netherlands in 1930 and the United States in 1975 made a distinction between chemical and biological weapons (BW) and limited their retaliation reservation to CW only.[9] Both states bound themselves not to use BW under any circumstances, even if BW were to be used against them.[10]

Biological Agents and Weapons

Prior to the 20th century, biological and chemical agents causing disease, incapacitation, and death were not well understood or distinguished from one another. However, with advancements in the chemical and biological sciences, states began to seriously consider biological agents that reproduce—principally, but not exclusively, bacteria and viruses—and the poisonous substances, or toxins, that some living agents produce, for weapons purposes. Throughout the 20th century, many governments investigated, developed, produced, and stockpiled biological and toxin weapons. However, few actually used biological agents to deliberately infect humans, animals, or plants with lethal and debilitating diseases. And herein lies a conundrum that remains unresolved.

Theoretically, any disease-causing microbe could be investigated for its weapons potential. Practical problems in production, storage, dissemination, and persistence of biological agents, however, have narrowed the number of biological agents that have made their way into actual weapons. Moreover, while some agents have the potential for use as a weapon against individuals—assassination weapons—their usefulness as a weapon to produce mass casualties is minimal. In addition, several states have developed antipersonnel agents that are not primarily lethal. Their intended purpose is to incapacitate their targets, whether those targets are military or civilian personnel. The bacteria that cause the diseases of anthrax, plague, brucellosis, and tularemia, the viruses that cause different types of encephalitis and dengue fever, and the rickettsiae that cause Rocky Mountain spotted fever, typhus, and Q-fever are among the agents that have been often been researched, tested, and weaponized. Each potential biological or toxin weapons agent has unique characteristics that make it more or less attractive for weapons use, or for different purposes as weapons.

One particular bacterium, *bacillus anthracis,* has several properties that are desirable for weapons purposes and has frequently been produced as a weapon. The bacterium forms very hardy spores that can be stored in bulk or in munitions for years without diminishing their ability to infect individuals. The spores are not readily destroyed by blast or sunlight and consequently are theoretically easier to deliver than many other bacteria and viruses that are easily rendered ineffective if delivered through munitions. Anthrax bacteria can be dispersed in a dry aerosol or in a wet slurry. It can be packaged into animal feed to infect cattle. Because the agent can persist in the soil for years or decades, it could be used to contaminate areas such as airports and fields, making them difficult to use.

Most naturally occurring anthrax in humans enters the skin through cuts or scrapes that allow the bacteria to enter the bloodstream. Cutaneous anthrax is rarely lethal. Eating the meat of animals that have been infected with anthrax is another route of human infection that is much more deadly than anthrax that enters the body through the skin. Anthrax weapons, however, have been designed to enter the airways of humans after the bacteria are sprayed or dispersed through aerosol munitions. One to six days after breathing anthrax spores, the victims' symptoms consist chiefly of fever, fatigue, and muscle pain. Two to three days later, patients infected with anthrax experience difficulty breathing, chest pain, and often, severe headache, vomiting, and neck pain due to inflammation of the covering of the brain and the spinal cord—meningitis. Shock and death usually occur 24–36 hours later. Taking antibiotics immediately following exposure can prevent the onset of the disease. Once a patient starts to exhibit symptoms, however, treatment with antibiotics is much less effective.[11] While inhalation of anthrax is very lethal—it kills a large percentage of people who develop the disease—it is not contagious. For some weapons purposes, a disease that does not spread from person to person is a desirable characteristic. Using an agent that causes a noncontagious disease would tend to limit the geographic spread of the disease.

Plague is a disease caused by the *Yersinia Pestis* bacteria. Most naturally occurring plague in humans occurs through the bites of fleas that have previously bitten infected rats. This route of transmission causes bubonic plague. Rarely, humans will inhale the bacterium, which leads to pneumonic, or inhalation, plague. Unlike anthrax, pneumonic plague is very contagious and patients suffer from cough, fever, chest pain, and shortness of breath. Pneumonia develops rapidly and death results from respiratory failure. As a weapon, plague can be disbursed through an aerosol, causing pneumonic plague or by disseminating infected fleas, leading to bubonic plague. Bubonic plague is cured relatively easily with antibiotics. If not treated with antibiotics, inhalation plague is nearly 100 percent lethal. Even with antibiotic treatment, approximately 50 percent of pneumonic plague victims die.[12]

Tularemia is a disease that usually occurs naturally in wild animals. Humans can contract the disease through skin lesions or by inhaling the bacteria. As a weapon, the tularemia bacterium would most likely be dispersed as an aerosol. Some people exposed to the bacteria would develop painful lesions on their skin and mucus membranes, including the membranes surrounding the eye. Others would develop a more severe disease, with less distinct symptoms such as fever, fatigue, and cough, eventually leading to pneumonia. Although patients with tularemia respond to antibiotic treatment, they frequently suffer relapses. Without antibiotics, a patient usually has weakness and fatigue for weeks or months.

Like tularemia and anthrax, brucellosis is most commonly an animal disease. Humans contract brucellosis through the eye, cuts in the skin, or by ingesting or inhaling the bacteria. Brucellosis causes an array of symptoms that vary with the individual, including fever, cough, muscle aches, fatigue, sweats, loss of appetite, headache, depression, and irritability. Brucellosis infections can lead to joint disease and infection of many different organs, including the bladder, kidney, lung, heart, and liver. Most of the deaths from brucellosis result from inflammation of the heart, its lining, and/or valves. Unless a six-week regimen of antibiotics is administered, patients can suffer a relapse. Brucellosis is not contagious and would usually lead to incapacitation rather than death.

Rickettsiae are microorganisms that fall somewhere between bacteria and viruses. Strictly considered a type of bacteria, they are very small and live within cells. The most common diseases that are caused by rickettsiae are Rocky Mountain spotted fever, typhus, and Q-fever. All three of the rickettsiae that cause these diseases have been studied, tested, or produced as biological weapons by one or another government. A sporelike form of the organism that causes Q-fever, like the spore that causes anthrax, is resistant to heat and dryness. Q-fever incapacitates humans with a variety of symptoms that include fever, chills, headache, fatigue, loss of appetite, and pain, but rarely leads to death. Very few bacteria are needed to produce disease in humans; indeed, a single bacterium has led to infection under laboratory conditions. Rocky Mountain spotted fever spreads to humans by the bite of ticks and can develop into a very serious disease involving many organs and can lead to paralysis. Like Rocky Mountain spotted fever, typhus spreads to humans through insect bites, usually fleas or lice. Like Q-fever, typhus is not contagious from person to person. Symptoms of typhus include pain, fever, rash, headache, among others.

Viruses, like rickettsiae, replicate within cells. Viruses infect humans through different bodily routes. Viruses that can be disseminated effectively through aerosols have been studied and produced as weapons, including those that cause encephalitis, hemorrhagic fevers, and smallpox. There are several different types of encephalitis caused by different viruses, and many of the viruses have been investigated for their weapons potential. Encephalitis is usually transmitted to humans through mosquito bites, but each of the viruses studied or produced as a weapon could be disseminated in an aerosol. Encephalitis can cause relatively mild symptoms of fever and headache, or can lead to paralysis, seizures, coma, or death. Like encephalitis, several different viruses can lead to hemorrhagic fevers that are very serious diseases. The hemorrhagic fevers, as the name implies, are often accompanied by severe bleeding in different bodily tissues. Rodents can naturally spread the hemorrhagic fevers to humans, but several of the viruses that cause these fevers are stable in aerosols and would likely be sprayed as a weapon.

Smallpox, caused by a virus that only affects humans, ravaged the human race century after century until it was eradicated worldwide through collaborative efforts of scientists throughout the world in the 1970s. The first vaccine against any disease was the one discovered by Edward Jenner in 1798. He infected people with a similar, but relatively harmless, virus that causes cow pox and that infection prevented people from contracting smallpox. After the eradication of smallpox, vaccinations of people with cowpox, which sometimes had serious side effects, was terminated. Nevertheless, the Soviet Union researched, produced, manipulated, and stockpiled smallpox weapons in the 1980s.

In addition to agents that replicate—bacteria, viruses, and rickettsiae—toxins also fall into the category of biological agents. Toxins are poisonous substances that are produced by plants, bacteria, or other living substances. Prohibitions against the possession of weaponized toxins are covered by both the Biological and Chemical Weapons Conventions. Toxins have been components of many biological weapons programs as lethal and capacitating agents. Botulinum toxin, ricin, saxitoxin, staphyloccal enterotoxin B, and others have been studied and stockpiled as weapons in various state BW programs.

Botulinum toxin, produced by bacteria, is one of the most lethal known substances. A very small amount of botulinum toxin can cause death through paralysis of the respiratory muscles. Death does not occur quickly after inhaling or ingesting the toxin. It can take from 12 to 72 hours for an individual to demonstrate symptoms of the poisoning.

Ricin is a toxin that can be refined from the seed of the castor plant. The seed is often referred to as a castor bean although it is not a true bean. Castor oil, used in medicine and industry, also comes from the castor seed. Ricin is relatively easy to produce and if inhaled could cause death from respiratory failure.

Saxitoxin is a powerful, lethal poison that can be extracted from shellfish—mussels, clams, and scallops. After inhaling saxitoxin, death can occur within minutes. The toxin paralyzes the respiratory muscles and a person exposed to saxitoxin suffocates.

Staphyloccal Enterotoxin B is produced by bacteria and has been weaponized as an incapacitating agent. The toxin affects people in very small amounts after a few hours, causing fever, abdominal pain, nausea, cough, headache, and respiratory symptoms. The symptoms last for several days. The toxin occasionally causes lethal toxic shock.

In addition to biological agents that kill or incapacitate humans, other agents that cause animal or plant diseases have also been researched as weapons. Several countries have studied agents that would cause various diseases in horses, cattle, and pigs. Plant agents that spoil or destroy wheat or rice crops are the most common anti-crop agents.

State BW Programs

The following is a short description of the biological weapons programs in the countries that have had the most sophisticated or extensive programs—at least those that are now publicly known. Indeed, information on all state BW programs is incomplete at best. All of the BW programs took place under intense secrecy, even those that took place when it was legal to produce BW. One argument for secrecy is to keep weapons details from potential enemies; another reason, of course, is shame.

Germany

During WWI, Germany conducted a large-scale sabotage operation directed at suppliers of the Allied Forces. Part of this sabotage operation involved the deliberate infection of livestock, most commonly horses and mules, with the bacteria that cause glanders and anthrax. The sabotage program targeted animals in the United States, Romania, Norway, Argentina, and probably Spain. As such, the German efforts were the first confirmed wartime use of BW and the first national offensive BW program.[13] France also had a biological veterinary sabotage program during WWI, although the evidence for this program is scant and may have largely been destroyed.[14]

During WWII, some Nazi officials were interested in biological warfare, but Hitler, who had been a victim of chemical warfare in WWI did not support those efforts. While some attempts were made to obtain certain pathogens from Japan, the two Axis powers did not cooperate on any BW development and it does not appear that Japan shared information about its program with the Germans. Thus, Germany was not prepared to engage in biological warfare during WWII and did not do so.[15]

Japan

An immense offensive BW program, this time employing agents causing disease in humans, accompanied Japan's rise as a formidable military power in the 1920s and 1930s. Japan produced vast quantities of the agents that cause many diseases including plague, anthrax, typhoid, cholera, and dysentery.[16] The Japanese BW program employed thousands of research scientists in institutions located first in Japan and later in Manchuria (known as Manchukuo during the Japanese occupation) and other areas of China. Japan's program was not limited to research, development, and production but included laboratory and field tests on humans, overwhelmingly Chinese prisoners. Shocking in retrospect, Japanese researchers tested lethal disease agents on the prisoners to determine effective dosages and to study the effects of different pathogens.

Thousands of test subjects died from the effects of the agents they were exposed to, or were killed by other means, and dissected. A few prisoners escaped.

Described as a field test, in July 1939, the doctor in charge of the BW program, Ishii Shiro, ordered that the river separating Manchuria from the Soviet Union and the area surrounding its shore be contaminated with bacteria causing typhoid and salmonella.[17] Fighting between Japanese and Soviet troops had been going on in this area, and Japan's troops had been experiencing losses. In the fighting, Japanese troops employed artillery shells filled with biological agents as well. Although disease outbreaks occurred following this so-called field test, it has never been conclusively determined that the outbreaks were a consequence of Japan's attempt to deliberately disseminate disease.

Following the test along the Manchurian–Soviet border, Ishii conducted many operations that involved the deliberate spread of disease in populated areas in China between 1939 and 1942. Although the Japanese once again referred to these undertakings as field tests, they are more appropriately labeled biological warfare. Outbreaks of typhoid, cholera, anthrax, and plague occurred, causing extensive casualties.[18] In addition to the agents causing human disease, the Japanese also employed the bacteria causing the animal disease of glanders, the same agent that Germany used to infect horses in WWI.

At the end of WWII, the victorious Allies were faced with decisions about what to do with those who had directed the Japanese BW program. The Soviet Union conducted a trial in Siberia of 12 men accused of "plotting to employ BW during World War II."[19] All 12 men, who were in Soviet custody, admitted their crimes in what was, to a remarkable degree, similar to the show trials of the Stalin era rather than the Nuremberg or other war crimes trials.[20]

In contrast, the United States did not conduct any trials of Japanese scientists and military personnel who directed or took part in the massive BW operation, which included, as described previously, human experimentation. In a Faustian bargain, the United States offered immunity to Ishii and others in command of the BW program in exchange for information gathered in the notorious experiments. Despite information from several sources that the Japanese BW program had conducted tests using Allied prisoners of war, including captured American soldiers, the value of the information from BW tests was considered more important and more valuable than prosecuting those responsible for the atrocities.[21]

Soviet Union

The BW program of the former Soviet Union began as early as the 1920s. While the Soviet Union pursued its BW research, development, and production before and throughout the Cold War, its clandestine activities following the implementation of the BWC have garnered the most publicity and condemnation. There was not, however, a break in the Soviet BW program; it simply continued apace, albeit with greater secrecy, after the Soviet Union pledged to destroy its weapon stocks and confine its activities to defense.

Allegedly unconvinced that the United States had abandoned its offensive BW, the Soviets did research and development on many bacteria and viruses including those that had made their way into the weapons programs of other countries, in place prior to the BWC ban; among them are the agents that cause anthrax, plague, tularaemia, brucellosis, Ebola, and many others. The Soviet Union's BW program involved approximately 17 major sites and employed tens of thousands of scientists, technicians, and administrative personnel. Among its most nefarious projects was producing tons of the smallpox virus for use in weapons after the disease had been eradicated throughout the world.

The BWC entered into force in 1975 when the science of genetic engineering was in its infancy. The Soviet scientists, unconstrained by a treaty without effective verification provisions, applied the new techniques of inserting foreign genes into potential weapons agents. They manipulated the genetic makeup of agents to make them more lethal, resistant to antibiotics, and exhibit other characteristics that they thought were desirable in a weapon.[22] In a particularly malicious series of experiments, they successfully engineered the bacterium that causes Legionnaire's disease. Among their creations was a germ that was able to infect people with many fewer cells. Moreover, the new creation affected the immune system, leading to paralysis and death after the initial bacterial infection was gone.[23] They conducted many tests on agents and munitions using baboons, guinea pigs, and other animals as test subjects. The Soviet Union also conducted research, developed, and produced anti-animal and anti-plant pathogens.

In 1992, Russian officials acknowledged that the Soviet BW activities constituted a violation of the BWC. Nevertheless, questions still linger as to whether or not prohibited activities still take place in the Russian Federation. The latest report from the U.S. Department of State declares that Russia has "not satisfactorily documented whether this program was completely destroyed or diverted to peaceful purposes in accordance with Article II of the BWC."[24] Russia maintains, however, that all of its activities are conducted in compliance with the BWC.

United Kingdom

As the Nazi party gained power in Germany, the United Kingdom began to receive intelligence about a German BW program. Although not particularly accurate, the intelligence spurred the development of a U.K. program to pre-pare to retaliate with BW if necessary. In 1940, the United Kingdom began work on biological warfare at its Chemical Defence Experimental Station at Porton Down. The program during the war was small, employing not more than a dozen qualified scientists. Nevertheless, the BW unit quickly concen-trated on the spores that cause anthrax and the powerful poison, botulinum toxin.

The bacterium that causes anthrax appears repeatedly in BW research and development and has made its way into the arsenals of nearly every country that produced BW. When the spores enter the body of humans or certain other animals through inhalation, ingestion, or cuts in the skin, the bacteria become active, multiply, and produce a toxin that is highly lethal. Anthrax is not contagious and responds to antibiotics. When anthrax spores are inhaled, antibiotics must be taken promptly following exposure. Once symptoms ap-pear, it is too late, the bacteria has produced sufficient toxins, and killing the bacteria will not prevent serious illness or death. Inhalation of anthrax is particularly deadly.[25]

Following laboratory research on the anthrax bacterium and field tests of bacterial spores that are similar to those that cause anthrax, the United King-dom conducted field tests of anthrax bombs on Guinard Island in Scotland and along the coast of Wales. On Guinard, sheep were tethered downwind of the bomb, which was not dropped from an airplane, but suspended on gallows and remotely detonated. Guinard remained contaminated and uninhabitable for decades after the tests. In other tests, bombs were dropped from planes. These tests, conducted in 1942 "showed unequivocally that biological warfare was feasible . . . and showed that, on a weight-for-weight basis, anthrax spores were 100–1000 times more potent than any effect obtainable under similar conditions with any chemical warfare agent of the time."[26] The United King-dom also produced and stockpiled cakes containing anthrax spores, which could be produced more quickly than munitions and then fed to cattle.

In addition to its work on anthrax spores, the United Kingdom conducted research on botulinum toxin, the deadliest known poison at the time, plague bacteria, and a few other agents. This research demonstrated that both bot-ulinum toxin and plague bacteria could be disseminated through aerosols. This research, however, was not particularly fruitful and did not lead to the development of these agents as weapons. Nevertheless, despite the apparent paucity of products—cattle cakes and an anthrax bomb that was never put into production—the wartime U.K. BW activities were significant. "Britain had launched an organized and concerted effort to produce biological weap-ons and had shifted from a defensive to an offensive oriented policy regime."[27]

During WWII, the United Kingdom, United States, and Canada collabo-rated closely with one another and shared information regarding their BW activities and exchanged personnel. This collaboration continued after the end of the war when the perceived BW threat from Germany transformed into a threat from the Soviet Union. In the post–WWII United Kingdom, the development of BW was given a priority equal to the development of nuclear weapons and the two were considered to be complementary.[28]

Developing biological bombs for retaliation and research to produce biological agents in bulk continued at Porton Down. Between 1949 and 1955, the United Kingdom conducted several operations to test pathological agents outdoors. A series of field tests involving several different disease-causing agents were carried out near islands in the Caribbean Sea, using guinea pigs, sheep, and monkeys. The trials were under the direction of the British, but the United States and Canada supplied scientific personnel and supplies.[29] Additional field tests were conducted off the Scottish Islands. Other trials, using stimulants—relatively benign agents that mimicked more dangerous pathogens—were conducted in U.K. government buildings and the London Underground.[30]

Gradually, nuclear weapons development and testing took precedence over BW projects in the United Kingdom and the BW emphasis shifted from work on a BW bomb to the potential for sabotage using biological agents. The United Kingdom continued to test agents in the field, but a focus on the vulnerability of the British Isles to large area germ warfare led U.K. researchers to eventually abandon offensive research and development to undertake strictly defensive endeavors in the 1960s and the 1970s.[31] The United Kingdom spearheaded international efforts that led to the BWC.

United States

The United States launched its offensive BW program during WWII amidst unconfirmed reports that Japan was waging biological warfare in China and concern that Germany considered biological warfare feasible. Lack of intelligence on German and Japanese programs stoked rather than dampened fears. Early research and development centered on anti-crop agents, but work on several human agents followed. Located initially in the War Research Service, by 1944 all biological warfare activities were undertaken by the Chemical Warfare Services.

Unlike the Axis Powers, the Allies shared information and personnel. The United Kingdom and Canada had an earlier start than the United States but the acquisition of data and information from the Japanese BW program spurred the U.S. efforts. By 1952, BW programs in the United States included "development of weapons, testing of potential agents, the development of dissemination techniques, warheads for missiles, decontamination procedures, detection devices and protective equipment."[32] Laboratory work in the United States examined numerous bacteria, viruses, toxins, and fungi. Scientists carried out work on lethal as well as disabling agents, antipersonnel, anti-animal, and anti-crop agents. The United States eventually made weapons from five different lethal agents, three incapacitating agents and two anti-plant agents. Field tests took place principally in Utah and Maryland using live agents. Other tests using stimulants took place in the San Francisco Bay area, Minneapolis, and Virginia.[33] While the United States conducted its early tests using animals, mostly monkeys, it eventually used human volunteers, exposing them to a variety of agents that cause disease. None of the volunteers died or experienced permanent disease or incapacitation.[34] Offensive BW operations continued throughout the 1960s and into the 1970s and, following the example of the British, tests took place in the New York subway, as well as bus terminals and airports.

Prior to the United States' unilateral renunciation of offensive BW by President Nixon in 1969, and of toxins in 1970, the United States investigated scores of agents for their weapons potential. The United States researched and developed many munitions for use with biological agents and stored tons of agents in liquid suspensions, as dried agent in frozen bulk pellets and in filled munitions. In 1970, the U.S. arsenal included lethal agents that cause anthrax and tularemia, incapacitating agents that cause encephalomyelitis and Q-fever, and lethal and incapacitating toxins including botulinum toxin, saxitoxin, and staphylococcus enterotoxin.

The United States planned to use BW in combination with nuclear weapons in retaliation to a Soviet nuclear attack. It also envisioned the use of incapacitating agents in other theatres of war, particularly in Laos or Korea. These plans were general and hypothetical except to include using BW in detailed plan to invade Cuba.[35] The United States abandoned its offensive BW program in 1969 and its toxin weapons program in 1970.

South Africa

Beginning in the 1980s, the individuals within the apartheid government of South Africa initiated a CBW program within the South African Defense Forces. In order to disguise the connection between the program and the government, shell companies were established to carry out the work. The CBW projects were carried out together and their purpose was primarily to work on agents and devices for clandestine assassination of individuals considered enemies of the apartheid state. The goal was to produce devices that would make it difficult or impossible to trace the assassinations back to the government.

Much of the information known about the program comes from the testimony of witnesses at the trial of Wouter Basson, the founder of the program.

Accounts of the program seem to come from the pages of Cold War spy novels. Among the products of the biological research and development were freeze-dried bacteria that cause cholera, anthrax, salmonella, and other diseases and several toxins, including botulinum toxin. Delivery devices ranged from cigarettes and chocolates laced with anthrax bacteria or botulinum toxin, to soda pop and beer bottles that had been injected with bacteria or toxins, to orange and sugar contaminated with salmonella bacteria.[36] The CBW program tested chemical poisons and biological agents on animals. Screwdrivers filled with poison were tested on pigs; dogs, baboons, and monkeys were other test subjects.[37]

Secrecy and deniability characterized the South African program. A front company, Roodeplaat Research Laboratories, carried out the bulk of the biological work, as well as a small amount of private legitimate work. While scientists supplied the assassination weapons, they did not know or select the targets of assassination. They operated on a strictly need-to-know policy. Orders for assassination employing biological agents were ordinarily given orally and elliptically so no paper trail could provide damning evidence. Despite the extensive research and development carried out on biological agents and toxins, the South African laboratory did not stockpile any agents or toxins for large scale use.

France

France's interest in BW dates to the period between the two World Wars. During the inter-war period, the French BW activities mirrored what it perceived as a possible BW threat from Germany, much as the United States and the Soviet Union attempted to counter each other's build up in nuclear weapons and missiles during the Cold War. Like other state BW programs, the French hid their interest in BW and their progress in research and development. As a party to the 1925 Geneva Protocol, France pledged not to use bacteriological (biological) weapons, except in retaliation. Nevertheless, the French did prepare to retaliate with BW if another state, particularly Germany, used BW first. The early French policy to explore research into biological warfare stemmed from its Commission for Chemical Studies and Experiments. The director of the Naval Chemical Research Laboratory compiled a report in 1922 that assessed intelligence on German BW activities, evaluated agents and delivery mechanisms for dispersal of biological agents, and defenses against biological warfare. The report concluded that a few diseases whose causative agents could have military potential included plague, cholera, typhoid, brucellosis, and glanders, among others. The report noted that the agent causing brucellosis could be cultured easily and persisted in the environment.[38] In 1922, the French established a commission within the war ministry to pursue BW research and development. The commission continued its work until France signed the armistice between Germany and France in 1940, after capitulating to the German invasion. France destroyed much of the information from its BW program in order to prevent Germany from obtaining it.

Following Germany's defeat in WWII, France resumed its interest in biological warfare. The French program performed research on several toxins as well as bacteria, viruses, and rickettsiae. Like other states, the French did work on the bacteria causing anthrax, glanders and botulinum, and other toxins. It studied the behavior of viruses in general and proposed various munitions for specific agents. The research included work on dispersal of agents using bombs, grenades, aerosols, mortars, antipersonnel mines, and insect vectors. It also conducted research on aerosols using dried agents and agents in liquid suspension. The program conducted trials using animals and different dispersal methods. The French program also focused on defensive measures, including agent detection and protections. The bulk of the French post-WWII activity took place between 1948 and 1956. Economic pressures and the French interest in nuclear weapons led to a waning of interest in BW. Although BW activities continued in France throughout the 1960s and shifted its focus to work on incapacitating rather than lethal agents, French activities never led to the production of stockpiles of biological or toxin weapons. While France intended to produce a BW arsenal, that policy was never implemented.[39]

Iraq

Iraq invaded neighboring Kuwait in 1991. After allied forces drove Iraq from Kuwait, the UN Security Council created the United Nations Special Commission (UNSCOM) to investigate Iraq's nuclear, chemical, biological, and missile programs. Information on Iraq's BW program was difficult to come by, but eventually the Commission and its successor, United Nations Monitoring, Verification and Inspection Commission (UNMOVIC), uncovered substantial information about the program from informers and documents. Iraq began development of BW in 1974. Initially limited to research, after the war between Iraq and Iran in the 1980s, Iraq intensified its efforts and developed weapons and tested dispersal devices.

Iraq produced botulinum toxin for use as a weapon and produced and tested the bacteria that causes anthrax. Other agents, including the toxins ricin and aflatoxin, were added to Iraq's arsenal, and it began to investigate viruses as well. Iraq destroyed its stockpiles of agents in 1991 and no evidence has emerged that Iraq restarted BW production while UNSCOM and UNMOVIC were active in Iraq, or prior to the U.S.-led invasion of Iraq in 2003.[40]

Others

In addition to these state programs, Hungary had a research and development program to examine the weapons potential of biological agents prior to WWII. The Soviet Union, however, did not want its Warsaw Pact allies engaged in BW activities. Thus, there is no evidence that the Hungarian program persisted after WWII. During the 1930s and 1940s, however, Hungary had an offensive BW program that included research on the bacterium that causes anthrax as well as agents that cause gangrene, dysentery, and diarrheal diseases. In addition to agents, Hungary tested various means of dispersing biological agents. While Canada never actually possessed BW, it cooperated with the British and U.S. programs during WWII and thereafter, including research on agents and field tests of munitions.[41]

CBW Arms Control

The linking of BW with CW that began with the 1925 Geneva Protocol persisted for nearly 50 years, but there was little progress on CBW disarmament. Nuclear arms control dominated the arms control agenda in the decades following WWII. Proposals dealing with CBW were typically viewed through their potential implications on nuclear policy and the Cold War. During the 1960s and early 1970s, CBW control and disarmament focused on the United States. At that time, the United States had not ratified the GP and was accused of using CW in Vietnam.

Throughout the 1960s, the United Kingdom's Ministry of Defence produced a series of papers assessing CW and BW policy. The paper summarizing the policy assessments emphasized three elements that motivated the U.K. BW policy initiative throughout the 1960s: (1) the United Kingdom was vulnerable to a BW attack, (2) BW had limited strategic and limited military tactical value, and (3) the Soviet Union was not a suitable BW target. Consequently, in 1968, the United Kingdom produced a working paper on microbiological warfare, describing the principle elements of a draft convention. These elements included:

- A common understanding that any use of microbiological warfare and in any circumstances was contrary to international law and a crime against humanity and therefore a complete prohibition of use.
- A ban on the production of agents for hostile purposes while recognizing the necessity of production of agents for peaceful purposes.
- A ban on the production of ancillary equipment.
- An obligation to destroy stocks of agents or equipment.
- A ban on research aimed at production of prohibited agents and equipment.

- Provisions for access by authorities to "all research which might give rise to allegations" of noncompliance.
- Openness of relevant research to international investigation and public scrutiny.[42]

The working paper recommended a "competent body of experts, established under the auspices of the United Nations," to investigate allegations of breaches of the convention and a commitment by parties to cooperate with any investigation.

The U.K. argument for a prompt ban on the use and possession of BW emphasized that:

1. BW "are regarded with general abhorrence, possibly more so than any other means of waging war."
2. "It seems unlikely that development or use of biological weapons is, at the moment, regarded by any state as essential to its security."
3. New technological developments could lead to BW becoming an integral part of some states' armaments.
4. It would be easier to achieve a ban before such armament took place than after.[43]

Arguments for separating biological from chemical weapons were based principally on political pragmatism. BW were at an earlier stage of development; therefore, prohibiting BW would face less opposition. The United States and the Soviet Union both had large stocks of CW. Moreover, differences between East and West during the Cold War concerning verification, and U.S. use of anti-crop and antipersonnel chemicals in Vietnam, made tackling CW disarmament a daunting political task.

Recognizing that verification as understood in the nuclear field was not feasible for BW, the United Kingdom recommended an approach for receiving complaints and investigating allegations of noncompliance that would allow very quick investigations to be automatically implemented as fast as possible.[44] Despite major skepticism from the U.K. ministry of defense that the Soviet Union, China, or the United States would ever accept an agreement that would ban research, development, and production on what would amount to an unverifiable basis, the Foreign and Commonwealth Office prevailed and introduced a Draft Convention in July 1969.

U.K. and Soviet Draft Conventions

The Biological Warfare Draft Convention tabled in 1969 contained stronger provisions than the 1972 BWC. Article I of the Draft Convention prohibited the use of biological agents for hostile purposes in any circumstances and explicitly outlawed the hostile use of BW against humans, other animals, or crops. Article II extended the prohibition on use to possession and re-search, and required parties to destroy or divert to peaceful purposes stocks of weapons agents, ancillary equipment, and vectors. Article III described the procedures for complaints of violation of the Convention, with allegations of use to be treated differently than other allegations of noncompliance. Allegations of use were to be taken to the UN secretary-general along with a recommendation for an investigation. Allegations of breaches of the Convention that did not involve use were to be taken to the Security Council along with a request for an investigation. Such requests, of course, would be subject to the veto power of the permanent members. Bifurcating the investigation procedures for allegations of the use of BW and allegations of other noncompliant activities would have great significance as the Draft Convention was altered through negotiations.

In September 1969, the Soviet Union responded to the U.K. Draft Convention by tabling its own Draft Convention, prohibiting the development and production of both chemical and biological weapons. In contrast to the U.K. Draft Convention, the Soviet Draft combined CW and BW, excluded an explicit prohibition against use and tabled the Convention at the UN General Assembly instead of at the Conference of the Committee on Disarmament (CCD).[45]

Meanwhile in Washington, DC, the U.S. government was in the midst of a review of all CBW policies.[46] Following the review, in November 1969, the United States announced its decision to unilaterally terminate its offensive BW program, to destroy its BW stocks, to place a moratorium on CW production, and to submit the 1925 Geneva Protocol to the U.S. Senate for ratification. The United States also declared its intention to support the U.K. Draft BW Convention. In February 1970, the United States extended its BW policy to toxins as well.

During 1970, Western delegations to the CCD concentrated their efforts on trying to convince others of the advisability of a Convention separating BW from CW. Then, on March 30, 1971, the Soviet Union unexpectedly tabled a second Draft Convention at the CCD, dropping its long-standing opposition to separating CW and BW.

The new Soviet draft differed from the U.K. draft in several crucial respects. First, it ignored Article I of the U.K. draft, which obligated parties never, in any circumstances, to use biological methods of warfare. Second, it omitted the U.K. draft's prohibition of research aimed at offensive production. Third, it required all complaints concerning a breach of obligation to go to the Security Council, including those of alleged use of BW. The Soviet draft included a few features absent from the U.K. draft. It required states to undertake legislative and administrative measures for prohibiting BW. It also created an obligation for states to facilitate the exchange of equipment, materials, and information for the use of biological agents and toxins for peaceful purposes.

Negotiating the BWC

Several states responded negatively to the attempt in the new Soviet Draft Convention to conform with the U.K. and U.S. desires to separate CW and BW. Sweden, Mexico, Morocco, and others expressed both dismay and doubt that effective controls on CW would ever be achieved if the two weapons were separated. The neutral and nonaligned countries, however, recognized that critical momentum was behind the initiative as soon as the Soviet Union and its Warsaw Pact allies tabled a Draft Convention that was similar to the U.K. draft supported by the United States.

Although an internal U.K. document raised a number of concerns about the Soviet Draft Convention, the United States, following consultations with its allies, decided to negotiate on the basis of the Soviet text. U.K. reservations of the Soviet draft were threefold. First, a concern that the Soviet Union might wish to retain the right to retaliate with BW since its draft excluded a prohibition on all use of BW. Second, the United Kingdom was worried that the Soviet Union might want to manufacture and stockpile the component parts of prohibited BW weapons. Third, the United Kingdom did not think that the language of consultation and cooperation procedures to resolve problems of implementation of the convention was a realistic deterrent to would-be violators.[47] For its part, the United States firmly rejected the Soviet interpretation of the Geneva Protocol—that the GP prohibited tear gas and herbicides. The United States preferred the advantages of a complaints procedure on use that went to the UN secretary-general rather than through the Security Council; yet it did not feel that those provisions were essential to its security interests.[48]

Ultimately the most contentious issues in the negotiations process concerned the references in the BWC to CW. U.S. national security advisor Henry Kissinger considered those references, in the Preamble and Articles VIII and IX of the BWC, to have been "the price for general support of a BW ban" from the nonaligned nations and the Soviets.[49]

On April 10, 1972, the Convention on the Prohibition of the Development, Production and Stockpiling of Bacteriological (Biological) and Toxin Weapons and on Their Destruction was signed in Washington, London, and Moscow. The Convention was the first to outlaw the possession, production, stockpiling, and development of an entire class of weapons. Despite the failure of efforts to strengthen the Convention, it still stands as a bulwark, as stated in the Preamble, against weapons that are "repugnant to the conscience of mankind."

The BWC entered into force in 1975 with 39 member states. That number has risen steadily to the current membership of 163 states parties. Nevertheless, the BWC has fewer member states than either the NPT or the CWC.

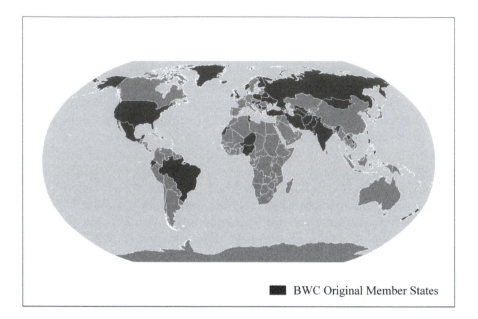

BWC Original Member States

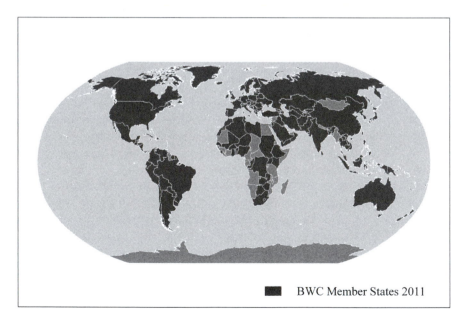

BWC Member States 2011

Implementation of the BWC

The strength of the BWC is its general-purpose criterion, the language of Article 1 that member states may not under any circumstances "develop, produce, stockpile or otherwise acquire or retain" biological agents or toxins *"that have no justification for prophylactic, protective or other peaceful purpose."* Despite challenges to the effectiveness of the BWC, this general-purpose criterion has stood the test of time, scientific advances in the biological sciences, and egregious violations of the Convention. The first challenge occurred at the first review conference of the Convention in 1981.

The 1980 RevCon was marked by two noteworthy events. The first was an unsuccessful effort, led by the Swedish delegation, to amend the Convention. Several states sought a better way to address questions about compliance with the treaty than going through the UN Security Council. The Soviet Union and its allies objected strenuously to the Swedish proposal on the grounds that a RevCon was not the proper forum to undertake amendments to the Convention. The second noteworthy event was the action taken by the U.S. Department of State asking for an explanation for the anthrax outbreak in the Soviet city of Sverdlovsk (now Ekaterinberg) in 1979. Initially, the U.S. embassy in Moscow followed the usual channels for resolving problems with arms control treaties and requested an explanation from the Soviets. The very next day, however, during the RevCon and without giving the Soviets an opportunity to reply, the United States made its suspicions public. It raised the allegation that the outbreak was due to a biological warfare accident, implicitly charging the Soviets with violating the BWC. The Soviets responded by acknowledging the existence of the epidemic and blamed it on the ingestion of tainted meat. The matter was not resolved at the RevCon and lingered until after the breakup of the Soviet Union, when a series of revelations indicated that indeed, the anthrax outbreak was caused by a leak from a facility conducting activities prohibited by Convention. Thus, it has been apparent since the first RevCon that the absence of provisions and procedures for states to demonstrate their compliance with the BWC, or conversely, to seek onsite investigations of events that could uncover noncompliant behavior by States, has plagued the Convention since its inception.

The second RevCon marked a point of cautious movement on the question of how to strengthen the Convention through greater transparency in biological activities relevant to the treaty and discussed obligations to call a consultative committee. Yet, the second RevCon established what would become a pattern: minor steps that could achieve consensus agreement among the states parties in attendance at the RevCon. The delegations adopted a provision in the final declaration that a consultative meeting will be called at the request of any party. In addition, the delegates established the initial political obligations of states parties to participate in an annual information exchange commonly referred to as Confidence Building Measures (CBMs). Information on research centers and laboratories that meet the highest international safety standards and those that specialize in permitted activities directly related to the Convention were among the declaration measures agreed to in 1986. In addition, states encouraged the open publication of biological research relevant to the Convention and promoted contacts between scientists engaged in Convention-relevant research.

Few could have imagined the changes in the world political landscape that unfolded between the second and third BWC RevCons. By September 1991, Eastern Europe was no longer under the boot of the Soviet Union; 14 Soviet Republics declared their intention to leave the Soviet Union and Mikhail Gorbachev had barely survived an August 1991 coup attempt. In early 1991, Operation Desert Storm had ousted Iraq from its invasion of Kuwait. Following the Iraqi exodus from Kuwait, the UN Security Council established the Special Commission on Iraq, authorizing the Commission and the IAEA to eliminate Iraq's weapons of mass destruction as well as missiles with a certain range. Although many Iraqi observers had long suspected that Iraq harbored a BW program, no solid evidence of the existence of the program came to light until 1995. Iraq signed the BWC in 1972, but did not ratify the Convention until June 1991 when it was forced to do so after its defeat in Kuwait. Thus, the third RevCon took place under optimism that the East–West stalemate on verification measures for the Convention could finally be overcome, and the weaknesses of Articles V and VI could be remedied.

The Conference made major changes in the Confidence Building Measures established in 1986. It amended and extended the measures agreed to in 1986 and added three additional measures. The additional CBMs included: (1) a declaration of legislation, regulations, and other measures, (2) a declaration on past activities in offensive and/or defensive biological research and development programs, and (3) a declaration of vaccine production facilities. The Conference also expanded and made more explicit the workings of any consultative meeting called to address concerns with the implementation of the Convention or compliance with its provisions.

Furthermore, the Conference established an Ad Hoc Group of Governmental Experts (AHG) to examine potential verification measures from a scientific and technical standpoint. The third RevCon set forth many details of the work of the group, which came to be known as VEREX.

Despite the accomplishments of the third RevCon, problems with the submission of the politically, but not legally, binding CBMs had already become apparent. Only a fraction of the states parties to the Convention had submitted the yearly declaration. In 1990, for example, only about one-third of the states parties submitted the declarations.

Overall, however, the RevCon was considered a success and delegations seriously embarked on the VEREX exercise. VEREX completed their work during four sessions in 1992 and 1993 and issued a consensus report at the conclusion of their work. VEREX examined 21 measures, including both onsite and offsite measures, both singly and in combination with other measures.

Paragraphs 31 and 32 of the VEREX Summary report issued at the conclusion of the final VEREX meeting state the conclusions of the expert group:

> 31. The Ad Hoc Group of Governmental Experts concluded that potential verification measures as identified and evaluated could be useful to varying degrees in enhancing confidence, through increased transparency, that States Parties were fulfilling their obligations under the BWC. While it was agreed that reliance could not be placed on any single measure to differentiate conclusively between prohibited and permitted activity and to resolve ambiguities about compliance, it was also agreed that the measures could provide information of varying utility in strengthening the BWC. It was recognized that there remain a number of further technical questions to be addressed such as identity of agent, types and quantities, in the context of any future work. Some measures in combination could provide enhanced capabilities by increasing, for example, the focus and improving the quality of information, thereby improving the possibility of differentiating between prohibited and permitted activities and of resolving ambiguities about compliance.
>
> 32. Based on the examination and evaluation of the measures described above against the criteria given in the mandate, the Group considered, from the scientific and technical standpoint, that some of the potential verification measures would contribute to strengthening the effectiveness and improve the implementation of the Convention, also recognizing that appropriate and effective verification could reinforce the Convention.

A Special Conference was convened in 1994 to review the VEREX findings and decide on further steps. The Conference established an AHG, open to all states parties. The objective of this AHG was "to consider appropriate measures, including possible verification measures, and draft proposals to strengthen the convention, to be included, as appropriate, in a legally binding instrument, to be submitted for the consideration of the States Parties."

The fourth RevCon was held in 1996. The need for more effective methods of dealing with compliance concerns was underscored by the revelations between the third and fourth RevCons of a massive offensive BW program in the former Soviet Union, and a much smaller, but significant program in Iraq. The conference essentially maintained a holding pattern while awaiting the conclusion of the work of the AHG. The conference reviewed the preamble and the Articles of the Convention, but took no action such as had taken place at the second and third RevCons.

The AHG began its meetings in 1995, and met regularly each year, developing a lengthy protocol to the Convention. In July 2001, the United States rejected the draft protocol that had been under negotiation for five years and rejected the mandate of the AHG. This rejection was due in part to the change in administrations in the United States.

The Fifth Review Conference

The fifth RevCon, opening in December 2001, took place shortly after the 9/11 terror attacks and the deliberate dissemination of letters containing anthrax spores to U.S. Senators and others. The United States and its allies had invaded Afghanistan and ousted the Taliban from governmental power; the Taliban, however, had retreated but not surrendered. In the United States, the arms control pendulum had swung to those who were skeptical or downright hostile to arms control. The George W. Bush administration was filled with many political appointees who viewed all arms control with suspicion. Many of them, including Vice President Cheney, had been on record as opposing U.S. ratification of the CWC. Moreover, although President Clinton had signed the CTBT, it had been withdrawn from the Senate because there was no support for its ratification among Republicans.

The initial session of the fifth RevCon also took place in the wake of the U.S. rejection of the AHG process. The United States sought to terminate the mandate of the AHG, but other countries were staunchly opposed. In an unprecedented move, the chairman suspended the conference for a year under very tense circumstances.

Ultimately, in lieu of a legally binding Protocol, the resumed fifth RevCon in December 2002 agreed to yearly meetings of two weeks duration each of experts and states parties. The topics were strictly constrained and none of the topics touched on Article I or verification of its provisions. Nevertheless, the implementation of the yearly meetings, with their discussions of topics pertinent to the treaty that had been neglected during the lengthy AHG process proved more beneficial than anticipated. States parties who favored the adoption of a legally binding Protocol, although disheartened by the stance of the United States—and presumably other states parties who to a great extent hid behind the U.S. rejection—made the most of the intercessional process.

The Sixth Review Conference

The Age of Terror mindset introduced at the fifth RevCon was alive and well during the sixth RevCon. Between the end of 2002 and December 2006, the date of the sixth RevCon, additional states parties had suffered terror-ist attacks; Spain, Indonesia, the United Kingdom, and others had experi-enced dramatic attacks. The UN Security Council had passed Resolution 1540 dealing with preventing nonstate actors from acquiring weapons of mass destruction.

Differences between 2002 and 2006 were also apparent. The U.S.-led co-alitions in Afghanistan and Iraq, rather than translating military success into stable governments, were bogged down in fighting insurgencies, a resurgent Al Qaeda, and its offshoots. The limits of military force to achieve desired outcomes in Afghanistan and Iraq were readily apparent.

With no hope of returning to a legally binding Protocol, states parties capitalized on a more cooperative atmosphere. The sixth RevCon decided to continue the yearly meetings of experts and states parties, on a reduced scale—two weeks in total rather than three. Once again, the topics of the meetings were sharply focused and limited. Arguably, the success of the inter-cessional process led directly to the establishment of a small, full-time Institu-tional Support Unit (ISU). The support staff of the intercessional process and the sixth RevCon, supplemented by an additional person, became the ISU. The ISU is not, however, permanent. Delegates debated at length over the size and mandate of the ISU, strictly limiting its functions.

While the establishment of the ISU was the most important formal deci-sion taken by the states parties, the emergence of a new negotiating group, the JACKSNNZ, marked a departure from the antiquated groupings of the Eastern Group, the Western Group, and the Non-Aligned and Others Group. Comprised of Japan, Australia, Canada, Korea (Republic of), Switzerland, Norway, and New Zealand, the new group broke the old mold by forming a group based on post–Cold War shared interests, rather than regional or other groupings.

The Seventh Review Conference

The months and years leading up to the Seventh RevCon saw an unprec-edented outpouring of meetings, reports, and academic articles making recom-mendations for ways that the states parties could improve the operation of the convention. Meeting in Geneva in December 2011, the conference opened with much optimism and ended with distinct resignation among the states parties. Despite high hopes, the states parties were able to agree on only a few minor changes to the CBMs, a continued schedule and topics for annual meetings, an increased mandate for the ISU—but no additional personnel to carry out the mandate. The worldwide economic crisis meant that many gov-ernments were unwilling to commit additional funds for the ISU or the annual meetings. The United States changed its position with regard to verification and compliance, but other governments insisted on returning to the AHG negotiations, which the United States refused to accept.[50] The disappointing outcome of the 7th RevCon has led to some pessimism that the RevCon process can lead to substantial improvement of the BWC yet it may open the door for increased action by NGOs.

Chemical Weapons Convention

The control of CW has been an important aspect of the international arms control agenda since their massive use in WWI. Article IX of the BWC obligated states parties to continue negotiations on the abolition of CW. The CCD negotiations on a CW ban continued at a leisurely pace, as many arms control agreements during the Cold War proceeded. Both the United States and the Soviet Union possessed vast arsenals of CW.

During the initial years of negotiations, onsite verification appeared to be an obstacle that could not be overcome. The U.S. negotiating position, along with its allies, was that onsite measures were necessary to verify destruction of chemical stockpiles and facilities and to ensure that the production of poisonous chemicals, whether by governments or private industry, was undertaken for peaceful purposes only. The Soviet negotiating position, on the other hand, systematically refused to allow onsite measures in arms control agreements.[51] In 1984, the United States introduced a draft Convention, for example, that the Soviet Union promptly rejected. A breakthrough on this issue was achieved only after the Soviet Union agreed to onsite inspections in 1987.

The behavior of Iraq during the 1980s provided significant impetus to the negotiations. In the Iran–Iraq war from 1980 to1988, Iran repeatedly accused Iraq of using CW. Other sources began to add their support to Iran's allegations, including a UN investigation team. In 1986, UN secretary-general Javier Perez de Cuellar formally accused Iraq of using CW. Then, in 1988, Saddam Hussein attacked his own Kurdish population in the town of Halabjah with CW, reportedly killing 5,000 people in the first hour. Furthermore, it was revealed that many nations, including several Western states, sold chemicals and equipment to Hussein's Iraqi government that enabled it to produce the deadly weapons.

The negotiations of the CWC were unique in the active role that the chemical industry played during the negotiations. Industry representatives, including the Chemical Manufacturers Association, were consulted regularly and helped shape the language of the treaty. Individual chemical companies hosted trial inspections during the negotiations to ensure that the managed access verification provisions of the Convention would not be onerous to the chemical industry, or expose it to the risks of losing trade secrets. The chemical industry and trade associations supported and worked to ratify the

CWC in the United States. The CWC's negotiations were also noteworthy in overcoming obstacles such as the use of riot control agents; these agents can be used for law enforcement but not as a method of warfare.

Provisions of the Convention

The text of the CWC contains 24 articles over more than 50 pages; with its annexes it is more than 180 pages. It is in many respects a very complex arms control agreement. The complexity is due, in part, to the scientific and industrial uses for chemicals that can cause harm. Virtually any chemical, if ingested at high enough doses, can cause illness, incapacitation, or death. At the same time, the CWC's prohibitions are broad and essentially simple. Each state party agrees never to use, develop, produce, acquire, or retain CW, to destroy any CW it possesses, controls, or has abandoned in another state's territory, and to destroy CW production facilities.

Unlike the BWC, the CWC contains many definitions, including, among others, those for chemical weapons, toxic chemical, and chemical weapons production facility. It also specifies "purposes not prohibited under this Convention." These permitted purposes include: (1) agricultural, industrial, medical, and pharmaceutical research; (2) protection against toxic chemicals and chemical weapons; (3) military purposes that are not the use of CW or do not depend on the use of the toxic properties of chemicals (i.e., chemicals used to illuminate the field of battle or enemy positions); and (4) "law enforcement including domestic riot control purposes."[52] This last permitted purpose has acquired different interpretations.

Conceptually, the CWC established three schedules of toxic chemicals based on several criteria. In doing so, the Convention sought to strike a balance between toxic chemicals that are widely used for commercial or industrial uses and those that have few commercial applications. Thus, the criteria for the different schedules focus first on whether a chemical has ever been developed, produced, stockpiled, or used as a weapon, or is closely related to such chemicals; second, whether a chemical is produced for commercial purposes, and if so, in what quantities; and third, whether a chemical could be developed as a weapon. Schedule 1 essentially includes all chemicals that had been developed, produced, stockpiled, or used as CW, certain precursor chemicals or components of CW, and other highly toxic chemicals, that have little or no use for commercial or other peaceful purposes permitted under the Convention. In addition to chemicals, there are two toxins on Schedule 1, ricin and saxitoxin, in spite of the fact that the BWC covers all toxins. The inclusion of these two toxins reflects some unease with the ability of the BWC to effectively control toxins. Schedule 2 chemicals are those that have the potential to be CW because of their lethal or incapacitating properties and are not produced in large quantities for commercial quantities. Schedule

3 chemicals may have been developed as weapons or precursors to weapons, but typically are produced in large commercial quantities for permitted purposes. Additions or changes to the chemicals enumerated in the schedules can be done through a procedure detailed in the Convention, and take effect if no state party objects.

The CWC is a true disarmament treaty; it requires all states parties that possess CW to destroy weapons stockpiles, munitions, and production facilities. Moreover, the CWC has elaborate measures to document and verify such destruction. All chemicals in any of the three schedules as well as facilities that produce, store, or are otherwise related to scheduled chemicals are subject to onsite inspection. Verification provisions are most burdensome for schedule 1 chemicals and least burdensome for schedule 3 chemicals.

Parties to the CWC are required to make detailed declarations of any CW they possess or control, old or abandoned CW, facilities that produce or have been designed to produce CW, and riot control agents that they possess.

The CWC created the Organization for the Prevention of Chemical Weapons (OPCW) to ensure implementation of the Convention and to provide a forum for consultation and cooperation among its parties. The OPCW consists of the Conference of States Parties (CSP), which ordinarily meets on an annual basis with each state party having one representative to the Conference. The Executive Council consists of 41 members distributed according to geographic regions. The members of the Council are elected for two year terms by the CSP. The EC, as its name implies, has executive responsibilities and takes substantive decisions by a two-thirds majority vote and procedural decisions by a simple majority. The Technical Secretariat, headed by a director general who serves a four-year term, conducts verification activities and assists the EC and the CP as requested. Its offices are in the Hague, the Netherlands. The OPCW has five divisions that report to the deputy director general and four offices and a policy secretariat that report directly to the director general. The OPCW has approximately 500 employees and an annual budget of more than €70 million for 2012.[53]

After a heated battle between the Clinton White House and the Republican-led Senate, the U.S. Senate ratified the CWC on a vote of 74 in favor to 26 against. While a slim majority of Republican Senators voted in favor of ratification, all 26 negative votes were cast by Republican senators even though the Convention was negotiated under the administration of President George H.W. Bush and signed by him in 1993. The Senate approved the treaty only after the Clinton administration agreed to a package of 23 conditions. One of the conditions asserted that the United States was not bound by Article XXII of the Convention, which did not allow states parties to attach reservations to their ratification documents. Another potentially damaging condition was the requirement that no samples taken from U.S. sites would be allowed to be taken out of U.S. territory for analysis.

CWC Implementation

The treaty text called for the Convention to enter into force 180 days after the 65th state ratified it.[54] On April 29, 1997, the CWC entered into force with 87 original states parties. Implementation of the treaty required each state party to establish a National Authority to submit initial declarations of relevant CW and chemical production facilities as well as other matters. Many aspects of the treaty required a longer time period to implement or complete than the CWC negotiators anticipated. According to one expert, writing about the 2003 RevCon, "since the Convention's entry-into-force, a large number of states parties has lagged behind in submitting even the most basic notifications and declarations to the OPCW. Although some of the gaps have closed over time, the state of affairs in this regard is still dismal."[55]

In the 15 years since its entry into force, many, but not all, of these delays have been rectified. By the end of 2011, 180 of the then 188 states parties had completed initial declarations.[56]

Universality

By the time of the first RevCon held in 2003, the CWC had 151 states parties and membership has continued to grow. As of May 15, 2012, states parties numbered 188. Nevertheless, significant states are among the eight that are not party to the treaty. Israel and Myanmar (Burma) have signed, but not yet ratified, the treaty while Angola, Egypt, North Korea, Somalia, South Sudan, and Syria have not signed or acceded to it.

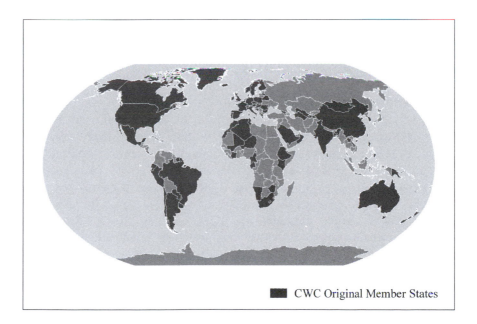

CWC Original Member States

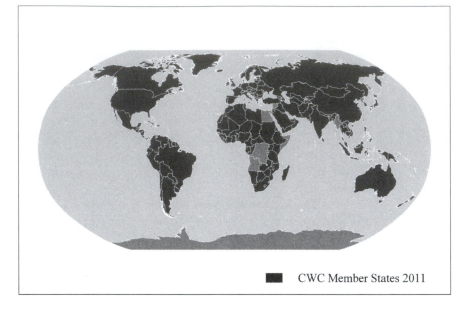

CWC Member States 2011

Chemical Weapons Stockpile and Production Facility Destruction

Seven states declared that they possessed CW that needed to be destroyed under the verification provisions of the CWC: Albania, India, Iraq, Libya, Russia, South Korea, and the United States. The United States and the Russian Federation had, by far, the largest stockpiles. Albania, India, and South Korea have completed the destruction of their stockpiles. A total of 71,194 metric tons of toxic CW agents were declared by these seven states; Russia declared 40,000 metric tons and the United States declared 27,771 metric tons. The conference of states parties in 2009 granted Libya's request for an extension of its destruction deadline to May 2011. Libya, however did not meet that deadline and requested another extension.[57] Iraq acceded to the CWC in 2009 and possesses old and neutralized CW left from Saddam Hussein's regime. Many states are assisting Iraq with its destruction obligations.[58] In 2006, the United States requested an extension of its destruction deadline, which was granted. As of January 23, 2012, the United States had destroyed 89.7 percent of its CW. The remaining 10 percent consists mainly of recovered chemical warfare material. The United States, however, has extended the deadline to destroy the remaining 10 percent until 2021. Russia has destroyed a smaller percentage of its weapons, roughly 50 percent, and announced that it will not complete the destruction until December 31, 2015. Russia has destroyed all of its category 2 and 3 CW and a substantial portion of its category 1 CW.

Because both the United States and Russia are unable to meet the 2012 deadline in destroying their CW, the OPCW is unlikely to punish either one. Experts recognize that the delays in destruction have not been deliberate. Some countries, such as Iran, may link the failure to meet the destruction deadline to Iran's nuclear program, arguing that the United States, in particular, has no right to criticize Iran when it does not meet its own CWC destruction obligations.[59] On the other hand, the former and current director generals of the OPCW accept that the United States and the Russian Federation are committed to destroying their CW arsenals.[60] As for munitions, 45.56 percent of the 8.67 million chemical munitions and containers have been destroyed as of March 30, 2012.[61]

Thirteen states declared that they had CW production facilities when they joined the treaty: Bosnia and Herzegovina, China, France, India, Iran, South Korea, Japan, Libya, Russia, Serbia, United Kingdom, and the United States. In total, these states declared 70 facilities. All of these facilities have been inactivated and 62 have been destroyed or converted to peaceful work.

Challenge Inspections

A critical component of the CWC, one that was vitally important to the negotiators, was the inclusion of the right of any state party to ask the OPCW to conduct a challenge inspection. Paragraph 8 of Article IX of the Convention reads,

> Each State Party has the right to request an on-site challenge inspection of any facility or location in the territory or in any other place under the jurisdiction or control of any other State Party for the sole purpose of clarifying and resolving any questions concerning possible non-compliance with the provisions of this Convention, and to have this inspection conducted anywhere without delay by an inspection team designated by the Director-General and in accordance with the Verification Annex.

In spite of this hard fought for right, no state has made use of this provision and called for a challenge inspection. The role of challenge inspections has thus been the subject of discussion at annual meetings and RevCons.

The CWC Review Conferences 2003 and 2008

The CWC has held two RevCons as well as yearly meetings of the states parties. These meetings have demonstrated a continuing tension between the disarmament aspects of the Convention—those that require the destruction of chemical stockpiles and production facilities—and the nonproliferation of aspects of the treaty. The nonproliferation provisions require that chemical production facilities that have not been designed to produce CW and have never been used for that purpose are subject to random inspections.

The vast majority of states parties did not have any CW when they joined the treaty and understandably believed that the verification of destruction of stockpiles and CW production facilities were of the highest priority. And demilitarization—the destruction of CW stockpiles and production facilities—has not been accomplished as rapidly as anticipated. At the same time, the perception of the global security environment, particularly in the United States, has change drastically. The United States and others are as or more concerned about nonstate actors acquiring CW or the means to produce them than they are about the likelihood that states will acquire and use CW. Thus, the nonproliferation aspects of the treaty have a greater priority in their eyes.[62]

Different interpretations of the role of challenge inspections were apparent at the first RevCon. On the one hand, some states parties felt that challenge inspections were a component of the fact-finding procedures and should only be initiated after other procedures had failed to clarify questions of noncompliance. Others challenged this interpretation and reiterated the importance of the right to call a challenge inspection at any time, without a requirement to go through other clarification procedures first.[63]

The second RevCon held in 2008 faced similar challenges as the first and was able to complete consensus documents by avoiding decisions on difficult issues such as the continuing disarmament and nonproliferation tension. Parties at the RevCon also couched disagreements about incapacitating chemical agents in weak language in the final document. Importantly, the United States responded to inquiries about its incapacitating chemical program by stating that it had no such program and that it had gotten rid of its incapacitating weapons.[64]

Discussion

The negotiation and implementation of the BWC and CWC illustrate two very different approaches to these dangerous weapons. The minimalistic BWC has been able to make progress in spite of the absence of verification mechanisms, a miniscule support staff, and political upheavals such as the suspension of the 2001 RevCon for a year. Nevertheless, the progress in the BWC, achieved overwhelming through the yearly meetings of experts and states parties, may be nearing the end of what it can accomplish without further steps. And the United States has precluded a return to the negotiations for legally binding mechanisms to strengthen compliance.

A number of experts have already made recommendations regarding a way forward to strengthen the BWC. Sims (2009) makes a strong case for a broad range of actions that would strengthen the BWC and improve its implementation without taking on the resumption of negotiations on a legally binding instrument. He proposes to remedy the institutional deficit of the BWC in several ways. First, he recommends increasing the size of the ISU and broadening its mandate to include an explicit role for the ISU in assisting new and existing states parties with comprehensive implementation of the Convention. He suggests that a voluntary fund could augment the UN scale budgetary assessments. This last suggestion could overcome the reluctance of some states parties, particularly Japan, who opposed a larger ISU with a broader mandate than it had in 2006. Sims goes on to suggest that a permanent Standing Secretariat with a broad mandate would have many benefits including increased flexibility to respond to scientific and political changes. Sims also recommends formalizing the annual meetings of the BWC. Canada called for the establishment of an accountability framework for the BWC at the 2006 RevCon. Sims strengthens the Canadian working paper by linking the concept of an accountability framework to the ways in which such a framework could take into account the multiple stakeholders in the BWC, not limited to states.[65]

Lentzos set the stage for a critical examination of the existing CBMs. Her work on improving the rate of submission of the annual exchange, as well as a more useful analysis of their contents has led to a series of meetings between government officials, NGOs, and others. The first meetings took place in August just prior to the 2009 Meeting of Experts, the second followed the December Meeting of states parties, and the third occurred in Berlin in April 2010. Early planning and widespread participation of interested parties at these meetings is likely to lead to strong support for its recommendations.[66]

McLaughlin focused on how to improve and increase the participation of scientists in BWC RevCons and annual meetings. Advances in science and technology are critical to understanding how effectively (or ineffectively) the BWC is operating. Moreover, McLaughlin rightly argues that a review of scientific and technological developments relevant to the Convention must occur more frequently given the rapid pace of developments in biological sciences and related technologies. Without such increased participation and timely review of scientific developments, the BWC's political achievements are likely to lag behind the science and risk becoming rapidly out of date.[67]

At the seventh RevCon of the BWC, however, the only forum for making decisions, none of the recommendations of the experts were acted on. A combination of the stultifying effect of need for consensus on every decision and budget constraints resulted in a RevCon that did little more than confirm that for the next five years there will be business as usual in the BWC arms control regime. Nevertheless NGO activities in the BWC arena may see the 7th RevCon as opportunity to increase their activities.

The CWC's challenges are intricately connected to its implementation. Will the challenge inspection mechanism become a vestigial organ of the

CWC, in existence, but of little utility? Will states use chemical agents other than riot control agents, such as incapacitating agents, in domestic law enforcement situations and will such use weaken the CWC's restraints?

Notes

1. The full title of the Hague Convention is "Convention (II) with Respect to the Laws and Customs of War on Land and Its annex: Regulations Concerning the Laws and Customs of War on Land. The Hague, 29 July 1899."

2. John S. Urbanetti, "Toxic Inhalational Injury," in *Medical Aspects of Chemical and Biological Warfare*, ed. Frederick R. Sidell, Ernest T. Takafuji, and David R. Franz (Washington, DC: Office of the Surgeon General, 1997), 255–60.

3. Jeffrey K. Smart, "History of Chemical and Biological Warfare: An American Perspective," in *Medical Aspects of Chemical and Biological Warfare*, ed. Frederick R. Sidell, Ernest T. Takafuji, and David R. Franz (Washington, DC: Office of the Surgeon General, 1997), 9–86.

4. Ibid.

5. Cathy Scott-Clark and Adrian Levy, "Spectre Orange," *The Guardian*, March 28, 2003, http://www.guardian.co.uk/world/2003/mar/29/usa.adrianlevy.

6. Nuclear Threat Initiative, "Former Yugoslavia," http://www.nti.org/country-profiles/former-yugoslavia/. Judith Miller, "U.S. Officials Suspect Deadly Chemical Weapons in Yugoslav Army Arsenal," *The New York Times*, April 16, 1999, http://partners.nytimes.com/library/world/europe/041699kosovo-chemwar.html. Human Rights Watch, "Were Chemical Weapons Used in Bosnia?" November 19, 1998, http://www.hrw.org/news/1998/11/18/were-chemical-weapons-used-bosnia.

7. The full text of the Geneva Protocol is available at: The United Nations Office for Disarmament Affairs, "Protocol for the Prohibition of the Use of Asphyxiating, Poisonous or Other Gases, and of Bacteriological Methods of Warfare. Geneva, 17 June 1925," http://www.un.org/disarmament/WMD/Bio/1925GenevaProtocol.shtml.

8. Nicholas Sims, *The Diplomacy of Biological Disarmament: Vicissitudes of a Treaty in Force, 1975–1985* (New York: St. Martin's Press, 1988), 60.

9. Full texts of the reservations are contained in D. Schindler and J. Toman, *The Laws of Armed Conflicts*, 3rd ed. (Dordrecht: Nijoff, 1988), 173.

10. For a more comprehensive discussion of the legal aspects of the Geneva Protocol, see N. Sims, "Chapter 16: Legal Constraints on Biological Weapons", in *Deadly Cultures: Bioweapons from 1945 to the Present*, ed. M. Wheelis, L. Rozsa, and M.R. Dando (Cambridge, MA: Harvard University Press, 2006), 329–54.

11. Arthur M. Friedlander, "Anthrax," in *Medical Aspects of Chemical and Biological Warfare*, ed. Frederick R. Sidell, Ernest T. Takafuji, and David R. Franz (Washington, DC: Office of the Surgeon General, 1997), 472.

12. Centers for Disease Control, "Plague Fact Sheet," http://www.cdc.gov/ncidod/dvbid/plague/resources/plagueFactSheet.pdf.

13. Mark Wheelis, "Biological Sabotage in World War I," in *Biological and Toxin Weapons: Research, Development and Use from the Middle Ages to 1945*, ed. Erhard Geissler and John Ellis van Courtland Moon (Stockholm: Stockholm International Peace Research Institute, 1999), 35–62.

14. Ibid, 56–57.

15. Erhard Geissler, "Biological Warfare Activities in Germany, 1923–45," in *Biological and Toxin Weapons,* ed. Erhard Geissler and John Ellis van Courtland Moon (Stockholm: Stockholm International Peace Research Institute, 1999), 91–106.

16. Sheldon Harris, "The Japanese Biological Warfare Programme: An Overview," in *Biological and Toxin Weapons,* ed. Erhard Geissler and John Ellis van Courtland Moon (Stockholm: Stockholm International Peace Research Institute, 1999), 138.

17. Ibid, 142.

18. Ibid, 142–145.

19. Sheldon H. Harris, *Factories of Death: Japanese Biological Warfare 1932–45, and the American Cover-Up* (London: Routledge, 1994), 226.

20. Ibid, 227.

21. Ibid, 173–223.

22. John Hart, "The Soviet Biological Weapons Program," in *Deadly Cultures: Biological Weapons Since 1945,* ed. Mark Wheelis, Lajos Rozsa, and Malcolm Dando (Cambridge, MA: Harvard University Press, 2006), 143–44.

23. Judith Miller, Stephen Engelberg, and William Broad, *Germs: Biological Weapons and America's Secret War* (New York: Simon & Shuster, 2001), 301.

24. United States Department of State, "Adherence To and Compliance with Arms Control, Nonproliferation, and Disarmament Agreements and Commitments," last modified August 2011, http://www.state.gov/documents/organization/170652.pdf.

25. Urbanetti, "Toxic Inhalational Injury," 468–72.

26. Gordon B. Carter and Graham S. Pearson, "British Biological Warfare and Biological Defence, 1942–1945," in *Biological and Toxin Weapons: Research, Development and Use from the Middle Ages to 1945,* ed. Erhard Geissler and John Ellis van Courtland Moon (Stockholm: Stockholm International Peace Research Institute, 1999), 179–80.

27. Brian Balmer, *Britain and Biological Warfare: Expert Advice and Science Policy, 1930—65* (Basingstoke: Palgrave, 2001), 53.

28. Brian Balmer, "The UK Biological Weapons Program," in *Deadly Cultures: Bioweapons from 1945 to the Present,* ed. M. Wheelis, L. Rozsa, and M.R. Dando (Cambridge, MA: Harvard University Press, 2006), 52.

29. Brian Balmer, "The UK Biological Weapons Program," 54–59.

30. Ibid, 60.

31. Ibid, 73–81.

32. John Ellis van Courtland Moon, "The US Biological Weapons Program," in *Deadly Cultures: Bioweapons from 1945 to the Present,* ed. M. Wheelis, L. Rozsa, and M.R. Dando (Cambridge, MA: Harvard University Press, 2006), 21.

33. John Ellis van Courtland Moon, "The US Biological Weapons Program," 24–25.

34. Ibid, 25–26.

35. Ibid, 29–30.

36. Marlene Burger and Chandre Gould, *Secrets and Lies: Wouter Basson and South Africa's Chemical and Biological Warfare Programme* (Cape Town: Zebra Press), 34–35.

37. Ibid.

38. Olivier Lepick, "French Activities Related to Biological Warfare," in *Biological and Toxin Weapons Research, Development and Use from the Middle Ages to 1945:*

A Critical Comparative Analysis, ed. Erhafd Geissler and J. E. van Courtland Moon, SIPRI Chemical and Biological Warfare Studies No. 18 (Oxford: Oxford University Press, 1999), 70–80, 73.

39. Olivier Lepick, "The French Biological Weapons Program," in *Deadly Cultures: Bioweapons from 1945 to the Present*, ed. M. Wheelis, L. Rozsa, and M. R. Dando (Cambridge, MA: Harvard University Press, 2006).

40. Graham S. Pearson, "The Iraqi Biological Weapons Program," in *Deadly Cultures: Bioweapons from 1945 to the Present*, ed. M. Wheelis, L. Rozsa, and M. R. Dando (Cambridge, MA: Harvard University Press, 2006).

41. Donald Avery, "The Canadian Biological Weapons Program and the Tripartite Alliance," in *Deadly Cultures: Bioweapons from 1945 to the Present*, ed. M. Wheelis, L. Rozsa, and M. R. Dando (Cambridge, MA: Harvard University Press, 2006).

42. Eighteen Nation Committee on Disarmament (ENCD) /231, "Working Paper on Microbiological Warfare."

43. Talking Points on Biological Warfare for the ENCD Informal Meeting on May 14, 1969, in I. F. Porter, United Kingdom Delegation to the 18 Nation Disarmament Conference, to Mulley, 31 March 1969, FCO 73/114, PRO.

44. Ibid.

45. The CCD succeeded the ENCD as the forum for disarmament negotiations in 1969; it in turn was succeeded by the Conference on Disarmament in 1978.

46. For a thorough account of the U.S. policy review, see J. Tucker, "A Farewell to Germs: The U.S. Renunciation of Biological and Toxin Weapons, 1969–1970," *International Security* 27 (summer 2002): 107–48.

47. Confidential Saving Telegram, Foreign and Commonwealth Office to Abidjan, 29 September 1969, DEFE 24/551, PRO.

48. Department of State Telegram, ACDA/IR:RLMCCORMACK, April 1971, NSC Files, Chemical, Biological Warfare (Toxins etc.) 4, pt. 1, box 312, National Archives and Records Administration.

49. Memorandum for Kissinger from Guhin, Convention Banning Biological Weapons and Toxins, September 17, 1971; ibid.

50. Conversation with U.S. government official, May 22, 2012.

51. Nuclear agreements were verifiable through what is known as "national technical means" (NTM). NTM consists of satellite imagery and other intelligence information.

52. CWC Article II, Paragraph 9.

53. "Programme and Budget for the OPCW 2012," Organization Conference of the States Parties, December 2, 2011 for the Prohibition of Chemical Weapons, http://www.opcw.org/index.php?eID=dam_frontend_push&docID=15226.

54. "OPCW Member States," Organization for the Prohibition of Chemical Weapons, http://www.opcw.org/about-opcw/member-states/.

55. Alexander Kelle, "The CWC after Its First Review Conference: Is the Glass Half Full or Half Empty?" *Disarmament Diplomacy* 71 (2003), http://www.acronym.org.uk/dd/dd71/71cwc.htm.

56. "Opening Statement by the Director-General to the Conference of the States Parties at its Sixteenth Session," OPCW, C-16/DG.18, November 28, 2011, *http://www.opcw.org/index.php?eID=dam_frontend_push&docID=15203.*

57. Ted Purlain, "Libya Misses Weapons Destruction Deadline," BioPrepWatch. com, last modified May 19, 2011, http://www.bioprepwatch.com/news/246187-libya-misses-weapons-destruction-deadline.

58. Statement by H. E. Ambassador Siamand Banaa Permanent Representative of the Republic of Iraq to the OPCW at the 60th session of the Executive Council, EC-60/NAT.10, April 20, 2010, http://www.opcw.org/index.php?eID=dam_fron tend_push&docID=13799.

59. Agent Destruction Status, U.S. Army Chemical Materials Agency, http:// www.cma.army.mil/aboutcma.aspx. "Russia Extends Scrapping of Chemical Weapons until 2016," RIA Novosti, May 21, 2012, http://en.ria.ru/russia/20110602/164394782. html. Martin Matishak, "One Year to U.S., Russian Chemical Weapons Disposal Deadline," Global Security Newswire, April 29, 2011, http://www.nti.org/gsn/article/ one-year-to-us-russian-chemical-weapons-disposal-deadline/.

60. Oliver Meier, "OPCW Chiefs Ponder Chemical Arms Deadlines," *Arms Control Today* 40 (2010), http://www.armscontrol.org/act/2010_01–02/OPCW.

61. Demilitarisation, OPCW, http://www.opcw.org/our-work/demilitarisation/.

62. Kelle, "The CWC after Its First Review Conference" and Oliver Meier, "CWC Review Conference Avoids Difficult Issues," *Arms Control Today* 38 (2008), http://www.armscontrol.org/act/2008_05/CWC.

63. Ibid.

64. Meier, "Avoids Difficult Issues".

65. Nicholas A. Sims, *The Future of Biological Disarmament: Strengthening the Treaty Ban on Weapons*, LSE International Studies (London and New York: Routledge, 2009).

66. Filippa Lentzos, "Reaching a Tipping Point: Strengthening BWC Confidence-Building Measures," *Disarmament Diplomacy* 89 (2008), http://www.acronym.org.uk/ dd/dd89/89fl.htm.

67. Kathryn McLaughlin, "Bringing Biologists on Board Report from the 2008 Meeting of BWC Experts," *Disarmament Diplomacy* 89 (2008), http://www.acronym. org.uk/dd/dd89/89bwc.htm.

CHAPTER 5

Controlling Antipersonnel Land Mines, Cluster Munitions, and Explosive Remnants of War

Although nuclear arms control dominated governments, scholarly research, and the headlines in the four decades following WWII, both bilateral and multilateral arms control negotiations also took place during this time concerning nonnuclear weapons. These negotiations yielded a number of important agreements[1] and set the stage for additional action following the end of the Cold War. As discussed in the introductory chapter, international humanitarian law and the humanitarian effects of these weapons was and continues to be a driving force behind their negotiation, entry into force, and implementation.

Antipersonnel Land Mines

Antipersonnel land mines earned a brutal reputation because they can remain active in the ground for decades after armed conflict has ceased. They are cheap and cause injury or death when stepped on. Their victims are overwhelmingly civilians and often children.[2] Land mines have killed more people than nuclear, chemical, and biological weapons combined.[3] The U.S. State Department, in 1994, estimated that 64 countries were littered with as many as 110 million land mines. According to a 1996 UN report, prepared before the land mines ban was negotiated, as many as 10 million mines covered Cambodia, and 3 million were scattered throughout Bosnia.[4] Crippled civilian victims of land mines made a lasting impression on policy makers and diplomats. The Canadian government, a champion of the effort to ban land mines, estimates that there have been more than a million land mine casualties since 1975 and that 300,000 to 400,000 people are still living with the pain and trauma inflicted by land mines. The visible victims of land mines were a constant reminder of the need to emphasize the humanitarian aspects of arms control as well as its security aspects.

The military utility of land mines is not controversial in most quarters. Land mines are typically buried in the soil to establish impenetrable borders or scattered across fields and countryside to prevent military action in those areas. The challenge to those governments and civil society organizations that advocated a total ban on land mines was to generate support that land mines were inhumane, in spite of their acknowledged military usefulness. Nevertheless, even some military commanders rejected the use of land mines. One U.S. commander in Korea and Vietnam has called them counterproductive and stated that "I did not allow my soldiers to use antipersonnel land mines because I believed them to be a net liability." Among other reasons, he has witnessed them backfire on soldiers they were ostensibly meant to protect.[5] Fifteen senior retired military commanders, including General H. Norman Schwarzkopf of 1991 Gulf War fame, urged President Clinton to support a complete mine ban, declaring that, "a permanent and total international ban on the production, stockpiling, sale, and use of anti-personnel mines was not only humane, but also militarily responsible." Banning mines worldwide, the commanders concluded "would not undermine the military effectiveness or safety of U.S. . . . armed forces."[6]

Post Cold War Arms Control

The end of the Cold War opened a new stage in arms control, characterized by a shift in emphasis toward negotiations to outlaw weapons that have claimed thousands upon thousands of victims. The new stage also placed a much higher emphasis on the humanitarian aspects of weapons, which sometimes outstripped any security rationale for retention of weapons that kill indiscriminately. These shifts reflected a growing realization that many weapons ended up in the hands of armed rebels, transnational groups, and other nonstate or substate actors. Finally, the process of achieving bans on antipersonnel land mines and cluster munitions involved an unprecedented involvement of organizations and people that were not formal representatives of governments. Recognizing the destructive nature of land mines, the International Committee of the Red Cross (ICRC) as early as 1993 hosted a meeting on land mines to explore ways to minimize their use. The extensive use of land mines in the intrastate conflicts in the former Yugoslavia and elsewhere following the Cold War were a stark reminder that sovereign states do not begin to fully control the manufacture and use of deadly weaponry. Sovereign states, however, were the formal participants in the arms control negotiations concerning land mines. While the negotiators represented nation states, they had to come to terms with the most effective way of preventing nonstate actors from acquiring and using land mines, often in civil wars against government militaries. One argument was that banning their manufacture and use, rather than restrictions or limitations on their use, was required to lessen the threat from nonstate actors.

The ICRC was instrumental in promoting the concept of weapons that cause superfluous suffering and unacceptable harm even though they have some military utility.[7] Rules of practice during war or conflict that are widespread and long-lasting eventually become what is known as Customary International Law. The humanitarian aspect of such law is called Customary International Humanitarian Law (CIHL) and applies to all—state and nonstate actors in the entire world—and covers intrastate as well as interstate conflict. The ICRC conducted a study of CIHL beginning in 1996 and identified 161 rules that form its core.[8] Rule 70 is the most relevant to the banning of land mines. The rule states: "The use of means and methods of warfare which are of a nature to cause superfluous injury or unnecessary suffering is prohibited." Antipersonnel land mines fit precisely under this rule. They produce superfluous injury by causing harm after a conflict has ended and their victims are overwhelmingly civilian. They cause unnecessary suffering because victims of land mines, if they survive, almost always require amputation of their feet and suffer injuries that demand extensive medical care and rehabilitation.

The influence of transnational civil society on governmental and international policy did not begin with the end of the Cold War, but the cessation of the decades-old superpower duel and the reprioritization of interests within states provided nongovernmental actors the opportunity to exercise persuasive powers in ways, and to a greater extent, than ever before.[9] Florini defines transnational civil society in three parts. First, "it includes only groups that are *not* governments or profit-seeking private entities. Second, it is transnational—that is, it involves linkages across national borders. Third, . . . it takes a variety of forms. Sometimes it takes the form of a single [international] NGO with individual members of chapters in several countries. . . . In other cases [it] consists of more informal border-crossing coalitions of organizations and associations."[10] Transnational civil society networks have organized to advance their goals in an array of issue areas, including the environment, sustainable development, anticorruption, fair trade, and security, to name but a few. Within the security arena, NGOs, one form of a civil society network, have long organized to promote peace, end wars, and limit the destructiveness of wars through, among other means, arms control.[11]

Mine Ban Treaty

The issue of antipersonnel land mines was on the arms control agenda before the end of the Cold War, but it did not occupy a particularly prominent position. The purpose of a 1996 book, *Arms Control: Toward the Twenty-First Century*, was meant to "give students of arms control the latest and best synthesis of lessons learned from the Cold War. More important, it points the way to a new millennium."[12] The issue of land mines merited less than one full page of discussion in this volume; and the editor concluded that "the [land mines] ban campaign has attracted substantial attention from governments and the press, but the test of its ultimate success is years away."[13] Nevertheless, by the end of 1997 following a whirlwind of activity, the Mine Ban Treaty (MBT) also known as the Ottawa Convention was completed and signed by 122 countries. The MBT entered into force less than 18 months later, "the fastest major international agreement ever to enter into force."[14] The rapid pace of the negotiations was attributed in part to the participation and influence of NGOs, particularly the International Campaign to Ban Land Mines (ICBL).

International efforts to regulate land mines following their extensive use in Vietnam and elsewhere led to Protocols I and II to the Geneva Conventions, and the Convention on Certain Conventional Weapons (CCW),[15] which were initially negotiated in the late 1970s. These agreements regulated the use of land mines, attempting to limit their indiscriminate effects rather than to ban them completely. Their impact on the use of land mines was an abject failure, however, in large part, because their provisions applied only to international conflicts, not civil wars. Between 1980 and 1990, combatants in civil wars around the globe, in Asia, Africa, South America, and Europe, littered the landscape with tens of millions of mines.[16]

Appalled by the ongoing casualties caused by land mines and the ineffective formal international response, several nongovernmental groups organized and developed a strategy to achieve a total ban on the production and use of antipersonnel land mines.[17] In October 1992, six NGOs, three U.S.-based groups, Human Rights Watch, Vietnam Veterans of America Foundation (VVAF), and Physicians for Human Rights, a German-based group, Medico International, French-based Handicap International, and a British group, Mines Advisory Group, formed the International Coalition to Ban Landmines (ICBL). Although the six groups approached the land mines issue from different perspectives—from an international human rights and humanitarian law perspective to the view from the field where demining operations took place—all eventually agreed to call for a global ban, constituted themselves as the steering committee, and appointed Jody Williams as the coordinator of the coalition.[18]

The ICBL declared a simple goal with three related elements: (1) "an international ban on the use, production, stockpiling, and sale, transfer or export of anti-personnel landmines," (2) "increased resources for humanitarian demining," and (3) "increased resources for landmine victim rehabilitation and assistance."[19] Any organization that agreed to this goal could join as a member of the campaign. A Chronology of the ICBL and the Ban Movement chronicles a flurry of activities by a host of NGOs, international organizations, and governments between 1993 and 1996, sparked by a 1993 international NGO conference on land mines to develop a strategy for the campaign.[20]

In April 1996, states parties to the CCW held a review conference to address—among other issues—the deficiencies of the restrictions on land mines and to implement stronger restrictions on the types of land mines and how they could be used.[21] During the review conference, the ICBL "provided newsletters and updates, lobbied government delegates, held public events and exhibits in the streets and the conference venue" (ICBL 2007). However, a global ban on land mines, the goal of the ICBL, was not on the agenda of the conference.[22]

Discouraged by the absence of a land mines ban on the CCW review conference agenda, the governments of a core group of medium-sized states—Austria, Belgium, Canada, Germany, Ireland, Mexico, Norway, Philippines, South Africa, and Switzerland—met in 1995 and 1996 to elaborate a strategy for developing a global land mines ban outside of the CCW process.[23] According to Sigal, these early meetings, comprised only of states favoring a ban on land mines, had four political aspects.[24] First, what would become the Ottawa process was a gathering of like-minded states in a stand-alone forum. That meant countries had to opt in and agree to a complete ban or opt out, and not be a party to the negotiations. Second, the NGOs were inside at last, in contrast to the Conference on Disarmament, where NGOs were rarely allowed to observe all of the proceedings, much less participate in them. Third, not just present and participating, NGOs were also influential in shaping policy, instrumental in attracting media attention to the ban, and undeterred from shaming governments into action. Fourth, the diplomats adopted the campaigners' way of framing the issue in moral terms, as a matter of basic human rights. The strategy of establishing a stand-alone forum led to a process where states that were reluctant to support a complete ban on land mines had no opportunity to weaken the provisions of a total ban or to delay the negotiations. Compromises that might have been necessary to appease those states were not even considered.

International celebrities also lent their names and fame to the ICBL, drawing attention to the plight of victims and raising money for the campaign. Princess Diana and Paul McCartney were among the most well known figures to support the antimine cause. The princess traveled to Angola and Bosnia to observe demining activities and visit with children who were maimed by land mines. The media attention that Diana attracted wherever she traveled ensured that the suffering of the children was well-covered in the international press. British officials criticized the princess at the time because her statements in Angola calling for a complete ban on land mines were not consistent with U.K. government policy at the time.[25]

Although some states that favored a ban sought to have the negotiations take place in the Conference on Disarmament (CD), the traditional forum for arms control talks, the foreign minister of Canada, Lloyd Axworthy, invited the governments to discuss the issue in Ottawa, thereby circumventing the CD. The choice of forum was significant. The Ottawa locale permitted Canada, the host government, to relax the typical norms of procedure that had developed during the Cold War and dominated the CD. In part, the relocation occurred because the ICBL shifted the frame of reference for the treaty from arms control to humanitarian law. A constantly repeated message of the ICBL was that land mines were a humanitarian, not an arms control, issue.[26] Consequently, the rationale for moving the negotiations out of a traditional arms control setting held sway.[27] According to Peter Herby of the ICRC, negotiations in the CD would be "likely to accentuate the security aspects of the landmine issue and to deemphasize humanitarian concerns. Neither the ICRC nor UN humanitarian agencies nor NGOs have access to CD negotiations."[28] The absence of deadlines and the leisurely pace of CD negotiations were another factor in Ottawa's favor. Herby predicted that,

> If conducted in good faith in a forum dedicated to [antipersonnel land mines], negotiations could be concluded in several sessions of a few weeks each. Such a process would highlight the urgency of the landmines crisis and could more effectively integrate humanitarian concerns.[29] The stand-alone forum also meant that active participation in the forum could be limited to those countries who favored a total ban, allowing for more rapid negotiations.[30]

The October 1996 meeting in Ottawa attracted 74 governments. Fifty governments agreed on the basic principle of a ban on land mines and the need to urgently complete the ban. The additional 24 governments had the status of observers. They could contribute, but not vote or block the ban. By all accounts, the participation of NGOs, above all the ICBL, was extensive and unprecedented in the Ottawa meeting and subsequent negotiations taking place in Brussels, Vienna, Bonn, and Oslo. Moreover, NGOs sat on the official governmental delegations of several countries. The ICBL participated as nonvoting delegates at several of the meetings. And, perhaps most importantly, NGOs had a high level of access to delegations.[31] According to one critic of the high level of NGO participation, "Once relegated to the hallways of official proceedings, the NGOs at the meeting called in Ottawa were front and center, advancing the agenda, drafting proposals, and pressing the delegates."[32]

In December 1997, Axworthy welcomed governments back to Ottawa to sign the completed treaty for global ban on land mines and 122 states did so. The treaty entered into force in March 1999. Article 1 of the MBT states:

1. Each State Party undertakes never under any circumstances:
   a) To use anti-personnel mines;
   b) To develop, produce, otherwise acquire, stockpile, retain or transfer to anyone, directly or indirectly, anti-personnel mines;
   c) To assist, encourage or induce, in any way, anyone to engage in any activity prohibited to a State Party under this Convention.
2. Each State Party undertakes to destroy or ensure the destruction of all anti-personnel mines in accordance with the provisions of this Convention.

In addition to the general obligations in Article 1, the MBT contains requirements to destroy mines in place, and establishes means to assist mine victims and increase awareness of mines. The treaty includes various transparency measures (Article 7) and methods to attempt to resolve compliance questions through clarification and fact-finding missions (Article 8). The treaty contains little in terms of traditional verification measures. As of April 2010, the MBT had 156 states parties, not including the United States, China, Russia, India, Pakistan, North, and South Korea.

Factors Contributing to the Success of the Ottawa Process

A number of scholars have analyzed the role of NGOs, particularly the ICBL, in the Ottawa Process and have drawn a number of conclusions about the factors that contributed to the influence of the NGOs. Jody Williams, the coordinator of the ICBL, attributed the success of the ICBL to a number of factors. First, the loose structure of the ICBL, a "true coalition made up of independent NGOs . . . there has never been an overarching, bureaucratic Campaign structure to dictate to the members how they should best strive to contribute [to the ICBL]. . . . This structure helped to insure (*sic*) that the ICBL 'belongs' to all of its members." Second, "clear and consistent communication has been critical to [the ICBL's] success. . . . [ICBL] gained strength by being able to speak with authority about all the efforts being made to address the issue. Sharing stories of their success and failures of the work, empowered all organizations and lessened the possibility of isolation of any one." Third, "the personal relationships that developed within the [ICBL] and between campaigners, and various government and military representatives."[33]

Nicola Short identified another set of elements that contributed to the success of NGOs in influencing government action on land mines. First, she observes that "there was a high resonance of goals between the core group governments, the ICBL and the ICRC." Even "at the outset of the Ottawa process it was clear that certain governments and NGOs had a common agenda," that of establishing a complete, global ban on the use, production, and sale of land mines. Second, Short notes that Canada acted as a patron to the ICBL. Thus, Canada served a role of granting legitimacy to ICBL and the ICBL in turn legitimized the land mines humanitarian crisis, "allowing [it] to be seen in terms of its social and economic consequences" rather than strictly as a security, military, or armaments issue. Third, many of the "founding organizations of the ICBL are large organizations with significant budgets." VVAF alone "contributed over $4.5 million" to the land mines campaign. In addition, "the morally unambiguous nature of the [anti-personnel mines] APM crisis may also have contributed to the availability of financing." Fourth, the indiscriminate nature of land mines and the impact of pictures of children and others who lost limbs to land mines allowed the ICBL to portray the use of land mines "as morally unambiguous . . . in a single visual image." Finally, Short emphasizes an important aspect of the Ottawa Process: "states were able to attend as full participants only" if they were committed to a ban of land mines. States that were opposed to a ban, who most likely would also be opposed to the active participation of NGOs in the process, were in attendance only as observers.[34]

Ken Rutherford, cofounder of the Landmine Survivors Network, a member of ICBL, describes seven trends that describe how NGOs exert influence. The rapid development and use of information technologies is common to all seven trends. The first trend is that "NGOs have acquired the expertise about specific issues and the technical ability to research and publicize information quickly and early enough in the international political arena where the process of setting an agenda takes place." Of particular importance is the ability of NGOs to "name names" of states that are deceptive, disingenuous, or behaving contrary to international norms, publicly shaming state action. The second and third trends echo Williams's emphasis on communication and dissemination of information. NGOs can gather and analyze information quickly and have "better flexibility than states in changing and addressing time-sensitive issues." NGOs use the media effectively to publicize their cause, recruit members, and affect public opinion. The fourth trend is that information technologies make it easier for NGOs to communicate quickly with states and their officials. Information technologies also allow the ICBL to have the loose structure that Williams describes. The ICBL resembles a virtual organization, made possible through fax, e-mail, and Internet communication. Moreover, these technologies lowered the costs of building and maintaining the coalition. According to Rutherford, this is especially important for "NGOs from the South such as Africa and Asia where non-Internet communication and logistical costs are barriers to working from state to state." Not coincidentally, millions of mines and tens of thousands of mine casualties come from such areas. Finally, information technologies make it easier for NGOs to monitor state behavior and report behavior that violates international obligations.[35]

In a separate article, Rutherford argues that the so-called New Diplomacy of the Ottawa process is not so new.[36] He compares the Ottawa Process to the First International Peace Conference in the Hague in 1899 and uncovers eight important similarities that led to their success:

"1. The negotiations . . . were convened at the invitation of an international political leader;
2. The regimes were negotiated by majority voting procedures;[37]
3. Both regimes were established without verification measures;
4. Both regimes were initiated for the broader purpose of a more peaceful international society;
5. Both regimes were negotiated on a fast-track process;
6. Both regimes were opposed by major powers;
7. Both regimes were encouraged and supported by public opinion and NGOs; and
8. Both regimes had clear, simple and consistent prohibitions."[38]

The success of the Ottawa Process is remarkable and deserving of significant attention; it was the model for the negotiation of the Treaty to Ban Cluster Munitions and is likely to have continued influence on multilateral arms control negotiations and implementation across many other substantive areas. As noted in the chapter on biological and chemical weapons, the example of the ICBL had led to the formation of an NGO coalition to support the CWC and the participation of NGOs in the annual BWC meeting has been growing.

There are a number of reasons why civil society has been increasingly active in the arms control arena. Frustration with the snail's pace of progress in the CD and other official arms control forums prompted thinking and action that could take place elsewhere. In addition, civil society organizations are typically more focused than governments, multinational in character and considered by many to be very trustworthy.

Civil society organizations are typically organized around a single goal or activity. As such, civil society organizations do not have the same extensive agendas as States or government ministries. They do not have competing priorities to contend with or to dilute their efforts. Being single-minded allows NGOs to be efficient in their actions and focused in their efforts. Similarly, civil society organizations characteristically lack the dense bureaucracies that can plague states and international organizations and delay action. Consequently, civil society can organize events and activities quickly and with a minimum of red tape. Though many civil society organizations exist within a single nation and concern themselves only with the activities therein, many others are comprised of actors from many countries and regions of the world. These civil society organizations are free from the sometimes more narrow single nation interests that, of necessity, are the province of national governments. This international characteristic of many civil society organizations enables them to act in an impartial fashion, which governments are frequently unable to do.

Although there are certainly exceptions, many governments and international organizations within the arms control community frequently view civil society organizations as trustworthy and effective partners in implementation. In nations that are beset with corruption and ineffective institutions, or those with an historical, and perhaps healthy, skepticism of government, civil society organizations are often able to gain the trust of those they serve. If seen as trustworthy, civil society organizations occasionally convert cynics and establish communication links with people and organizations that are oftentimes reluctant to share their information with governments. Moreover, many governments and government personnel who question the motives or the priorities of other nations or plurilateral endeavors may give civil society organizations the benefit of the doubt. Indeed, in the implementation of the Land Mines Ban, the ICBL has taken a strong and effective leadership role not only in the drafting and negotiation of the ban, but also in its implementation.

Implementation of the Land Mines Ban

The implementation of the Land Mines Ban is different from most other multilateral arms control agreements. Destroying land mines, clearing land mines from mined areas, monitoring compliance, and providing secretarial support are conducted primarily by two independent organizations: the Geneva International Centre for Humanitarian Demining (GICHD) and the ICBL, which publishes the annual *Landmine Monitor Report*. Since 2001, the GICHD has hosted a small Implementation Support Unit (ISU) to provide secretariat services to the treaty's standing committees, the meetings of states parties, and RevCons. In contrast, the work of implementing the Nuclear NPT and the CWC is performed by large international organizations. The CTBT is also served by an international organization, even though the treaty has not yet entered into force. Several international NGOs, including VERTIC (the Verification Research, Training and Information Centre) and the BioWeapons Prevention Project, as well as academic supporters such as the University of Bradford and the University of Hamburg share implementation tasks for the BWC with the very small, three-person, implementation support unit of the Convention headquartered at the UN in Geneva.

Landmine Monitor

Established as an initiative of the ICBL, the *Landmine Monitor* is the de facto monitoring regime for the MBT. It is not a technical verification organization; rather the Monitor gathers, analyzes, and reports on extensive open source information regarding all aspects of land mines and publishes its reports annually. Its editorial board consists of representatives of five different NGOs and its funding is provided by donor governments and organizations.[39] It is published yearly.

Production and Use of Land Mines

Since the MBT entered into force in 1998, the use of antipersonnel land mines has fallen dramatically. The 2009 Landmine Monitor estimated that 21 states used land mines in the early years of the treaty, but only four since 2004 and only two between 2007 and 2009, Myanmar and Russia. Russia was dropped from the list of land mines users in 2010, leaving only Myanmar as a government still laying land mines.[40] Sadly, in 2011, however, Israel and Libya were added to the list. Equally important, perhaps, the norm of nonuse of land mines has extended beyond governments to armed groups that are not national militaries. Fifty-nine of these nonstate armed groups have renounced the use of land mines. The 1999 and 2000 Monitors reported that approximately 20 partisans and rebels used land mines.[41] By 2011, the use of land mines by nonstate actors was recorded in only four countries: Afghanistan, Colombia, Myanmar, and Pakistan, down from six the previous year.[42] The reduction in the use of land mines and concerted efforts to remove mines from contaminated minefields has also radically decreased the number of mine casualties. From an estimate of 26,000 yearly casualties before the MBT went into effect, the yearly totals of mine casualties in 2010 and 2011 were just over 4,000.[43]

The production of land mines has also fallen dramatically since the MBT has been implemented. Thirty-nine of 51 states that were known to produce land mines have ended production. There is also evidence that the norm against the production and use of land mines extends beyond the treaty parties. Egypt and Israel, neither of whom is a party to the treaty, have ceased production of land mines and Finland, which has signed but not yet ratified the ban, has also ceased production. In addition, although 12 states still reserve the right to produce land mines and consequently are considered potential producers of land mines, active production of land mines in 2011 was limited to only three states—India, Myanmar, and Pakistan.[44]

Demining and Other Mine Action

Removing land mines from mined areas—areas of land known or suspected of containing land mines—is one of the principle obligations of
parties to the ban. Although each state party is responsible for removing
land mines, the Geneva International Center for Humanitarian Demining
(GICHD), a nonprofit foundation consisting of international experts, assists many states in their demining efforts. The mission of GICHD includes
working "for the elimination of anti-personnel mines and for the reduction
of the humanitarian impact of other land mines and explosive remnants of
war."[45] The GICHD was founded by Switzerland and a group of countries
in 1998. In addition to experts in demining who work with states in their
demining and stockpile destruction efforts, GICHD provides educational
materials, assistance to victims, and advocacy. The GICID receives funding from donor governments and organizations. These include the governments of Australia, Canada, Denmark, Finland, France, Germany, Italy,
Japan, Norway, Sweden, Switzerland, and the United States, as well as the
European Union, United Nations organizations, foundations, and private
contributors.[46]

A total of 72 states are still affected by the presence of land mines on their
territories. Most of these, 64 in all, are parties to the ban, and under the terms
of the treaty, states are required to remove land mines from their territories
within 10 years of becoming a party to the treaty. As of June 2010, 18 states
completed demining. Nevertheless, 22 states have asked for and been granted
extensions beyond their original 10-year deadlines; according to the *Landmines Monitor*, extensions beyond the 10-year destruction deadline is becoming the norm and only Nicaragua, which completed demining in 2010, has
accomplished its task after receiving an extension.[47] More than 1,100 square
kilometers have been cleared of mines since the treaty entered into force, destroying more than 2.2 million antipersonnel mines and 250,000 antivehicle
mines. The pace of demining has also increased, with 2009 and 2010 recording the largest areas cleared of mines each year, approximately 200 square
kilometers. Unfortunately, accurate mapping of mined areas has not yet been
completed and early estimates of mined areas have been proven to be quite
inaccurate.

Among its other activities, the GICHD educates populations in mine-
affected areas about the risks of land mines to lower the number of potential
casualties. The number of states with education programs increased from just
14 in 1999 to 57 in 2008. As more states complete demining or have smaller
areas of their territories with active mines, educational programs on the risks
are not needed as extensively.

Assistance to victims of land mines was an integral part of the MBT, but its implementation has been disappointing. Funding for victim assistance has not been sufficient to accomplish the goals stated in the treaty, relating to medical care, rehabilitation, and social and economic reintegration of victims into society. Assistance has focused mainly on medical and physical rehabilitation. In the short run, that is perhaps appropriate, but over time and over the long haul, self-reliance of survivors and reintegration into the economies and communities become more compelling goals.

Universality

As of May 2012, the Land Mines Ban had 160 states parties. Thirty-six states were not party to the treaty; in addition, Poland and the Marshall Islands have signed but not yet ratified the ban. Although Poland stated that it would ratify the MBT in 2010, it has not yet done so. Poland had confirmed that it plans to ratify the ban in 2012 and it has submitted annual transparency reports since 2003.[48] Many powerful and influential states are among the holdouts to the ban, including China, India, Iran, Israel, both Koreas, Pakistan, Russia, and the United States. Nevertheless, discussions with diplomats to the treaty negotiations revealed that only 16 percent of them felt that implementation of the ban would be negatively affected by those states who declined to join the treaty.[49]

The success of the MBT and its implementation has been nothing short of remarkable. Few could have envisioned much less predicted the accomplishments achieved through cooperation between governments, international organizations such as the Red Cross, the coalition of NGOs that comprise the ICLB, and the organizations that it has spawned. Moreover, many aspects of the ban mines campaign have influenced other arms control groups and initiatives, most directly the Cluster Munitions Convention.

Despite this rosy picture, there are a few ominous clouds on the horizon. There are unresolved reports that the Turkish army may have used land mines in 2009, even though Turkey is a member of the treaty. Although the laying of the mines may have been done on the personal initiative of a single field commander, the Turkish government has the obligation under the treaty to investigate the allegations, determine responsibility, and report its findings.[50]

Two states, Belarus and Greece, have still not completed destruction of their land mine stocks. Under Article IV of the treaty, states parties are obligated to destroy their antipersonnel land mine stockpiles no later than four years after the treaty enters into force for that party.[51] Belarus is more than a year late and Greece is more than three years behind schedule.[52] Of the 22 states that have been granted extensions on their deadlines to complete

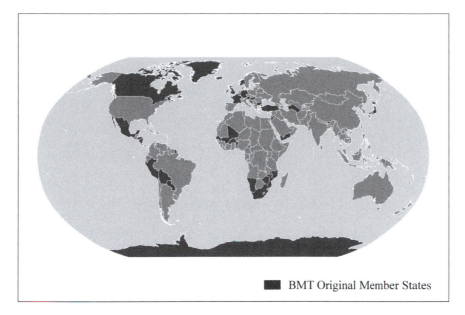

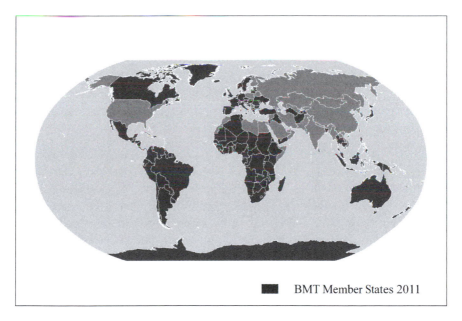

demining, only six are listed in the 2011 Monitor as being "on track": Denmark, Guinea-Bissau, Mauritania, Mozambique, Tajikstan, and Venezuela. The remaining 14 are listed as "falling behind," "status unclear," or "no information."[53]

In contrast to treaties that compel states to comply with onsite monitoring requirements, the MBT requires states to submit an initial report to the UN secretary-general with detailed information on many aspects of treaty implementation, including mine stockpiles, areas that contain mines, mine production, and status information. States are required to update this information annually. The 2011 Monitor reported that the annual transparency reports were at an all time low, with only 52 percent of states complying with this obligation.[54]

Although the United States has ceased producing and using land mines and provides monetary support for demining activities and victim assistance, its position vis-à-vis the land mines treaty remains troubling. President Obama ordered a review of U.S. land mine policy in 2009, but more than two years later the review has not yet been concluded. There are still more than 11 million antipersonnel mines in the U.S. stockpile, although the United States has destroyed more than 3 million. In the meantime, according to at least one press report, the Obama administration had received letters from 68 senators supporting the treaty, one more than enough to secure Senate ratification if the administration would submit it to the Senate for its advice and consent.[55]

In sum, in order to sustain the stellar progress achieved in the first 10 years of the MBT, governments and NGOs must continue to stress the importance of achieving a total land mines ban. Indications that compliance with all aspects of the land mines ban is falling among states is evidence of land mines dropping in the priority list of nations' arms control policies. A renewed effort is needed to maintain momentum.

Cluster Munitions

Cluster munitions are a type of weapon dropped from the air or exploded from the ground. These weapons are designed to fragment and disperse numerous submunitions or bomblets and cover a large surface area. Like land mines, cluster munitions are not, and cannot be, designed to differentiate between military and civilian targets.[56] If the submunitions fail to detonate immediately as planned, they can and do remain in the area and cause harm later on, essentially having the potential to cause injuries similar to land mines. Cluster munitions fall into the category of explosive remnants of war (ERW) when they fail and are left behind after the cessation of hostilities.

The negotiations on the Convention on Cluster Munitions (CCM), like that of many arms control and disarmament treaties, have a long history, yet were rapidly completed when the political conditions were ripe and the Ottawa Process provided a model to follow. Once again, the International Committee for the Red Cross spearheaded early discussions on cluster munitions as weapons that should be outlawed by international humanitarian law because of their effects on civilians and their tendency to be a risk for harm long after active hostilities have ceased or abated, despite any security benefits that they may have.[57] Thus, we see once again a push to consider the cost in humanitarian terms of these weapons weighed against security benefits. Protocol II of the CCW restricted land mines but not cluster munitions.[58]

Following the completions of the MBT, many advocates for that agreement turned their attention to outlawing cluster munitions and other ERW. Nevertheless, a new coalition—the Cluster Munition Coalition (CMC)—was formed to press for a treaty banning cluster munitions, as many in the ICBL worried that taking on a new initiative would dilute efforts needed for successful implementation of the MBT.

The use of cluster munitions in warfare during the early years of the 21st century generated momentum to ban their use completely, like land mines, rather than merely restricting the types of munitions that could be used. The United States, the United Kingdom, and their coalition partners used cluster munitions in the 2001–2002 war to oust the Taliban from power in Afghanistan. Despite injuries to civilians in Afghanistan, the United States again used cluster munitions in its invasion of Iraq in 2003. The United States and the United Kingdom ignored warnings from Human Rights Watch that the use of cluster munitions would "result in grave dangers to civilians and friendly combatants . . . [that are] both foreseeable and preventable."[59] In addition, both Israel and Hezbollah employed cluster munitions during their conflict during the summer of 2006. Many Israeli munitions were designed to self-destruct if not properly detonated on launching, supposedly circumventing the problem of unexploded munitions. Despite these designs, however, many munitions did not explode and did not self-destruct. Reports on unexploded munitions underscored the problem the CCW parties faced in trying to restrict cluster munitions to those that theoretically self-destruct.[60]

The Oslo Process

The negotiation process leading to the ban on Cluster Munitions is termed the Oslo Process because of the leadership of the Norwegian government. The emergence of that leadership was a gradual development. Norway was an active participant in the MBT and the final negotiations for that agreement took place in Oslo. Yet for some period of time Norway supported constraints on certain types of cluster munitions rather than a total ban. NGOs in Norway, including the Norwegian Red Cross, Norwegian Church Aid, and Save the Children, were influential in convincing the government to change its position and organize an international conference to ban the use, stockpiling, production, and transfer of these munitions.

The Third RevCon of the CCW was held shortly after the conflict be-tween Israel and Hezbollah in southern Lebanon, in November 2006. The day before the conference was to end, Norway announced that it would con-vene a conference to discuss an outright ban on cluster munitions, insofar as the CCW RevCon was unable to reach an agreement on these weapons.[61] Similar to the Ottawa Process to ban land mines, the Oslo Process was in-tended to bring together states that supported the principle that production, use, and transfer of all cluster munitions should be outlawed on humanitarian grounds that they cause superfluous injury and unnecessary suffering.

Once again NGOs, primarily members of the Cluster Munitions Coali-tion, worked long and hard with members of governments and international organizations to make the CCM a reality in record time. The first conference in Oslo in February 2007 attracted 46 countries with a follow-on conference in Lima, Peru, in May 2007. In the meantime, national governments took steps to support the Oslo Process. Even before the Norwegian government launched the Oslo Process, in early 2006 the Belgian government passed leg-islation banning cluster munitions, much as it had done in 1995 to ban land mines.[62] Peru announced that it would seek a zone free of cluster munitions in Latin America. Hungary and Switzerland declared moratoriums on the weapons and Belgium and Costa Rica hosted regional meetings. Additional meetings were held in Vienna, Austria, in December 2007, and Wellington, New Zealand, in February 2008.[63]

In May 2008, more than 100 countries gathered in Dublin to finalize and adopt the CCM and it opened for signature in Oslo the following month. The swiftness of the treaty's completion belies some of the difficulties in the negotiations. Governments struggled with the definition of cluster munitions to make sure that the ban was sufficiently broad. While the Oslo Process was gathering steam, the CCW was continuing to negotiate a Protocol on cluster munitions that would have been weaker than the ban sought through the Oslo Process. Ultimately, the Oslo Process would achieve a Convention, but to some extent at the price of having a smaller number of states accede to the ban.

Convention on Cluster Munitions

Using language similar to the BWC, the CWC, and the MBT, parties to the CCM undertake "never under any circumstances to a) use cluster mu-nitions; b) develop, produce, otherwise acquire stockpile, retain or trans-fer to anyone, directly or indirectly, cluster munitions; c) assist, encourage or induce anyone to engage in any activity prohibited . . . under this Convention."[64]

The Convention also requires members to destroy any existing stockpiles of cluster munitions within eight years after entry into force of the treaty or to request an extension if unable to meet the destruction deadline. Similar to the MBT, the CCM requires clearing of areas that have unexploded munitions, provision of education about the dangers of cluster munitions, and provision of assistance to victims. Transparency measures in the CCM are also similar to those in the MBT.

Implementation

The CCM entered into force on August 1, 2010, and as of January 2012 the Convention had 67 states parties and an additional 44 states have signed, but not yet ratified the Convention. Since WWII, cluster munitions were used in conflicts in 36 countries as well as four territories whose sovereignty was disputed. At least 28 states are believed to be contaminated with cluster munitions. Nine of those states have ratified the CCM and seven more are signatories. Thus, 16 of the 28 contaminated states are CCM parties committed to decontamination. While 34 states have produced cluster munitions, nearly half, 16, have already joined the Convention. However, 19 of the producers have sold or transferred these weapons to more than 60 countries, all prior to 2010. One mark of the Convention's rapid influence and success is that there were no reported transfers of cluster munitions in 2010, the most recent year for which information is available. Following entry into force, states also rapidly began or continued the destruction of their stockpiles. The United Kingdom and Germany, for example, destroyed half of their stockpiles by mid-2011. At 39 million and 67 million, these states had two of the largest stockpiles of cluster munitions prior to the CCM. Twelve states and 8 signatories have destroyed their stockpiles completely, some of them prior to the Oslo process or the entry into force of the CCM.[65]

One hundred twenty-one states as well as numerous civil society groups and international organizations attended the first meeting of states parties to the CCM in April 2011. Since the treaty entered into force, only two instances of new use of cluster munitions have been reported. One instance was in Libya by forces loyal to Muammar Gaddafi. The president of the meeting issued a press statement expressing "serious concern" over the use of cluster munitions in the second use, the conflict on the Thai–Cambodian border.

The implementation of the CCM is in its very early years, yet work on the CCM is likely to follow the path of other treaties, encouraging signatories to ratify the convention and encouraging those states outside the convention to accede to the treaty. At the same time, the CCM membership and supporters will seek to internationalize the norm of nonuse, nonproduction, and nonpossession of these munitions. It is premature to suggest that the CCM will follow the path of the MBT and enjoy initial rapid success, followed by what may appear to be lack of enthusiasm or political commitment to the ban. Nevertheless, supporters of the Convention need to be on the lookout for such an eventuality.

Conclusion

The negotiations on a land mines ban and a ban on cluster munitions broke the mold. The supporters of these conventions eschewed the moribund CD, the long-established forum for multilateral arms control negotiations. Instead, civil society and sympathetic governments joined forces in creating new fora for the negotiations under the sponsorship of governments and new methods of negotiating. The new methods included the active participation of NGOs in the drafting of the conventions and the sustained support of international organizations such as the ICRC in laying the groundwork and building support for a total ban. In addition, the meeting organizers would not allow the participation of any governments that were unwilling to espouse the overarching goal of a complete ban.

Despite the unpredicted and rapid success of these negotiations in producing international treaties banning these weapons that lead to superfluous injury and unnecessary suffering, each Convention faces challenges in convincing hold-outs to the treaties to join on. Nevertheless, the MBT has achieved astonishing success in constructing a robust norm against the manufacture and use of land mines in a remarkably short period of time. It remains to be seen if this trend will continue and whether the CCM will be able to repeat the success of the MBT.

Notes

1. E.g., The Conference on Security and Cooperation in Europe, the Conventional Forces in Europe Treaty, and the Biological and Toxin Weapons Convention.

2. Richard Price, "Reversing the Gun Sights: Transnational Civil Society Targets Land Mines," *International Organization* 52, no. 3 (1998): 613–44, 618.

3. Ibid.

4. UNICEF, "Landmines: Hidden Killers," State of the World's Children, May 8, 1996, http//www.unicef.org/sowc96pk/hidekill.htm.

5. Lt. General Robert G. Gard Jr. (U.S., Ret.) "Past Time to Join the Landmine Treaty" *Huffington Post World,* March 18, 2009, http://www.huffingtonpost.com/lt-general-robert-g-gard-jr-/past-time-to-join-the-lan_b_176335.html.

6. Maxwell A. Cameron, Robert J. Lawson, and Brian W. Tomlin, "To Walk without Fear," in *To Walk without Fear: The Global Movement to Ban Landmines,* ed. Maxwell A. Cameron, Robert J. Lawson, and Brian W. Tomlin (Ontario: Oxford University Press, 1998), 88.

7. Louis Maresca and Stuart Maslen, *The Beginning of Anti-Personnel Landmines: The Legal Contribution of the International Committee of the Red Cross 1955–1999* (Cambridge: Cambridge University Press, 2008).

8. "Customary International Humanitarian Law: 29-10-2010 Overview," *International Committee of the Red Cross,* http://www.icrc.org/eng/war-and-law/treaties-customary-law/customary-law/overview-customary-law.htm.

9. Ann Florini, "Lessons Learned," in *The Third Force: The Rise of Transnational Civil Society,* ed. Ann Florini (Washington, DC: Carnegie Endowment for International Peace, 2000), 217.

10. Ann Florini and P. J. Simmons, "What the World Needs Now," in *The Third Force: The Rise of Transnational Civil Society,* ed. Ann Florini (Washington, DC: Carnegie Endowment for International Peace, 2000), 7–8.

11. Thomas C. Schelling and Morton H. Halperin, *Strategy and Arms Control* (New York: Twentieth Century Fund, 1961), 2. Schelling and Halperin define arms control as "all the forms of military cooperation between potential enemies in the interest of reducing the likelihood of war, its scope and violence if it occurs, and the political and economic costs of being prepared for it." They chose "arms control" over "disarmament" in order to broaden the term.

12. Ronald F. Lehman II, Foreword to *Arms Control and Cooperative Security,* ed James A. Larsen and James J. Wirtz (Boulder, CO: Lynne Rienner Publishers, 2009), vii–xii.

13. Jeffrey A. Larsen, *Arms Control toward the Twenty-First Century* (Boulder, CO: Lynne Rienner Publishers, 1996).

14. Kenneth R. Rutherford, "Nongovernmental Organizations (NGOs) and International Politics in the Twenty-First Century," *American Foreign Policy Interests* 23, no. 1 (2001): 23.

15. "The Convention on Prohibitions or Restrictions on the Use of Certain Conventional Weapons which May Be Deemed to Be Excessively Injurious or to Have Indiscriminate Effects," United Nations Office at Geneva, http://www.unog.ch/80256EDD006B8954/(httpAssets)/40BDE99D98467348C12571DE0060141E/$file/CCW+text.pdf.

16. Leon V. Sigal, *Negotiating Minefields: The Landmines Ban in American Politics* (New York: Taylor and Francis Group, 2006), 11–13.

17. Landmine Monitor Report 2000, (Washington, DC: Human Rights Watch, 2000), http://www.the-monitor.org/index.php/content/view/full/18734. According to the 2000 edition of the Land Mines Monitor, the "long standing and widely used" estimate of yearly casualties prior to the MBT was 26,000.

18. Sigal, *Negotiating Minefields,* 1–3.

19. Nicola Short, "The Role of NGOs in the Ottawa Process to Ban Landmines," *International Negotiation* 4, no. 3 (1999): 483.

20. "Ban Movement Chronology," International Campaign to Ban Landmines. http://www.icbl.org/index.php/icbl/About-Us/History/Chronology.

21. Michael J. Matheson, "Filling the Gaps in the Conventional Weapons Convention," *Arms Control Today* 31 (2001), http://www.armscontrol.org/act/2001_11/mathesonnov01.

22. Kenneth R. Rutherford, "The Hague and Ottawa Conventions: A Model for Future Weapons Ban Processes," *Non-Proliferation Review* 6, no. 3 (1999) 36–50, 37.

See Sigal, *Negotiating Minefields*, 9–55 for a detailed discussion of the preparatory meetings of the Review Conference and the ICBL's strategy.

23. Short, "The Role of NGOs."

24. Sigal, *Negotiating Minefields*.

25. BC, "1997: Princess Diana Sparks Landmines Row," http://news.bbc.co.uk/onthisday/hi/dates/stories/january/15/newsid_2530000/2530603.stm.

26. Short, "The Role of NGOs," 483.

27. Sigal, *Negotiating Minefields*; Short, "The Role of NGOs," 486.

28. Sigal, *Negotiating Minefields*, 98.

29. Ibid, 99–100.

30. Ibid, 100.

31. Short, "The Role of NGOs," 486–87.

32. David Davenport, "The New Diplomacy," *Policy Review* 116 (2002): 20.

33. Jody Williams, "The International Campaign to Ban Landmines—A Model for Disarmament Initiatives?," Nobel Peace Prize 1997, International Campaign to Ban Landmines, http://www.nobelprize.org/nobel_prizes/peace/laureates/1997/article.html.

34. Short, "The Role of NGOs," 491–94.

35. Rutherford, "Nongovernmental Organizations (NGOs) and International Politics in the Twenty-First Century," 1, 23–29, 26.

36. Rutherford, "The Hague and Ottawa Conventions: A Model for Future Weapons Ban Processes," 37.

37. A vote was never called for in the Ottawa Process, but delegations knew that any nonconsensus issues could be resolved by resorting to a supermajority vote.

38. Ibid.

39. "Introduction," Landmine & Cluster Munitions Monitor, http://www.the-monitor.org/index.php.

40. "Major Findings," Landmine Monitor 2010, Toward a Mine Free World, http://www.the-monitor.org/index.php/publications/display?url=lm/2010/es/Major_Findings.html.

41. The language in the Monitor sometimes refers simply to "rebels," "various rebel groups," "opposition forces," or "various factions" in assessing landmine use in many countries. "Banning Antipersonnel Mines," Landmine Monitor: Toward a Mine Free World, 1999, http://www.the-monitor.org/index.php/publications/display?url=lm/1999/english/exec/Execweb1–02.htm#P184_13658.

42. Landmine Monitor 2011, 1, http://www.the-monitor.org/lm/2011/resources/Landmine%20Monitor%202011.pdf.

43. Ibid.

44. Ibid, 13.

45. "Mission," Overview and Strategic Chart, Geneva International Center for Strategic Demining, http://www.gichd.org/about-gichd/overview/.

46. Geneva International Centre for Humanitarian Demining, Annual Report 2010, 13, http://www.gichd.org/fileadmin/pdf/about_gichd/activity_reports/GICHD-Annual-Report-2010-en.pdf.

47. Landmine Monitor 2011, 2.

48. Landmine Monitor, Executive Summary 2009.

49. Cameron, *To Walk without Fear*, 10.

50. ICBL, "Grave Concern over Allegations of Landmine Use by Turkish Army," Press release, Geneva, April 19, 2010, http://www.icbl.org/index.php/icbl/Library/News-Articles/Work/pr-19April2010.

51. Convention on the Prohibition of the Use, Stockpiling, Production and Transfer of Anti-Personnel Mines and on Their Destruction, http://www.icbl.org/index.php/icbl/Treaty/MBT/Treaty-Text-in-Many-Languages.

52. ICBL, http://www.icbl.org/index.php/icbl/Universal/MBT/States-Parties.

53. Landmine Monitor 2011, 23.

54. Ibid, 2.

55. Jesuit Refugee Service/USA, "Civil Society Frustrated by U.S. Landmine Policy Review," December 4, 2011, http://jrsusa.org/news_detail?TN=NEWS-2011120 2020709.

56. John Borrie, *Unacceptable Harm: A History of How the Treaty to Ban Cluster Munitions Was Won*, United Nations Publications (United Nations Institute for Disarmament Research, 2008), 8–9.

57. Ibid, 27–30, 44–45.

58. United Nations Office at Geneva, Disarmament, the Convention on Certain Conventional Weapons, http://www.unog.ch/80256EE600585943/%28httpPage s%29/4F0DEF093B4860B4C1257180004B1B30?OpenDocument. Protocol II of the Convention on Certain Conventional Weapons entered into force in 1981 and was amended in 1996.

59. John Borrie, *Unacceptable Harm*, 50. Human Rights Watch, 2003, quoted in Borrie (2008), 50.

60. Borrie, *Unacceptable Harm*, 97–98.

61. Ibid, 139.

62. Ibid, 64–70.

63. Wade Boese, "Cluster Munitions Control Efforts Make Gains," *Arms Control Today* 37 (2007), http://aphdressingroom.livejournal.com/1141604.html?thread=173 728356#t173728356.

64. "Diplomatic Conference for the Adoption of a Convention on Cluster Munitions," Dublin, 2008, http://www.clustermunitionsdublin.ie/pdf/ENGLISHfinaltext.pdf.

65. All statistics in this section are taken from the Cluster Munition Monitor 2011, http://www.the-monitor.org/cmm/2011/pdf/Cluster_Munition_Monitor_2011.pdf.

CHAPTER 6

Conclusion

Arms control and disarmament, particularly involving nuclear weapons and delivery systems, played a vital role in the relationship between the United States and the Soviet Union during the Cold War. They continue to do so in the sometimes turbulent relationship between the United States and Russia, now that the Cold War is history. Furthermore, multilateral arms control geared toward constraining the proliferation of nuclear weapons, eliminating CBW, land mines, and cluster munitions, is woven into the fabric of international relations among the vast majority of nations in the world. Arms control has moved well beyond its game-theoretic framework of cooperation between potential enemies to encompass cooperation among friends and allies as well as conflict management among potential enemies. In light of recent advances in technology and violent conflict, the drive to control arms is necessarily being extended to nonstate actors.

This book has set forth the prominent features of the arms control landscape over roughly the last half-century, highlighting agreements, disagreements, accomplishments, and failures. The challenge in this final chapter is to draw reasonable conclusions from the array of instruments that have been studied and whose implementation has been explored. Across the agreements that are the subject of this book, several trends and challenges have become apparent.

Political Opportunities and Constraints

Throughout the Cold War, nuclear arms control policy was not considered an end in itself; rather it was considered to be an instrument to achieve other policy objectives. Following the appalling destructiveness and lethality of WWII, the main policy objective in controlling arms was to enhance security, to make it less likely that the United States, the Soviet Union, and their allies would go to war with each other, and if they did go to war, to make wars less costly. Because arms control was one component of achieving national security, arms control initiatives remained on the agendas of states and international multilateral forums, such as the CD. Nevertheless, because arms control was only one component contributing to national security and rarely, if ever, the most important component, arms control almost never made it to the top of the priority list. In many instances, policy makers were willing to forego achieving arms control and disarmament treaties for the sake of what they regarded as more important political goals. At the same time, when the political stars align correctly, durable arms control agreements can be completed rather quickly.

During the Cold War, the relationship between the United States and the Soviet Union varied from active hostilities to détente. At times, during increased hostilities, such as the Soviet invasion of Afghanistan, support for arms control fell. Public ire in the United States against the Soviet Union following its Afghan invasion prevented U.S. Senate ratification of the nuclear SALT II agreement, one in a series of nuclear agreements between the superpowers. Conversely, other critical events like the Cuban Missile Crisis increased awareness of the contributions of arms control efforts in reducing the risk of war. Political leaders and the public alike renewed their commitment to arms control in the aftermath of crises. For example, amidst increasing tensions and great suspicion of the intentions of each other regarding nuclear missiles in Europe, changes in leadership in the Soviet Union and the United States led to the Intermediate Range Nuclear Forces Agreement, a breakthrough effort supported by President Reagan and Soviet premier Gorbachev. The tragedy of the war in the former Yugoslavia, although not closely related to superpower rivalry, also catalyzed arms control efforts. The extensive placement of land mines exposed once again their enduring destructiveness and spurred international efforts to ban them.

While bilateral nuclear arms control garnered the lion's share of attention in the United States during the Cold War, it was not the only game in town. National security demanded that the proliferation of nuclear weapons, predicted by President Kennedy in 1963 to be within the reach of some 20 nations by 1975, be halted. A recently declassified U.S. National Intelligence Estimate from 1957 claimed that Sweden would likely produce a nuclear weapon around 1961, that a French nuclear weapon would spur arguments in Germany for nuclear weapons, and that Japan and Canada would seek nuclear capability in the 1960s.[1] By 1966, an updated National Intelligence

Estimate listed India as "likely to undertake a nuclear weapons program" and that Belgium, Denmark, Italy, the Netherlands, Norway, Portugal, Spain, Argentina, Brazil, Czechoslovakia, and East Germany "could produce a few weapons in the next ten years, although the constraints against them acquiring a nuclear capability were numerous and compelling." India, Israel, Sweden, Japan, West Germany, Switzerland, Australia, South Africa, Taiwan, Pakistan, Indonesia, and Egypt—known as the United Arab Republic at the time—had less compelling constraints and were considered potential NWS.[2] The threat of proliferation of nuclear weapons and apprehension that the Soviet Union might be pulling ahead in the arms race was widely noted and discussed; concerns about the so-called missile gap, for example, played a prominent role in the 1960 presidential campaign.

Given the prospect of a hair-trigger world and the number of states armed with nuclear weapons continually increasing, all the known NWS at the time, the United States, Soviet Union, China, France, and the United Kingdom, were united in seeking an agreement to keep the dire predictions of nuclear proliferation from becoming reality. Their shared interest provided impetus to the Nuclear NPT negotiations. The NPT also took center stage in 1995. The terms of the agreement stipulated that the treaty would last for 25 years, after which a special conference would determine its future. An intense diplomatic effort on the part of the United States and others resulted in extending the duration of the NPT indefinitely, in spite of dissatisfaction among many of the nonnuclear weapon states with the slow pace of nuclear disarmament.

The Vietnam War, the top U.S. international priority at its peak, gave rise to criticism of the U.S. use of chemical herbicides, especially Agent Orange. The international and to some extent domestic uproar surrounding allegations that the United States was using chemical warfare in Vietnam contributed to President Nixon's review of chemical and biological warfare policy soon after he took office in 1969.[3] The review, in turn, promoted a proposed ban on the possession of biological and toxin weapons on the U.S. political agenda and within three short years, the Biological Weapons Convention (BWC) was open for signature. During the same time period, however, a similar proposed ban on the possession of chemical weapons (CW) languished in the CD, while U.S. and Soviet differences on onsite verification held up completion of the treaty for nearly another 20 years.

The end of the Cold War opened up new arms control opportunities. The collapse of Communism in the Soviet Union and Eastern Europe ended the ideological struggle between the United States and the Soviet Union that had fed the arms race. Deep reductions in the nuclear arsenals of the two Cold War powers were now possible. In addition, there was new potential in multilateral arms control negotiations. Disagreements between the United

States and the Soviet Union were no longer the focal point of multilateral negotiations. A breakthrough in the negotiations to ban CW occurred when the Soviet Union dropped its long-standing objection to onsite inspections. Middle powers, such as Canada and Norway, in partnership with international organizations and coalitions, provided the leadership to garner agreement to ban land mines and cluster munitions.

The September 11, 2001, terrorist attacks, however, led to more militant politics in the United States. The George W. Bush administration turned away from arms control and sought other means to bolster national security. The Bush administration had already rejected the legally binding protocol to the BWC. It followed the invasion of Afghanistan with an invasion of Iraq, ostensibly to counter Saddam Hussein's quest for weapons of mass destruction. The UN commissions to uncover and destroy Iraq's CBW programs, its missile program, and its rudimentary attempts to acquire nuclear material had already crippled Iraq's weapons programs and the U.S. invaders found no evidence of hidden weapons stockpiles or programs. Furthermore, the United States chose the route of the UN Security Council to address possible terrorist acquisition of weapons of mass destruction. It sponsored and championed Resolution 1540 to impose restrictions on the transfer of materials that could be used for weapons purposes.

In April 2004, the Security Council passed Resolution 1540, a concise but broad agreement that buttressed various nonproliferation agreements, including the BWC, the CWC, and the NPT. Most importantly, Resolution 1540 expanded the scope of prior nonproliferation accords to better guard against the possibility of weapons, materials, or their means of delivery spreading to nonstate actors. Motivated by the specter of international terrorism, Resolution 1540 aims to prevent the acquisition of weapons, materials, or means of delivery by any private persons or institutions. The Resolution calls for all member states to withhold their support for any nonstate actors in the process of, or seeking to, acquire, produce, ship, or use chemical, biological, or nuclear weapons, and calls on all states to explicitly prohibit and penalize all such activities through their own legal mechanisms. Later sections elaborate that a nonproliferation investigation and enforcement infrastructure must be established, particularly in the arena of border controls, as well as heightened safety protocols for the storage and transport of any chemical, biological, or nuclear weapons, materials, or means of delivery. The resolution also promotes the compilation, in conjunction with relevant industry, academia, and international organizations, of lists of materials, technologies, and means of delivery that should be forbidden or, in the case of dual-use items, monitored and restricted. Given that many states may require or benefit from assistance in carrying out Resolution 1540's provisions, the resolution includes a call for nations to work with each other, regional groups, relevant international organizations, and the Security Council Committee established to oversee and facilitate implementation. The Committee is also responsible for helping to coordinate assistance between nations, maintaining reports and information on progress and best practices that countries develop, conducting media education and outreach about the goals and progress of Resolution 1540, and preparing comprehensive reviews on the status of ongoing implementation.

The ever-changing political landscape may continue to provide an opportunity to search for what presently seem to be unlikely or impossible arms control agreements: a zone free of weapons of mass destruction in the Middle East, for example, or the total elimination of nuclear weapons. Governments and other arms control experts need to be prepared to seize the moment if such political opportunities present themselves.

The Enduring Role of Arms Control in International Relations

Arms control is here to stay. At least for the foreseeable future, the agenda for new arms control agreements includes a ban on the production of fissile material, complete nuclear disarmament, the explosive remnants of war, regulation of small arms, space weapons, and cyber warfare. The implementation of arms control is also deeply embedded in the civic culture of many countries, and is likely to grow rather than recede. In addition, the implementation and management of multilateral arms control agreements has been carried out by international organizations that develop expertise among international staff members and dedication to the purposes of the treaties. The organizations also provide a focus for interaction among treaty parties, other relevant international organizations, and national and international NGOs and academics with an interest in successful treaty implementation.

Despite this array of forces aligned to support the furthering of the arms control agenda, completion of agreements on any or all of the topics listed previously is not imminent, nor even likely, in the near term. Political opportunities that led to the culmination of the MBT and the CCM could lead to the speedy conclusion of an agreement on the explosive remnants of war or on small arms, but that is by no means assured. The technical and political obstacles facing an agreement on small arms, for example, are formidable. A Fissile Material Cut-Off Treaty (FMCT) has been in the offing for decades, but is hung up in the CD because Pakistan refuses to agree to negotiations while it enlarges its nuclear arsenal. Because the CD operates by consensus, any member of the body can block action.[4] Nonnuclear weapons states have called for its early completion and it has considerable support. Yet, even if the treaty is concluded and open for signature, its fate could to be similar to the CTBT, which opened for signature since 1996 and has not yet entered into force. Proponents of FMCT might be able to avoid the problems of the CTBT, however, if they refrain from including unrealistic requirements on the number of states needed to ratify the agreement before it enters into force.

Furthermore, the regime changes that have taken place in Egypt, Libya, and Tunisia in the 2011 Arab Spring could have ripple effects on arms control negotiations. What those effects might be, however, remain to be seen. A more democratic Egypt could accede to the CWC and ratify the CTBT. On the other hand, the military and conservative religious leaders in Egypt may have a chilling effect on any arms control proposals. And once again, the new governments that emerge in the area are unlikely to have arms control as a high priority. It is likely, however, that arms control advocates within newly democratizing states in North Africa and the Middle East will view regime change as an opportunity to push an arms control agenda. And groups outside these nations will do so as well, hoping for a breakthrough in the region that could also support progress in the Arab–Israeli conflict. It is simply too soon to tell whether these national and international arms control supporters meet with support or resistance.

Interplay across Agreements

An examination across arms control agreements shows that negotiations for each agreement do not occur in a vacuum. Rather, each new agreement is in the position to benefit from lessons from previous treaties, to incorporate successful language and ideas from them, and to avoid pitfalls and failures. Each of the strategic nuclear agreements between the United States and the Soviet Union, and subsequently Russia, built on the language and experience of earlier treaties. The series of treaties from the SALT to the START to the SORT and the New START treaties all relied on the experiences of previous agreements and their implementation.

Moreover, arms control experience in one weapons system spills over into accords in other substantive areas. Language on access to nuclear technology for peaceful purposes that appears in the NPT, for example, finds its way to the BWC and CWC, with some alterations. Verification measures similar to those in the CWC were incorporated in the Protocol to strengthen the BWC, although that instrument failed to attract consensus among the negotiating governments. The interplay is facilitated by diplomatic personnel going from one negotiating forum to another. In most small countries, a limited number of diplomats typically shoulder the entire arms control portfolio and are able to easily make comparisons across weapons systems. Delegations from larger countries include experts from relevant ministries or departments that may take part in negotiations across different weapons systems and are ultimately coordinated at a higher level that seeks to ensure that agreements are consistent with a nation's interests and national goals.

The process of conducting negotiations changes across time and from agreement to agreement, but never completely. Procedures, habits, and norms of operating continue to influence arms control negotiation, although sharp departures from previous practices also occur. Bilateral Cold War nuclear negotiations could at times be complex and protracted with many experts, defense, and political components; at other times, such as at the conclusion of the INF agreement, leaders agreed to broad policy objectives and agreements were swiftly drafted.

Ideas about the negotiating process established by prior negotiations often linger and perhaps limit the thinking of nations about how to organize their deliberations. The Cold War practice of alternating Eastern and Western bloc chairs and cochairs of important committees in negotiations and review conferences has continued after the end of the Cold War in the absence of an acceptable alternative. Although the alignments have changed dramatically, this structure remains in place even though some members of the former Eastern bloc, particularly former members of the Warsaw Pact that have joined NATO, have become members of the Western Group.

Coalitions formed in the context of negotiating one agreement may have staying power and influence the course of negotiations in future agreements. The recent emergence of the JACKSNNZ (Japan, Australia, Canada, South Korea, Switzerland, Norway, and New Zealand) in the meetings of the BWC adds a new twist. The formation of the JACKSNNZ demonstrates the ability of nations to form temporary negotiating coalitions based on similar interests and positions in the negotiations. These coalitions are unlikely to be as stable as those that existed during the Cold War but, ironically, may garner more attention because of their novelty and achieve rapid success because of the commitment and energy of their members. They are also likely to exhibit more flexibility than the traditional negotiating groups and less likely to be burdened with decades-old routines of procedure.

One aspect of historical arms control negotiations has gone by the wayside. The nonaligned movement (NAM) countries no longer have a superpower rivalry not to be aligned with one side or the other. Their members appreciate that more than nonalignment unites many of them. They have become an influential group even if fissures are apt to occur in such a large group with divergent interests. Because so many of the NAM are small or relatively weak states, they recognize that they can achieve more of what they desire in coalition with other like-minded states.

The connections between the NPT, the CTBT and the proposed FMTC are explicit and continuing. The nonnuclear member states that are party to the NPT persistently demanded that the nuclear states negotiate, ratify, and comply with an agreement that bans nuclear weapons testing and cease the production of new fissile material. Despite these demands, and the completion of the CTBT shortly after the 1995 NPT review conference, six countries that must ratify or accede to the CTBT before it enters into force have not done so. China, Israel, and the United States have signed but not ratified the CTBT. North Korea, India, and Pakistan have not signed the treaty. U.S. president Obama has repeatedly stated his intention to submit the CTBT for Senate ratification, but as of the date of publication has not done so. So the CTBT remains in a kind of limbo, with a substantial international organization employing more than 250 people who work under a cloud of uncertainty to build an effective verification regime and to promote the treaty and the norm that it embodies. The norm against nuclear testing, however, appears to be robust.

Skepticism Unjustified

Arms control skeptics have always been prevalent inside and outside of government. Nevertheless, their predictions regarding arms control in general or with reference to a specific agreement have often not been borne out by subsequent events. Skeptics within the British government, for example, did not envision any possibility for an agreement banning BW, yet the agreement was open for signature four years after the United Kingdom submitted an influential working paper on BW disarmament at the CD. The Working Paper proposed severing BW from CW in order to promote negotiations on the weapons system that had not been used extensively in warfare. The tactic worked, somewhat to the surprise of U.K. diplomats.

New arms control agreements continue to be negotiated and implemented. Similarly, a prediction in 1996 that a treaty on antipersonnel land mines was years off underestimated the momentum that would accumulate behind the MBT, which opened for signature only a year later.[5] Simultaneously, arms control agreements continue to attract new states parties. The preceding chapters on multilateral agreements—the NPT, the BWC, the CWC, the MBT, and the Cluster Munitions Treaty—all demonstrate that adherents to these treaties have increased over time. Even the CTBT, which has not yet taken effect, has increased its membership substantially over time. While none of these agreements has universal membership, the observance of the norms associated with these treaties—especially the nonuse of the proscribed weapons—has been surprisingly consistent. The norms appear to have an effect on nonparties as well as treaty parties. No state has used nuclear weapons since 1945. While some accusations persist, there has been no conclusive proof that any state has used BW or CW since their respective treaties entered into force. Furthermore, although India and Pakistan both tested nuclear weapons in 1998, only North Korea has tested nuclear weapons since the completion of the CTBT. Yet even North Korea may consider joining the less formal and widespread moratorium on nuclear testing that is in place among other nuclear weapons states.[6] The use and production of land mines have fallen dramatically since the completion of the Landmines Ban. Thus, even when arms control norms are not binding on sovereign states, empirical evidence supports the notion that they exert influence on their behavior.

Verification

How can any state be sure that others are doing, or refraining from doing, what they have promised? Verification as an arms control concept is complex and, at times, confusing. Some states refer to verification as the activities that states or international organizations engage in to come to a conclusion as to whether other states are in compliance with their obligations. In the United States, in particular, successive governments consider verification to be the judgment of the government as to whether states are living up to agreements, rather than the activities. Thus, verification as activities versus verification as a governmental judgment is one source of confusion.

Verification activities, or the means of verifying compliance with obligations, vary from one agreement to the next. Many nuclear agreements use national technical means, which includes satellite imagery and seismic monitoring. Many agreements require states to make initial and periodic declarations of relevant facilities or activities as one of the factors that would make the judgment of whether a state is in compliance less difficult and more reliable. In contrast to national technical means and declarations, both of which occur without a physical presence in another sovereign state, onsite activities are required to verify some arms control agreements, such as the CWC and the NPT. Onsite activities include monitors that relay information and inspections by national or international personnel. During the Cold War, some arms control negotiations were stalemated because the Soviet Union typically refused onsite measures and the United States insisted on them.[7]

In addition to verification activities, there are also differences of opinion on the degree of certainty regarding others' compliance with arms control strictures. While the impossibility of absolute, or certain, verification is readily accepted, there is not an international consensus on the degree of tolerable uncertainty regarding others' level of compliance. The United States declares that the BWC, for example, cannot be verified, and continues to oppose any effort to include legally binding measures such as onsite inspection of its biodefense facilities and programs. Meanwhile, the United Kingdom supported a proposed legally binding protocol to the Convention chock full of verification measures. For the United States, participation with those measures would not reduce uncertainty of compliance to an acceptable level.

Nevertheless, verification activities have changed a great deal over time. The intrusive measures to verify the destruction of CW stockpiles, for example, would have been unattainable during the years of the Cold War. Moreover, in an earlier or different political environment, an NGO would not have been entrusted with responsibility for verification activities and reports. Yet, the International Campaign to Ban Landmines (ICBL) has been delegated the responsibility to verify compliance with the provisions of the CCM based on its exemplary work with land mines and its annual report *Landmines Monitor*. It now publishes an annual *Cluster Munitions Monitor* as well. Such a prominent role for an NGO would likely have been not only impossible but considered ludicrous in some other contexts. NGOs also learn from one another's work, just as governments and treaty implementation organizations do. The BioWeapons Prevention Project issued the first *BioWeapons Monitor* in 2010 to report on biological capacities and capabilities in four countries and a second with double the number of countries in a report in 2011. The process to produce the *BioWeapons Monitor* was modeled after the *Landmines Monitor*, and the government of Norway has agreed to provide funding for at least the next two years.

The Importance of Science and Technology

Scientific and technological achievements have affected many aspects of arms control. In the nuclear arena, for example, advances in distinguishing seismic events from nuclear explosions have made states confident that they would be able to detect nuclear tests above a threshold that would have grave security consequences, contributing to the completion of the CTBT. Such a distinction was impossible in the 1960s when states were able to ban atmospheric, but not underground, nuclear tests.

Advances in science and technology do not always lead to progress in arms control, however. The ability to produce biological agents in smaller laboratories, the diffusion of scientific knowledge throughout a larger portion of the population, and the ability to create synthetic analogs of naturally occurring toxins have all contributed to skepticism regarding whether the BWC can be effectively verified.

While we do not know how the next set of discoveries will affect arms control, it is safe to assume that future scientific advances in telemetry, synthetic biology, nanotechnology, and other areas will continue to provide both opportunities and challenges to various arms control measures. The ability of the international processes to come to terms with and evaluate the relevance of scientific and technical developments in a timely fashion, however, is limited and inadequate. The BWC and to a lesser extent the CWC are especially ill-equipped to come to terms with the rapid advances in chemistry and biology, the overlap of the two sciences, and their partial convergence. As yet, recent discoveries have not led to catastrophic disease epidemics or widespread outbreaks from the accidental or deliberate release of agents engineered to be extra virulent or more easily transmissible, but arms control is not well prepared to address such possibilities

Roles for Governments, Business, and Civil Society

The early days of modern arms control were pretty strictly a government affair. Some scientific organizations, notably the Pugwash Conferences on Science and World Affairs, worked to influence governments to terminate the nuclear arms race. One of the goals of Pugwash was to enhance contact between U.S. and Soviet physicists, on the theory that greater familiarity could make a lasting and beneficial contribution to nuclear arms control. The Pugwash agenda included all aspects of nuclear arms issues including testing and later expanded to include CW and BW as well. The Nobel committee recognized that contribution by awarding the Pugwash organization and its founder, Joseph Rotblat, the 1995 Peace Prize. But other scientific and civil society groups were notably absent from many negotiations. Organizations such as the Nuclear Freeze Movement tried to influence the arms race and certainly made the issue a household word, but they did not attain success in freezing nuclear production or even generating negotiations among nations on the topic.

The negotiation of the CWC changed the practice of negotiations conducted by diplomats only. Because the worldwide chemical industry produces and works with toxic chemicals that would be regulated by the Convention, it became heavily involved in the negotiations. Chemical societies developed industry positions and worked with many governments to advance positions within the negotiations that would protect trade secrets but still allow international inspectors to conduct onsite activities in commercial facilities. Chemical industry representatives served on the negotiating teams of several countries and otherwise influenced the process. It is unlikely that the CWC would have come to fruition without the support of industry and certainly would not have been ratified in the United States without that support.

Civil society organizations, notably the umbrella organization, the ICBL, took involvement a step further. Not content to advise governments, the ICBL took on an unprecedented organizing and advocacy role. The ICBL insisted on working only with governments that supported a total land mines ban and some governments criticized it for interfering with work that was within the purview of governments. Nevertheless, once again the Nobel committee honored a civil society group and its coordinator, Jody Williams, with the Peace Prize. The ICBL built on its success with land mines by tackling cluster munitions and achieving success on that front as well.

Globalization and electronic communication has made it much easier for civil society groups to interact and support each other and the causes that they believe in. There are other reasons that civil society groups have become more influential and important over time. Civil society organizations are typically organized around a single goal or activity. As such, civil society organizations do not have the same extensive agendas as states or government ministries. They do not have competing priorities to contend with or dilute their efforts. Being single-minded allows them to be efficient in their actions and focused in their efforts. Secondly, many civil society organizations are comprised of actors from many states and regions of the world. They are free from the sometimes more narrow state interests. Thus, civil society organizations can act in an impartial fashion, which governments are frequently unable to do. Thirdly, many states that are beset with corruption and/or ineffective institutions have populations that rely on civil society organizations for reliable information about arms control issues. Civil society organizations are able to gain the trust of the general population who may distrust or have a healthy skepticism of governments. Civil society organizations can convert cynics and establish communication links with people and organizations that are typically reluctant to share their information with governments. And governments and government personnel who question the motives or priorities of other states or multistate endeavors may give civil society organizations the benefit of the doubt.

International organizations such as the World Health Organization, the International Committee for the Red Cross, and others are also frequent advocates for and leaders in arms control. Even more than civil society, these organizations are typically respected, trusted, and viewed as neutral arbiters in the conflicts among states over negotiating positions or posturing.[8]

Thus, arms control is no longer solely a governmental function and is not likely to ever become so again. There are too many stakeholders in the arms control field, in business, civil society, and elsewhere that will not allow that to happen. These groups have legitimate interests in the form and outcomes of arms control negotiation processes. They will continue to keep a sharp eye on governments and communicate with each other and the general public easily. They are here to stay.

Persistent Challenges

Problem States

The picture for international arms control is by no means all rosy. North Korea's withdrawal from the NPT and its subsequent tests of nuclear weapons is an ominous series of events. Despite years of negotiations, deals and reneging on deals, sanctions, and defiance, North Korea now has demonstrated its ability to launch a nuclear attack. It conducted underground nuclear tests in 2006 and 2009. North Korea has not signed the CTBT and is not likely to do so. Moreover, it is not a member of the CWC, the MBT, or the CCM although it has been a member of the BWC since 1987. The ability to persuade or coerce North Korea is limited by its isolation; neither sticks nor carrots have had much effect.

Iran may be following in North Korea's footsteps and may be receiving assistance from North Korea in its missile program.[9] Iran seems to be equally defiant and meetings hosted by the European powers have not made headway with Iran. It continues to enrich uranium and continues to insist that the program is intended for peaceful purposes. The reaction of other states if Iran also withdraws from the NPT is unknown. One possibility is that nuclear proliferation would end with Iran. Another, of course, is that one by one other states would reassess their commitments to the NPT and explore the possibilities of developing their own nuclear weapons. It is impossible to ascertain how many withdrawals the NPT could sustain. North Korea conducted its first nuclear test in 2006; five years later, the NPT had a modestly successful review conference. The member states of the NPT seem to have concluded that they can live with a few nuclear weapons in North Korea, just as they have come to live with a nuclearized India, Pakistan, and Israel. A nuclear-armed Iran, however, could be the straw that breaks the camel's back. If diplomacy, sanctions, or threatened military action do not prevent Iran from producing nuclear weapons, other nations may follow suit, and seek their own nuclear weapons.

Furthermore, as long as there are nuclear-armed states outside the NPT, the five nuclear weapon states inside the NPT are unlikely to fulfill their ultimate commitment to end the arms race and get rid of their own nuclear weapons. As U.S. president Obama has suggested, we may not see a nuclear weapons-free world in our lifetimes. In that case, the NPT is likely to continue, albeit in a weakened state.

Universality

The problems associated with North Korean withdrawal from the NPT and Israeli, Indian, and Pakistani refusal to join at all are part of a larger problem. None of the multilateral treaties discussed in this volume have universal membership. And as long as Israel, for example, stays outside the NPT, other states like Egypt are unwilling to join the CWC. Clearly, a comprehensive peace in the Middle East is a prerequisite to solving a portion of the universalization issues with the NPT, CWC, and perhaps the BWC.

The BWC has fewer parties than the NPT and the CWC even though the CWC is a more recent convention and it has strict verification requirements. In part, the Organization for the Prevention of Chemical Weapons has vigorously pursued a policy to increase membership. The Implementation Support Unit of the BWC would like to do the same but does not have sufficient resources to carry out a comprehensive program of education and advocacy.

The MBT and the CCM are still in the process of building their membership. Both are likely to continue to attract additional parties, but serious obstacles remain. Regional or bilateral conflicts such as between India and Pakistan, or North and South Korea, are likely to remain obstacles to universality in these regimes. The Obama administration announced in 2009 that it would not sign the MBT. U.S. refusal to join the MBT gives cover to other states who also wish to continue to possess or use land mines.

Response to Noncompliance

Writing in *Foreign Affairs* in 1961, Fred Iklé asked the question "After Detection, What?"[10] Although Iklé focused on the then Soviet Union, his question remains relevant today. North Korea could not hide its nuclear weapons program after its development reached a certain stage and therefore withdrew from the NPT. Despite UN sanctions, North Korea appears undeterred from continuing its nuclear program. The member states of the BWC took no action when details of the former Soviet BW program in violation of the BWC were reported.[11] The consequences of the U.S. invasion of Iraq based on the premise that it was in violation of its arms control agreements, particularly concerning hidden BW, does not bode well for military action against another state. What are the alternatives?

The answer may depend on the treaty whose violation is in question. A detection of a violation of the CWC would likely be taken up by the Executive Council of the Organization for the Prevention of Chemical Weaponry. More frequent inspections and greater scrutiny of required declaration would likely ensue. Although the BWC has a mechanism to address allegations of noncompliance, the only time the mechanism was used, when Cuba accused the United States of deliberately disseminating crop-destroying insects over the island, no conclusion was reached.

Iklé suggested that world opinion and domestic opinion might have some effect, but that ultimately deterring arms control violations was likely to be more effective than dealing with violations once they occur. His prescriptions are relevant but limited. His central question remains, "After Detection, What?" Fifty years after he asked the question, there is still no definitive answer.

The world has endured for more than 65 years without experiencing the effects of another nuclear blast. CW, which once caused thousands of casualties, have been brought under significant international control. BW are considered "repugnant to the conscience of mankind."[12] Land mines and cluster munitions, which have killed and maimed hundreds of thousands of civilians, are now being cleared from conflict sites. One lesson of the 20th-century history of arms control is that advocates inside and out of government are motivated and persistent. Further, negotiators continue to find new methods and processes to make warfare and other violent conflicts less deadly. As science allows more sophisticated weaponry, new ways of containing the effects of that weaponry are imagined and in some cases brought to fruition.

Notes

1. National Intelligence Estimate Number 100-6-57, "Nuclear Weapons Production in Fourth Countries Likelihood and Consequences," June 18, 1957, The National Security Archive, http://www.gwu.edu/~nsarchiv/NSAEBB/NSAEBB155/index.htm.

2. National Security Estimate Number 4-66, "The Likelihood of Further Nuclear Proliferation," January 20, 1966, 2, The National Security Archive, http://www.gwu.edu/~nsarchiv/NSAEBB/NSAEBB155/index.htm.

3. Jonathan B. Tucker, "A Farewell to Germs: The U.S. Renunciation of Biological and Toxin Weapons, 1969–1970," *International Security* 27 (summer 2002), 107–48.

4. Peter Crail, "Pakistan's Nuclear Buildup Vexes FMCT Talks," *Arms Control Today* (March 2011), http://www.armscontrol.org/act/2011_03/Pakistan.

5. Jeffrey A. Larsen, *Arms Control toward the Twenty-First Century* (Boulder, CO: Lynne Rienner Publishers, 1996).

6. Seth Mydans and Choe Sang-Hun, "North Korea Said to Weigh Nuclear Test Moratorium," *The New York Times*, August 24, 2011, http://www.nytimes.com/2011/08/25/world/europe/25siberia.html.

7. See Alan B. Sherr, *The Other Side of Arms Control: Soviet Objectives in the Gorbachev Era* (Boston, MA: Unwin Hyman, 1988), 242–72, for a thorough discussion of Soviet attitudes toward verification activities including national technical means and onsite activities.

8. Much of this discussion is drawn from a report the author prepared on behalf of the BioWeapons Prevention Project and delivered in a statement to the United Nations 1540 committee in October 2009, http://www.stanleyfoundation.org/publications/working_papers/ChevrierBWPPSC1540.pdf.

9. AlertNet, A Thomson Reuters Foundation Service, "N. Korea, Iran Trade Missile Technology," May 15, 2011,http://www.trust.org/alertnet/news/exclusive-nkorea-iran-trade-missile-technology-un.

10. Fred Charles Iklé, "After Detection What?" *Foreign Affairs* 39, no. 2 (1961): 208–20.

11. Ken Alibek (with Stephen Handelman), *Biohazard: The Chilling True Story of the Largest Covert Biological Weapons Program in the World—Told from Inside by the Man Who Ran It* (New York: Random House, 1999).

12. Preamble, Convention on the Prohibition of the Development, Production and Stockpiling of Bacteriological (Biological) and Toxin Weapons and on Their Destruction, http://www.opbw.org/.

Guide to Treaties

Common Name	Acronym	Full Name	Major Provisions	Year Open for Signature	Year of Entry into Force	Number of Parties as of May 15, 2012
Anti-Ballistic Missile Treaty	ABM	Treaty between United States of America and the Union of the Soviet Socialist Republics on the Limitation of Anti-ballistic Missile Systems	Permitted the United States and the Soviet Union to deploy only two ABM systems each, which were limited to 100 missile interceptors and coverage of an area with a radius of 150 kilometers; allowed one system to defend the capital of the nation and the other to protect an offensive ICBM site. Prohibited developing, testing, and deploying any ABM system or its components in the sea, the air, or space. Limited the number of intercept launchers at the allowed ABM sites and limited those launchers to one intercept each. Established a Standing Consultative Commission to resolve any ambiguities with implementation of the treaty, provide a forum to exchange information between the two parties, and discuss any relevant changes in the strategic situation that might warrant amendments or other changes to the treaty.	1972	1972, U.S. withdrew in 2002	N/A

		Full Name	Year	Year	Parties	Description
Biological Weapons Convention	BWC	Convention on the Prohibition of the Development, Production, and Stockpiling of Bacteriological (Biological) and Toxin Weapons and on Their Destruction	1972	1975	165	Bans developing, producing, stockpiling, or otherwise acquiring or retaining microbial or other biological agents, or toxins *"that have no justification for prophylactic, protective or other peaceful purpose."* Research is not prohibited. Supported by a three-person Implementation Support Unit.
Chemical Weapons Convention	CWC	Convention on the Prohibition of the Development, Production, Stockpiling, and Use of Chemical Weapons and on their Destruction	1993	1997	188	Prohibited use, development, production, acquisition, or retention of chemical weapons. Required states parties to destroy any chemical weapons they possess, control, or have abandoned in another state's territory and to destroy chemical weapons production facilities. Permitted (1) research: agricultural, industrial, medical, and pharmaceutical; (2) protection against toxic chemicals and chemical weapons; (3) military purposes that are not the use of chemical weapons or do not depend on the use of the toxic properties of chemicals (i.e., to illuminate the field or battle or enemy positions); and (4) "law enforcement including domestic riot control purposes." Created the Organization for the Prevention of Chemical Weapons (OPCW) to ensure implementation of the Convention and to provide a forum for consultation and cooperation among its parties.

(Continued)

175

Common Name	Acronym	Full Name	Major Provisions	Year Open for Signature	Year of Entry into Force	Number of Parties as of May 15, 2012
Convention on Cluster Munitions	CCM	Convention on Cluster Munitions	Prohibited under any circumstances to use cluster munitions or develop, produce, otherwise acquire, stockpile, retain, or transfer to anyone, directly or indirectly, cluster munitions.	2008	2010	68
Convention on Certain Conventional Weapons	CCW	Convention on Prohibitions or Restrictions on the Use of Certain Conventional Weapons which May be Deemed to Be Excessively Injurious or to Have Indiscriminate Effects	Restricted use of certain weapons that are considered to cause unnecessary or unjustifiable suffering to combatants or to affect civilians indiscriminately. Provisions applied only to international conflicts, not civil wars, and did not include land mines.	1981	1983	103
Comprehensive Test Ban Treaty	CTBT	Comprehensive Nuclear Test Ban Treaty	Prohibited all nuclear explosions. Established the Comprehensive Nuclear Test Ban Treaty Organization.	1996	–	182
Intermediate-Range Nuclear Forces Treaty	INF Treaty	Treaty Between the United States of America and the Union of Soviet Socialist Republics on the Elimination of Their Intermediate-Range and Shorter-Range Missiles	Eliminated all U.S. and Soviet ballistic and cruise missiles in Europe; allowed the United Kingdom and France to retain their nuclear-armed ballistic missiles.	1987	1988	2

		Required removal of 1,667 Soviet and 429 U.S. warheads and required that the missiles be removed from European soil and that the missiles' guidance systems be destroyed.			
		Established a forum, called the Special Verification Commission, which was to meet at the request of either of the two parties to the treaty.			
Fissile Material Cut-Off Treaty	FMCT	Treaty Banning the Production of Fissile Materials for Nuclear Weapons or Other Nuclear Explosive Devices	Proposed treaty	–	–
		Would ban the production of fissile material for nuclear weapons or other nuclear explosive devices. Does not include a production ban on plutonium and HEU for nonexplosive purposes.			
Limited Test Ban Treaty	LTBT	Treaty Banning Nuclear Weapon Tests in the Atmosphere, in Outer Space and Under Water	Prohibited nuclear weapons tests or other nuclear explosions in the atmosphere, in outer space, and under water.	1963	1963	3
			Prohibited nuclear explosions that cause "radioactive debris to be present outside the territorial limits of the State."			
Mine Ban Treaty	MBT	Convention on the Prohibition of the Use, Stockpiling, Production, and Transfer of Antipersonnel Mines and on Their Destruction	Prohibited, under any circumstance, the use of antipersonnel mines and banned the development, production, acquisition, stockpiles, retention, or transfer of antipersonnel mines. Required the destruction of all antipersonnel mines.	1997	1999	160

(Continued)

Common Name	Acronym	Full Name	Major Provisions	Year Open for Signature	Year of Entry into Force	Number of Parties as of May 15, 2012
			Established means to assist mine victims and increase awareness of mines.			
			Established transparency measures and methods to attempt to resolve compliance questions through clarification and fact-finding missions.			
New Strategic Arms Limitation Talks	New START	Treaty between the United States and the Russian Federation on Measures for the Further Reduction and Limitation of Strategic Offensive Arms	Placed limits on both the United States and Russia of no more than 700 deployed strategic nuclear delivery vehicles—ICBMs, SLBMs, and heavy bombers—and 1,550 deployed strategic warheads, which can be distributed among the delivery vehicles as each of the parties sees fit. Allowed an additional 100 nondeployed delivery vehicles.	2010	2011	2
			Restricted where the deployed and nondeployed delivery vehicles may be located and tested.			
			Enhanced verification to include national technical means and established the rights of each party to conduct inspections to confirm the accuracy of data declarations that each side is obligated to provide to the other.			

				1968	1970	189
			Enhanced transparency by requiring exchange of telemetry (missile flight test data).			
			Did not limit missile defenses or long-range conventional strike capabilities.			
Nuclear Non-Proliferation Treaty	NPT	Treaty on the Non-Proliferation of Nuclear Weapons	Established separate obligations for nuclear weapons states and nonnuclear weapons states.			
			Nuclear weapons states obligated to not transfer or give control of nuclear weapons to any recipient, or help nonnuclear weapons states acquire the weapons. Nuclear weapons states also agreed to pursue nuclear disarmament and negotiations to end the nuclear arms race.			
			Nonnuclear weapons states obligated to not to manufacture, acquire, or receive nuclear weapons. They were obliged to accept safeguards on their nuclear energy facilities.			

(Continued)

Common Name	Acronym	Full Name	Major Provisions	Year Open for Signature	Year of Entry into Force	Number of Parties as of May 15, 2012
Strategic Arms Limitation Treaty (I)	SALT (I)	Interim Agreement between the United States and the Union of the Soviet Socialist Republics on Certain Measures with Respect to the Limitation of Strategic Offensive Arms	Limits on fixed, land-based ICBMs, freezing them to the number already deployed or in construction. Limits on submarines and SLBMs. The Soviet Union was allowed to have 950 SLBMs, the United States 710. SALT I agreement did not involve dismantling any of the existing warheads, did not reduce the number of deployed ICBMs or SLBMs, did not involve any cooperative measures for verification, nor did it contain any provisions for onsite monitoring or inspection.	1972	1972	2
Strategic Arms Limitation Treaty (II)	SALT (II)	Treaty between the United States and the Union of the Soviet Socialist Republics on the Limitation of Strategic Offensive Arms	Limited each side to a ceiling of 2,400 weapons launchers. Each side could distribute its ceiling among ICBMs, SLBMs, heavy bombers, and long-range air-to-surface missiles. Limited number of launchers with MIRVs to no more than 1,300. U.S. missiles based in Europe were not included in the ceilings. Banned construction of additional fixed ICBM launchers. Banned air-to-surface ballistic missiles, a limit of 10 warheads on a new type of permitted ICBM. Limited the number of cruise missiles per heavy bomber.	1979	N/A	2

			Banned new weapons systems such as long-range ballistic missiles on surface ships and ballistic missiles and cruise missiles on the seabed, and limited the throw weight of strategic ballistic missiles. Ten-year agreement.		
Strategic Arms Reduction Treaty (I)	START (I)	Treaty between the United States and the Union of the Soviet Socialist Republics on the Reduction and Limitation of Strategic Offensive Arms	Required each country to reduce its aggregate number of deployed ICBMs, SLBMs, and heavy bombers to 1,600 and to reduce the number of warheads associated with those delivery vehicles to 6,000. Obligated each side to reduce its delivery capabilities by one-third and its warheads by roughly one half.	1991	1994, expired 2009
Strategic Arms Reduction Treaty (II)	START (II)	Treaty between the United States and the Russian Federation on Further Reduction and Limitation of Strategic Offensive Arms	Required the two parties to reduce their total deployed deployed nuclear warheads from 6,000 to no more than 3,500 and established limits within the overall maximum for warheads deployed on ICBMs and SLBMs. Established an upper limit of 3,600 metric tons on missile throw weight. START II also prohibited all MIRVs on ICBMs.	1993	1993, Russia withdrew 2002
Strategic Offensive Reduction Treaty	SORT	Treaty between the United States and the Russian Federation on Strategic Offensive Reductions	Required each side to reduce the aggregate number of deployed nuclear warheads in its arsenal to 1,700–2,000. No limit on the number of delivery vehicles for the warheads; permitted parties to store warheads that were not deployed. No provisions for assessing compliance.	2002	2003	2

Bibliography

"1997 Helsinki Joint Statement." Nuclear Threat Initiative, http://www.nti.org/db/nisprofs/fulltext/treaties/abm/abm_heje.htm.

"A Fissile Material Cutoff Treaty." The International Panel on Fissile Materials, http://www.fissilematerials.org/ipfm/pages_us_en/fmct/fmct/fmct.php.

"About the OPCW." Organization for the Prohibition of Chemical Weapons, http://www.opcw.org/about-opcw/.

Achen, Christopher H., and Duncan Snidal. "Rational Deterrence Theory and Comparative Case Studies." *World Politics* 41, no. 2 (1989): 143–69.

The Acronym Institute for Disarmament Diplomacy. "Conference on Disarmament," http://www.acronym.org.uk/un/aboutcd.htm.

Adams, David. *The American Peace Movements*. New Haven, CT: Advocate Press, 2002.

Ahmed, Ali. "Pakistan's 'First Use' in Prescriptive," http://www.idsa.in/idsacomments/PakistansFirstUseinPerspective_aahmed_120511.

AlertNet, A Thomson Reuters Foundation Service. "N. Korea, Iran Trade Missile Technology." May 15, 2011, http://www.trust.org/alertnet/news/exclusive-nkorea-iran-trade-missile-technology-un.

Alibek, Ken, with Stephen Handelman. *Biohazard: The Chilling True Story of the Largest Covert Biological Weapons Program in the World—Told from Inside by the Man Who Ran It*. New York: Random House, 1999.

"Anti-Ballistic Missile Treaty." *Nuclear/Strategic Treaties and Agreements, Naval Treaty Implementation Program*, http://www.ntip.navy.mil/abm_treaty.shtml.

Archive of Nuclear Data. Natural Resources Defense Council, http://www.nrdc.org/nuclear/nudb/datainx.asp.

Arms Control Association, http://www.armscontrol.org/factsheets/dprkchron.

Associated Press, "North Korea Would Use Nuclear Weapons in a 'Merciless Offensive.'" *The Independent*, June 9, 2009, http://www.independent.co.uk/

news/world/asia/north-korea-would-use-nuclear-weapons-in-a-merciless-offen sive-1700590.html.

Atomic-Archive. Operation Castle: 1954 Pacific Proving Ground, May 2006, http:// nuclearweaponarchive.org/Usa/Tests/Castle.html.

Atomic-Archive. Operation Sandstone 1948, July 10, 1997, http://nuclearweaponar chive.org/Usa/Tests/Sandston.html.

Avery, Donald. "The Canadian Biological Weapons Program and the Tripartite Alliance." In *Deadly Cultures: Bioweapons from 1945 to the Present*, edited by M. Wheelis, L. Rozsa, and M.R. Dando, 84–107. Cambridge, MA: Harvard University Press, 2006.

Balmer, Brian. *Britain and Biological Warfare: Expert Advice and Science Policy, 1930—65*. Basingstoke: Palgrave, 2001.

Balmer, Brian. "The UK Biological Weapons Program." In *Deadly Cultures: Bioweapons from 1945 to the Present*, edited by M. Wheelis, L. Rozsa, and M.R. Dando, 47–83. Cambridge, MA: Harvard University Press, 2006.

"Ban Movement Chronology," International Campaign to Ban Landmines. http:// www.icbl.org/index.php/icbl/About-Us/History/Chronology.

Barenblatt, Daniel. *A Plague upon Humanity: The Hidden History of Japan's Biological Warfare Program*. New York: HarperCollins, 2004.

The Baruch Plan, Presented to the United Nations Atomic Energy Commission June 14, 1946. The Atomic Archive, http://www.atomicarchive.com/Docs/Deterrence/ BaruchPlan.shtml.

BBC. "1997: Princess Diana Sparks Landmines Row," http://news.bbc.co.uk/onthisday/ hi/dates/stories/january/15/newsid_2530000/2530603.stm.

Board of Governors, International Atomic Energy Agency, Implementation of the NPT Safeguards Agreement and Relevant Provisions of Security Council Resolution 1737 (2006) in the Islamic Republic of Iran, http://www.iaea.org/ Publications/Documents/Board/2010/gov2010–62.pdf.

Boese, Wade. "Cluster Munitions Control Efforts Make Gains." *Arms Control Today* 37 (2007), http://www.armscontrol.org/act/2007_07–08/Cluster.

Borrie, John. *Unacceptable Harm: A History of How the Treaty to Ban Cluster Munitions Was Won*. United Nations Institute for Disarmament Research, United Nations Publications, 2008.

"Brief Chronology of START II." Arms Control Association, http://www.armscon trol.org/factsheets/start2chron.

Brodie, Bernard. *Strategy in the Missile Age*. Princeton, NJ: Princeton University Press, 1959, 1965.

Bull, Hedley. *The Control of the Arms Race: Disarmament and Arms Control in the Missile Age*. New York: Frederick A. Praeger Publishers, 1961.

Bundy, McGeorge. *Danger and Survival: Choices about the Bomb in the First Fifty Years*. New York: Random House, 1988.

Burger, Marlene, and Chandre Gould. *Secrets and Lies: Wouter Basson and South Africa's Chemical and Biological Warfare Programme*. Cape Town: Zebra Press, 2002.

Cameron, Maxwell A., Robert J. Lawson, and Brian W. Tomlin, "To Walk without Fear." In *To Walk without Fear: The Global Movement to Ban Landmines*, edited by Maxwell A. Cameron, Robert J. Lawson, and Brian W. Tomlin. Ontario: Oxford University Press, 1998.

Carter, Gordon B., and Graham S. Pearson. "British Biological Warfare and Biological Defence, 1942–1945." In *Biological and Toxin Weapons: Research, Development and Use from the Middle Ages to 1945*, edited by Erhard Geissler and John Ellis van Courtland Moon. Stockholm: Stockholm International Peace Research Institute, 1999.

Center for Nonproliferation Studies. "Comprehensive Nuclear Test Ban Treaty," http://nti.org/e_research/official_docs/inventory/pdfs/ctbt.pdf.

Centers for Disease Control. "Plague Fact Sheet," http://www.cdc.gov/ncidod/dvbid/plague/resources/plagueFactSheet.pdf.

"Chemical Weapons," Global Security.org, http://www.globalsecurity.org/wmd/world/iran/cw.htm.

Chevrier, Marie. A statement delivered to the United Nations 1540 committee in October, 2009. BioWeapons Prevention Project, http://www.stanleyfoundation.org/publications/working_papers/ChevrierBWPPSC1540.pdf.

Clinton, Bill. President. "Confronting the Challenges of a Broader World." Address to the UN General Assembly, September 27, 1993, available in *Dispatch Magazine*. Georgetown, TX: United States Bureau of Public Affairs, 1993, http://dosfan.lib.uic.edu/ERC/briefing/dispatch/1993/html/Dispatchv4no39.html.

Cohen, Avner, and William Burr. "Israel Crosses the Threshold." *Bulletin of the Atomic Scientists* 62, no. 3 (2006): 22–30.

Committee on National Security and Arms Control, National Academy of Sciences. *Nuclear Arms Control: Background and Issues*. Washington, DC: National Academy Press, 1995, http://www.nap.edu/openbook.php?record_id=11&page=109.

Confidential Saving Telegram, Foreign and Commonwealth office to Abidjan, September 29, 1969, DEFE 24/551, PRO.

"Convention on Cluster Munitions," http://www.clusterconvention.org/.

"Convention on the Prohibition of the Development, Production and Stockpiling of Bacteriological (Biological) and Toxin Weapons and on Their Destruction." April 10, 1972, http://www.un.org/disarmament/WMD/Bio.

"Convention on the Prohibition of the Development, Production, Stockpiling and the Use of Chemical Weapons and on Their Destruction." Organization for the Prohibition of Chemical Weapons, http://www.opcw.org/index.php?eID=dam_frontend_push&docID=6357.

"The Convention on Prohibitions or Restrictions on the Use of Certain Conventional Weapons which May Be Deemed to Be Excessively Injurious or to Have Indiscriminate Effects." United Nations Office at Geneva, http://www.unog.ch/80256EDD006B8954/(httpAssets)/40BDE99D98467348C12571DE0060141E/$file/CCW+text.pdf.

"Convention on the Prohibition of the Use, Stockpiling, Production and Transfer of Anti-Personnel Mines and on Their Destruction." September 18, 1997, http://www.un.org/Depts/mine/UNDocs/ban_trty.htm.

"Convention on the Prohibition of the Use, Stockpiling, Production and Transfer of Anti-Personnel Mines and on Their Destruction," http://www.icbl.org/index.php/icbl/Treaty/MBT/Treaty-Text-in-Many-Languages.

Cornwell, Susan. "Obama Administration to Push for Test Ban Treaty." Reuters, May 10, 2011, http://www.reuters.com/article/2011/05/10/us-nuclear-usa-testing-idUSTRE7496M020110510.

Crall, Peter. "Pakistan's Nuclear Buildup Vexes FMTC Talks." *Arms Control Today* (2011), http://www.armscontrol.org/act/2011_03/Pakistan.

CRS Issue Brief. "Pakistan–U.S. Relations," http://www.fas.org/spp/starwars/crs/94–041.htm.

CTBTO."Timeline of CTBT," http://ctbto.org/the-treaty/.

"Customary International Humanitarian Law: 29-10-2010 Overview." International Committee of the Red Cross, http://www.icrc.org/eng/war-and-law/treaties-customary-law/customary-law/overview-customary-law.htm.

Dahl, Fredrik. "Iran Shows U.N. Official All Nuclear Sites: Envoy." Reuters, August23,2011,http://www.reuters.com/article/2011/08/23/us-iran-nuclear-idUSTRE77M6ZW20110823.

Davenport, David. "The New Diplomacy." *Policy Review* 116 (2002): 17–30.

Decision 1: Strengthening the Review Process for the Treaty, NPT/CONF.1995/32 (Part I), Annex (1995), http://www.un.org/disarmament/WMD/Nuclear/1995-NPT/pdf/NPT_CONF199532.pdf.

Decision 2: Principles and Objectives for Nuclear Non-Proliferation and Disarmament (1995), http://www.un.org/disarmament/WMD/Nuclear/1995-NPT/pdf/NPT_CONF199501.pdf.

Decision 3: Extension of the Treaty on the Non-Proliferation of Nuclear Weapons (1995), http://www.un.org/disarmament/WMD/Nuclear/1995-NPT/pdf/NPT_CONF199503.pdf.

"Declaration Renouncing the Use, in Time of War, of Explosive Projectiles under 400 Grammes Weight." International Humanitarian Law—Treaties & Documents, International Committee of the Red Cross, http://www.icrc.org/ihl.nsf/FULL/130?OpenDocument.

Department of State Telegram, ACDA/IR:RLMCCORMACK, April 1971, NSC Files, Chemical, Biological Warfare (Toxins etc.), vol. 4, pt. 1, box 312. National Archives and Records Administration.

DeYoung, Karen. "Pakistan Doubles Its Nuclear Stockpile." *The Washington Post,* January 31, 2011, http://www.washingtonpost.com/wp-dyn/content/article/2011/01/30/AR2011013004682.html.

"Diplomatic Conference for the Adoption of a Convention on Cluster Munitions." Dublin, 2008, http://www.clustermunitionsdublin.ie/pdf/ENGLISHfinaltext.pdf.

Du Preez, Jean, and William Potter. "North Korea's Withdrawal from the NPT: A Reality Check." In *The Center for Nonproliferation Studies*. Monterey Institute of International Studies, 2003, http://cns.miis.edu/stories/030409.htm.

Eighteen Nation Disarmament Committee (ENDC) /231. "Working Paper on Microbiological Warfare."

Eisenhower, Dwight D. Address by Mr. Dwight D. Eisenhower, president of the United States, to the 470th Plenary Meeting of the United Nations General Assembly, 1953, http://www.iaea.org/About/history_speech.html.

Erhard Geissler. "Biological Warfare Activities in Germany, 1923–45." In *Biological and Toxin Weapons*, edited by Erhard Geissler and John Ellis van Courtland Moon. Stockholm: Stockholm International Peace Research Institute, 1999.

Federation of American Scientists. "Memorandum of Understanding," http://www.fas.org/sgp/othergov/mou-infoshare.pdf.

"The Final Document of the 2000 Review Conference of the Parties to the Treaty of the Non-Proliferation of Nuclear Weapons." Arms Control Association, www.armscontrol.org/act/2000_06/docjun.

Fischer, David. *History of the International Atomic Energy Agency: The First Forty Years*. Vienna: The International Atomic Energy Agency, 1997.

Fisher, Max. "What If Kim Jong Il's Successor Isn't Ready?" *The Atlantic*, December 19, 2011, http://www.theatlantic.com/international/archive/2011/12/what-if-kim-jong-ils-successor-isnt-ready/250169/.

Flauraud, Valentin. "Iran Six 'disappointed' by nuclear talks in Istanbul". RIA Novosti, January 22, 2011. http://en.rian.ru/world/20110122/162251094.html?id=.

Florini, Ann. "Lessons Learned." In *The Third Force: The Rise of Transnational Civil Society*. Washington, DC: Carnegie Endowment for International Peace, 2000.

Florini, Ann, and P. J. Simmons, "What the World Needs Now." In *The Third Force: The Rise of Transnational Civil Society*. Washington, DC: Carnegie Endowment for International Peace, 2000.

Fordan, Geoffrey. "Reducing a Common Danger: Improving Russia's Early-Warning System." *Policy Analysis*, no. 399. The Cato Institute. http://www.cato.org/pubs/pas/pa399.pdf.

Friedlander, Arthur M. "Anthrax." In *Medical Aspects of Chemical and Biological Warfare*, edited by Frederick R. Sidell, Ernest T. Takafuji, and David R. Franz, 467–78. Washington, DC: Office of the Surgeon General, 1997.

Gard Jr., Robert G. Lt. General (U.S., Ret.). "Past Time to Join the Landmine Treaty." *Huffington Post World*, March 18, 2009, http://www.huffingtonpost.com/lt-general-robert-g-gard-jr-/past-time-to-join-the-lan_b_176335.html.

Geneva International Centre for Humanitarian Demining. Annual Report 2010, 13, http://www.gichd.org/fileadmin/pdf/about_gichd/activity_reports/GICHD-Annual-Report-2010-en.pdf.

George, Alexander L., and Richard Smoke. *Deterrence in American Foreign Policy: Theory and Practice*. New York: Columbia University Press, 1974.

"Global Fissile Material Report 2010," International Panel on Fissile Materials, http://www.fissilematerials.org/ipfm/site_down/gfmr10.pdf.

Goldblat, Jozef. *Arms Control: The New Guide to Negotiations and Agreements.* Oslo: International Peace Research Institute, 2002.

Grabosky, P. N. "A Toxic Legacy: British Nuclear Weapons Testing in Australia." In *Wayward Governance: Illegality and Its Control in the Public Sector.* Canberra: Australian Institute of Criminology, 1989.

Graham Jr., Thomas, Ambassador. "A Return to Arms Control and Non-Proliferation Process," Testimony before the Subcommitte on Oversight of Government Management, the Federal Workforce, and the District of Columbia, Committee on Homeland Security and Government Organization, U.S. Senate, May 15, 2009. http://hsgac.senate.gov/public/_files/GrahamTestimony051508.pdf.

Harris, Sheldon H. *Factories of Death: Japanese Biological Warfare 1932–45, and the American Cover-Up.* London: Routledge, 1994.

Harris, Sheldon. "The Japanese Biological Warfare Programme: An Overview." In *Biological and Toxin Weapons*, edited by Erhard Geissler and John Ellis van Courtland Moon. Stockholm: Stockholm International Peace Research Institute, 1999.

Hart, John. "The Soviet Biological Weapons Program." In *Deadly Cultures: Biological Weapons Since 1945*, edited by Mark Wheelis, Lajos Rozsa, and Malcolm Dando. Cambridge, MA: Harvard University Press, 2006.

"IAEA Chief 'Concerned' about Iran's Nuclear Ambitions." VOA News, http://www.voanews.com/english/news/middle-east/UN-Nuclear-Chief-Concerned-About-Irans-Nuclear-Ambitions—129648218.html.

ICBL, http://www.icbl.org/index.php/icbl/Universal/MBT/States-Parties.

ICBL. "Grave Concern over Allegations of Landmine Use by Turkish Army." Press release. Geneva, April 19, 2010, http://www.icbl.org/index.php/icbl/Library/News-Articles/Work/pr-19April2010.

Iklé, Fred Charles. "After Detection What?" *Foreign Affairs* 39, no. 2 (1961): 208–20.

"India Profile," Nuclear Threat Initiative, 2003, http://www.nti.org/e_research/profiles/India/Nuclear/.

International Atomic Energy Agency Board of Governors, Report by the Director General. "Implementation of the NPT Safeguards Agreement and Relevant Provisions of Security Council Resolutions in the Islamic Republic of Iran," Resolution adopted by the Board of Governors on November 8, 2011. GOV/2011/65, http://www.iaea.org/Publications/Documents/Board/2011/gov2011-65.pdf.

International Atomic Energy Agency Board of Governors. "Implementation of the NPT Safeguards Agreement and Relevant Provisions of United Nations Security Council Resolutions in the Islamic Republic of Iran," Resolution adopted by the Board of Governors on November 18, 2011. GOV /2011/69, http://www.iaea.org/Publications/Documents/Board/2011/gov2011-69.pdf.

International Atomic Energy Agency. The Semipalatinsk Test Site, Kazakhstan, August 30, 2008, http://www-ns.iaea.org/appraisals/semipalatinsk.htm.

The International Committee of the Red Cross, International Humanitarian Law—Treaties & Documents, Declaration (IV, 2) Concerning Asphyxiating Gases. The Hague, July 29, 1899, http://www.icrc.org/ihl.nsf/FULL/165? OpenDocument.

"Introduction," Landmine & Cluster Munitions Monitor, http://www.the-monitor. org/index.php.

"Iran Moving Centrifuges to Fordow," SIS Iran in Brief, http://www.isisnucleariran. org/brief/detail/iran-moving-centrifuges-to-fordow/.

Israel Special Weapons Guide: Nuclear Weapons. Federation of American Scientists, 2007, www.fas.org/nuke/guide/israel/index.html.

Jesuit Refugee Service/USA. "Civil Society Frustrated by U.S. Landmine Policy Review," December 4, 2011, http://jrsusa.org/news_detail?TN=NEWS-2011 1202020709.

Johnson, Rebecca. *Unfinished Business: The Negotiation of the CTBT and the End of Nuclear Testing.* New York: United Nations Publications, 2009.

Kalshoven, Frits, and Liesbeth Zegveld. *Constraints on the Waging of War: An Introduction to International Humanitarian Law.* Geneva: International Committee on Red Cross, 2001, http://www.loc.gov/rr/frd/Military_Law/pdf/Constraints-waging-war.pdf.

Kelle, Alexander. "The CWC after Its First Review Conference: Is the Glass Half Full or Half Empty?" *Disarmament Diplomacy* 71 (2003), http://www.acronym.org. uk/dd/dd71/71cwc.htm.

Kerr, Paul. "The IAEA's Report on Iran: An Analysis." *Arms Control Today* 33 (2003), http://www.armscontrol.org/act/2003_12/IAEAreport.

Kimball, Daryl G. "Impact of the US–Indian Nuclear Deal on India's Fissile Production Capacity for Weapons." Press release, Arms Control Association, 2006, http://www.armscontrol.org/pressroom/2006/20061115_Indian_Fissile.

Kissinger, Henry. "NATO: The Next Thirty Years," *Survival,* November/December 1979.

Krasner, Stephen D. *International Regimes.* Ithaca, NY: Cornell University Press, 1983.

Krepon, Michael. "The Conference on Disarmament: Means of Rejuvenation." *Arms Control Today* 36 (2006), http://www.armscontrol.org/act/2006_12/Krepon.

Krepon, Michael. "LOOKING BACK: The 1998 Indian and Pakistani Nuclear Tests." *Arms Control Today* 38 (2008), http://www.armscontrol.org/act/2008_05/ lookingback.

Landmine and Cluster Munition Monitor 2011. http://www.the-monitor.org/index. php/publications/display?url=lm/2011/es/Casualties_and_Victim_Assistance. html.

Landmine Monitor 2010. Toward a Mine Free World, "Major Findings," http:// www.the-monitor.org/index.php/publications/display?url=lm/2010/es/Major_ Findings.html.

Landmine Monitor 2011. http://www.the-monitor.org/lm/2011/resources/Landmine%20Monitor%202011.pdf.

Landmine Monitor Report 2000. Washington, DC: Human Rights Watch, http://www.the-monitor.org/index.php/content/view/full/18734.

Landmine Monitor: Toward a Mine Free World, 1999. "Banning Antipersonnel Mines," http://www.the-monitor.org/index.php/publications/display?url=lm/1999/english/exec/Execweb1–02.htm#P184_13658.

Larsen, Jeffrey A., ed. *Arms Control: Cooperative Security in a Changing Environment.* Boulder, CO: Lynne Rienner Publishers, 2002.

Larsen, Jeffrey A. *Arms Control toward the Twenty-First Century.* Boulder, CO: Lynne Rienner Publishers, 1996.

Lavoy, Peter R. "Predicting Nuclear Proliferation: A Declassified Documentary Record," *Strategic Insights* 3, no. 1 (2004), http://www.fas.org/man/eprint/lavoy.pdf.

Lebow, Richard Ned, and Janice Gross Stein. "Deterrence and the Cold War." *Political Science Quarterly* 110, no. 2 (1995): 157–81.

Lehman II, Ronald F. Foreword to *Arms Control and Cooperative Security,* edited by James A. Larsen and James J. Wirtz. Boulder, CO: Lynne Rienner Publishers, 2009.

Lentzos, Filippa. "Reaching a Tipping Point: Strengthening BWC Confidence-Building Measures." *Disarmament Diplomacy* 89 (2008), http://www.acronym.org.uk/dd/dd89/89fl.htm.

Lepick, Olivier. "The French Biological Weapons Program." In *Deadly Cultures: Bioweapons from 1945 to the Present,* edited by M. Wheelis, L. Rozsa, and M.R. Dando. Cambridge, MA: Harvard University Press, 2006.

Mardor, Munya M. Rafael. Tel Aviv: Misrad Habithaon, 1981, 120–21, as quoted in Avner Cohen, *Israel and the Bomb,* New York: Columbia University Press, 1998.

Maresca, Louis, and Stuart Maslen. *The Beginning of Anti-Personnel Landmines: The Legal Contribution of the International Committee of the Red Cross 1955–1999.* Cambridge: Cambridge University Press, 2008.

Matheson, Michael J. "Filling the Gaps in the Conventional Weapons Convention." *Arms Control Today* 31 (2001), http://www.armscontrol.org/act/2001_11/mathesonnov01.

McLaughlin, Kathryn. "Bringing Biologists on Board Report from the 2008 Meeting of BWC Experts." *Disarmament Diplomacy* 89 (2008), http://www.acronym.org.uk/dd/dd89/89bwc.htm.

Meerburg, Arend, and Frank N. Von Hippel. "Complete Cutoff: Designing a Comprehensive Fissile Material Treaty." *Arms Control Today* 39 (2009), http://www.armscontrol.org/print/3546.

Meier, Oliver. "CWC Review Conference Avoids Difficult Issues." *Arms Control Today* 38 (2008), http://www.armscontrol.org/act/2008_05/CWC.

Meier, Oliver. "OPCW Chiefs Ponder Chemical Arms Deadlines." *Arms Control Today* 40 (2010), http://www.armscontrol.org/act/2010_01–02/OPCW.

Memorandum for Kissinger from Guhin, Convention Banning Biological Weapons and Toxins. September 17, 1971.

Miller, Judith, Stephen Engelberg, and William Broad. *Germs: Biological Weapons and America's Secret War*. New York: Simon & Shuster, 2001.

Ministry of Foreign Affairs, India. "Address by Foreign Secretary at NDC on 'Challenges in India's Foreign Policy,'" November 19, 2010, http://www.mea.gov.in/mystart.php?id=530116703.

"Mission," Overview and Strategic Chart, Geneva International Center for Strategic Demining, http://www.gichd.org/about-gichd/overview/.

Mistry, Dinshaw. "India and the Comprehensive Test Ban Treaty." ACDIS Research Reports, 1998, http://acdis.illinois.edu/publications/207/publication-Indiaandthe ComprehensiveTestBanTreaty.html.

Muller, Richard R. "The Origins of MAD: A Short History of City-Busting." In *Getting MAD: Nuclear Mutual Assured Destruction Its Origins and Practice*, edited by Henry D. Sokolski. Carlisle Barracks, PA: The Strategic Studies Institute, November 2004, http://www.strategicstudiesinstitute.army.mil/pdffiles/pub585.pdf.

Mydans, Seth, and Choe Sang-Hun. "North Korea Said to Weigh Nuclear Test Moratorium." *The New York Times*, August 24, 2011, http://www.nytimes.com/2011/08/25/world/europe/25siberia.html.

"Napalm," Global Security.org, http://www.globalsecurity.org/military/systems/munitions/napalm.htm.

National Intelligence Estimate Number 100-6-57. "Nuclear Weapons Production in Fourth Countries Likelihood and Consequences," June 18, 1957, The National Security Archive, http://www.gwu.edu/~nsarchiv/NSAEBB/NSAEBB155/index.htm.

National Resources Defense Council, Archive of Nuclear Data Table of USSR/Russian Nuclear Warheads 1949–75 | 1976–2002, http://www.nrdc.org/nuclear/nudb/datab10.asp.

National Security Council Report 68. "A Report to the National Security Council—NSC 68," President's Secretary's File, Truman Papers, April 12, 1950, http://www.trumanlibrary.org/whistlestop/study_collections/coldwar/documents/pdf/10–1.pdf.

National Security Estimate Number 4-66. "The Likelihood of Further Nuclear Proliferation," January 20, 1966, 2. The National Security Archive, http://www.gwu.edu/~nsarchiv/NSAEBB/NSAEBB155/index.htm.

National-Archives, Operation Hurricane: The Explosion of the First British Bomb, http://www.nationalarchives.gov.uk/films/1951to1964/filmpage_oper_hurr.htm.

"No First Use Policy of the Declared Nuclear Weapons States," April 5–6, 1995, http://www.nuclearfiles.org/menu/key-issues/nuclear-weapons/issues/policies/ no-first-use_1995–04–05.htm.

"North Korea—Denuclearization Action Plan, February 13, 2007." The Acronym Institute, Disarmament Documentation, http://www.acronym.org.uk/docs/ 0702/doc01.htm.

"Nuclear Successor States of the Soviet Union." The Monterey Institute for International Studies and the Carnegie Endowment for International Peace. Monterey, CA; Washington, DC, and Moscow, March 1998, http://cns.miis.edu/ reports/pdfs/statrep.pdf.

Nuclear Suppliers Group. "What Is the NSG," http://www.nuclearsuppliersgroup.org/ Leng/default.htm.

Nuclear Weapon Stockpile Chart, July 2005. Carnegie Endowment for International Peace, http://www.carnegieendowment.org/publications/?fa=view&id=19238.

Nye, Joseph. "The Superpowers and the Non-Proliferation Treaty." In *Superpower Arms Control: Setting the Record Straight*, edited by Albert Carnesale and Richard N. Haass. Cambridge, MA: Ballinger Publishing Company, 1987.

"OPCW Member States." Organization for the Prohibition of Chemical Weapons, http://www.opcw.org/about-opcw/member-states/.

Pearson, Graham S. "The Iraqi Biological Weapons Program." In *Deadly Cultures: Bioweapons from 1945 to the Present*, edited by M. Wheelis, L. Rozsa, and M.R. Dando. Cambridge, MA: Harvard University Press, 2006.

Pinkston, D.A., "Implementing the Agreed Framework and Potential Obstacles." In *12th Pacific Basin Nuclear Conference 2000, Center for Nonproliferation Studies*. Seoul: Monterey Institute of International Studies, http://cns.miis.edu/reports/ kaeri.htm.

Preamble. Convention on the Prohibition of the Development, Production and Stockpiling of Bacteriological (Biological) and Toxin Weapons and on Their Destruction, http://www.opbw.org/.

Price, Richard. "Reversing the Gun Sights: Transnational Civil Society Targets Land Mines." *International Organization* 52, no. 3 (1998): 613–44.

"Protocol for the Prohibition of the Use in War of Asphyxiating, Poisonous or Other Gases, and of Bacteriological Methods of Warfare." June 17, 1925, http://www. un.org/disarmament/WMD/Bio/pdf/Status_Protocol.pdf.

Public Papers of the Presidents of the United States: John F. Kennedy 1963–1964. Washington, DC: U.S. Government Printing Office.

Purkitt, Helen, and Stephen Burgess. *South Africa's Weapons of Mass Destruction*. Indianapolis, IN: Indiana University Press.

Purlain, Ted. "Libya Misses Weapons Destruction Deadline." BioPrepWatch.com, http://www.bioprepwatch.com/news/246187-libya-misses-weapons-destruction- deadline.

Rappert, Brian. *Controlling the Weapons of War: Politics, Persuasion, and the Prohibition of Inhumanity*. London: Routledge, 2006.

Rauf, Tariq. "An Unequivocal Success? Implications of the NPT Review Conference." *Arms Control Today* 30 (2000), http://www.armscontrol.org/act/2000_07–08/raufjulaug.

Report of the OPCW on the Implementation of the Convention on the Prohibition of the Development, Production, Stockpiling and Use of Chemical Weapons and on Their Destruction in 2009, C-15/4, last modified November 30, 2010, http://www.opcw.org/documents-reports/annual-reports/.

Review Conference of the Parties to the Treaty on the Non-Proliferation of Nuclear Weapons Final Document, NPT/CONF /35/1, http://www.un.org/disarmament/WMD/Nuclear/pdf/finaldocs/1975%20-%20Geneva%20%20NPT%20Review%20Conference%20-%20Final%20Document%20Part%20I.pdf.

Roberts, Guy B. "This Arms Control Dog Won't Hunt: The Proposed Fissile Material Cut-Off Treaty at the Conference on Disarmament." Institute for National Security Studies, U.S. Air Force Academy, Occasional Paper 36, January 2001, http://www.dtic.mil/cgi-bin/GetTRDoc?Location=U2&doc=GetTRDoc.pdf&AD=ADA435059.

"The Role of the Parliament in the Ratification of International Treaties and Agreements." The Knesset—Research and Information Center, http://www.knesset.gov.il/mmm/data/pdf/me00647.pdf.

Rutherford, Kenneth R. "The Hague and Ottawa Conventions: A Model for Future Weapons Ban Processes." *Non-Proliferation Review* 6, no. 3 (1999): 36–50.

Rutherford, Kenneth R. "NGOs and International Politics in the Twenty-First Century." *American Foreign Policy Interests*, 23, no. 1 (2001): 23–29..

Sagan, Scott D. *The Limits of Safety: Organization, Accidents, and Nuclear Weapons.* Princeton, NJ: Princeton University Press, 1993.

Sanders, Jackie W. Remarks to the Conference on Disarmament, The Acronym Institute for Disarmament Diplomacy, 2004, http://www.acronym.org.uk/docs/0407/doc08.htm.

Schelling, Thomas C. "An Astonishing 60 Years: The Legacy of Hiroshima." *Proceedings of the National Academy of Sciences of the United States of America* 103, no. 16 (2006), http://www.pnas.org/content/103/16/6089.full.pdf+html.

Schelling, Thomas C., and Morton H. Halperin. *Strategy and Arms Control.* New York: Twentieth Century Fund, 1961.

Schindler, D., and J. Toman. *The Laws of Armed Conflicts*, 3rd ed. Dordrecht: Nijoff, 1988.

Schwartz, Stephen I., ed. *Atomic Audit: The Costs and Consequences of U.S. Nuclear Weapons since 1940.* Washington, DC: Brookings Institution Press, 1998.

Scott-Clark, Cathy, and Adrian Levy. "Spectre Orange." *The Guardian*, March 28, 2003, http://www.guardian.co.uk/world/2003/mar/29/usa.adrianlevy.

"The Secret History of The ABM Treaty, 1969–1972," in National Security Archive, Electronic Briefing Book No. 60, www.gwu.edu~nsarchiv/NSAEBB/NSAEBB60.

Short, Nicola. "The Role of NGOs in the Ottawa Process to Ban Landmines." *International Negotiation* 4, no. 3 (1999).

Siamand Banaa, H. E. Ambassador. Statement by the Permanent Representative of the Republic of Iraq to the OPCW at the Sixtieth Session of the Executive Council. EC-60/NAT.10, April, 20, 2010, http://www.opcw.org/search/?search=Iraq.

Sigal, Leon V. *Negotiating Minefields: The Landmines Ban in American Politics.* New York: Taylor and Francis Group, 2006.

Sims, Jennifer E., "The Arms Control Process: The U.S. Domestic Context." In *Arms Control: Toward the 21st Century,* edited by Jeffrey A. Larsen and Gregory J. Rattray. Boulder, CO: Lynne Rienner Publishers, 1996.

Sims, Nicholas A. *The Diplomacy of Biological Disarmament: Vicissitudes of a Treaty in Force 1975–1985.* New York: St. Martin's Press, 1988.

Sims, Nicholas A. *The Future of Biological Disarmament: Strengthening the Treaty Ban on Weapons.* LSE International Studies. London and New York: Routledge, 2009.

Sims, Nicholas A. "Legal Constraints on Biological Weapons." In *Deadly Cultures: Bioweapons from 1945 to the Present,* edited by M. Wheelis, L. Rozsa, and M. R. Dando. Cambridge, MA: Harvard University Press, 2006.

Smart, Jeffrey K. "History of Chemical and Biological Warfare: An American Perspective." In *Medical Aspects of Chemical and Biological Warfare,* edited by Frederick R. Sidell, Ernest T. Takafuji, and David R. Franz. Washington, DC: Office of the Surgeon General, 1997.

Smith, Grant. "Oil Climbs as European Union Agrees on Sanctions against Iran." *Bloomberg Businessweek,* January 31, 2012, http://www.businessweek.com/news/2012-01-23/oil-climbs-as-european-union-agrees-on-sanctions-against-iran.html.

Statute of the IAEA, 1956, www.iaea.org.

Stoiber, Carlton. "The Evolution of NPT Review Conference Final Documents, 1975–2000." *The Nonproliferation Review* 10, no. 3 (2003): 126–66, http://cns.miis.edu/npr/pdfs/103stoi.pdf.

Talking Points on Biological Warfare for the ENDC Informal Meeting on May 14, 1969, in I. F. Porter. United Kingdom Delegation to the 18 Nation Disarmament Conference, to Mulley, March 31, 1969, FCO 73/114, PRO.

Trachtenberg, Mark. "Making Grand Strategy: The Early Cold War Experience in Retrospect." *SAIS Review* 9, no. 1 (1999): 33–40, http://www.sscnet.ucla.edu/polisci/faculty/trachtenberg/cv/grandstrat%28sais%29.html.

"Treaty between the United States of America and the Union of Soviet Socialist Republics on the Limitation of Anti-Ballistic Missile Systems," signed in Moscow, May 26, 1072, http://www.state.gov/t/isn/trty/16332.htm.

"Treaty on the Cessation of Production of Fissile Material for Use in Nuclear Weapons or Other Nuclear Explosive Devices," http://www.reachingcriticalwill.org/political/cd/speeches06/18MayDraftTreaty.pdf.

"Treaty Texts & Fact Sheets: Intermediate-Range Nuclear Forces (INF) Treaty," Defense Treaty Inspection Readiness Program, http://dtirp.dtra.mil/tic/treatyinfo/inf.aspx.

Tucker, Jonathan B. "A Farewell to Germs: The U.S. Renunciation of Biological and Toxin Weapons, 1969–1970." *International Security* 27 (summer 2002): 107–48.

U.S. Department of State. "Treaty between the United States of America and the Russian Federation on Measures for the Further Reduction and Limitation of Strategic Offensive Arms," April 8, 2010, http://www.state.gov/documents/organization/140035.pdf.

U.S. Policy Leading into the NPT Conference, in Occasional Papers on International Security Policy. British American Security Information Centre, 1995.

"U.S. Secretary of Defense Frank Carlucci on Nuclear Deterrence and Strategic Defenses, January 17, 1989," http://nuclearfiles.org/menu/key-issues/nuclear-weapons/history/cold-war/strategy/report-carlucci-deterrence_1989–01–17.htm.

UN Document. 48/70 Comprehensive Test-Ban Treaty, http://daccess-dds-ny.un.org/doc/RESOLUTION/GEN/NR0/711/54/IMG/NR071154.pdf?OpenElement.

UN Document. A/RES/50/245 Comprehensive Test Ban Treaty, http://www.un.org/documents/ga/res/50/a50r245.htm. See also vote summary at http://www.un.org/depts/dhl/resguide/r50.htm.

UNICEF. "Landmines: Hidden Killers," State of the World's Children, May 8, 1996, http//www.unicef.org/sowc96pk/hidekill.htm.

United Nations General Assembly Resolution. "Prevention of the Wider Dissemination of Nuclear Weapons," A/RES/1665/XVI, 1961.

United Nations General Assembly Resolution 48/75L. "Prohibition of the Production of Fissile Material for Nuclear Weapons or Other Nuclear Explosive Devices," December 16, 1993, http://daccess-dds-ny.un.org/doc/RESOLUTION/GEN/NR0/711/59/IMG/NR071159.pdf?OpenElement.

United Nations Institute for Disarmament Research and the Geneva Forum. "The Conference on Disarmament and Negative Security Assurances," http://unidir.org/pdf/activites/pdf3-act593.pdf.

United Nations Office at Geneva. Disarmament, the Convention on Certain Conventional Weapons, http://www.unog.ch/80256EE600585943/%28httpPages%29/4F0DEF093B4860B4C1257180004B1B30?OpenDocument.

United Nations Security Council. Resolution 255, 1968. "Question Relating to Measures to Safeguard Non-Nuclear-Weapon States Parties to the Treaty on the Non-Proliferation of Nuclear Weapons." June 19, 1968, http://www.securitycouncilreport.org/atf/cf/%7B65BFCF9B-6D27-4E9C-8CD3-CF6E4FF96FF9%7D/Disarm%20SRES255.pdf

United Nations Security Council. Resolution 284 S/RES/984, 1995, http://daccess-dds-ny.un.org/doc/UNDOC/GEN/N95/106/06/PDF/N9510606.pdf?OpenElement.

United States Department of State. "Adherence To and Compliance with Arms Control, Nonproliferation, and Disarmament Agreements and Commitments," http://www.state.gov/documents/organization/170652.pdf.

United States Department of State. "Treaty Banning Nuclear Weapon Tests in the Atmosphere, in Outer Space and under Water," http://www.state.gov/t/isn/4797.htm.

Urbanetti, John S. "Toxic Inhalational Injury." In *Medical Aspects of Chemical and Biological Warfare*, edited by Frederick R. Sidell, Ernest T. Takafuji, and David R. Franz. Washington, DC: Office of the Surgeon General, 1997.

"US Reviewing FMCT Policy," *Arms Control Today* 33 (2003), http://www.armscontrol.org/node/3247.

Van Courtland Moon, John Ellis. "The US Biological Weapons Program." In *Deadly Cultures: Bioweapons from 1945 to the Present*, edited by M. Wheelis, L. Rozsa, and M. R. Dando. Cambridge, MA: Harvard University Press, 2006.

Walzer, Michael. "World War II: Why Was This War Different?" *Philosophy & Public Affairs* 1, no. 1 (autumn 1971), http://www.jstor.org/stable/pdfplus/2265089.pdf.

Weber, Steve. *Cooperation and Discord in US–Soviet Arms Control*. Princeton, NJ: Princeton University Press, 2006.

Wheelis, Mark. "Biological Sabotage in World War I." In *Biological and Toxin Weapons: Research, Development and Use from the Middle Ages to 1945*, edited by Erhard Geissler and John Ellis van Courtland Moon. Stockholm: Stockholm International Peace Research Institute, 1999.

Wiese, Rachel A. "Russia, U.S. Lag on Chemical Arms Deadline." *Arms Control Today* 39 (2009), http://www.armscontrol.org/act/2009_07–08/chemical_weapons.

Wilson, Ward. "A-Bomb v. H-bomb," http://wardhayeswilson.squarespace.com/a-bomb-v-h-bomb/.

Index

About the Author

MARIE ISABELLE CHEVRIER, PhD, is a professor of public policy and administration at Rutgers University–Camden. Dr. Chevrier is a member and former chair of the Scientists Working Group on Biological and Chemical Weapons in Washington, DC. She served as the chair of the board of directors of the Bio Weapons Prevention Project from 2007 to 2011. In 2004, she received a Fulbright Fellowship to teach at the Nelson Mandela Center for Peace and Conflict Resolution at Jamia Millia Islamia University in New Delhi, India. She received her undergraduate degree from the University of Nebraska and her PhD in public policy from Harvard University where she was a fellow at the Belfer Center for Science and International Affairs at the Kennedy School of Government. In 1997–1998, she was the associate director of the Harvard-Sussex Program on Chemical and Biological Armaments and Arms Limitation. She lives in Philadelphia, Pennsylvania, with her husband Paul Jargowsky and is the proud mother of Isabelle and Zackary Jargowsky.